USDA

United States
Department of Agriculture

Forest Service

Pacific Northwest
Research Station

General Technical Report
PNW-GTR-806
May 2010

Aspen Biology, Community Classification, and Management in the Blue Mountains

David K. Swanson, Craig L. Schmitt, Diane M. Shirley, Vicky Erickson, Kenneth J. Schuetz, Michael L. Tatum, and David C. Powell

Author

David K. Swanson was an area ecologist, U.S. Department of Agriculture, Forest Service, P.O. Box 907, Baker City, OR 97814, is now an ecologist with the U.S. Department of the Interior, National Park Service, 4175 Geist Rd., Fairbanks, AK 99709. **Craig L. Schmitt** is a zone pathologist, U.S. Department of Agriculture, Forest Service, 1401 Gekeler Lane, La Grande, OR 97850. **Diane M. Shirley** is a forestry technician, U.S. Department of Agriculture, Forest Service, Umatilla National Forest, P.O. Box 158, Ukiah, OR 97880. **Vicky Erickson** is the regional geneticist, and **David C. Powell** is a forest silviculturalist, U.S. Department of Agriculture, Forest Service, Umatilla National Forest, 2517 Hailey Avenue, Pendleton, OR 97801. **Kenneth J. Schuetz** (deceased) was a forest wildlife biologist, and **Michael L. Tatum** is a forest silviculturist, U.S. Department of Agriculture, Forest Service, Malheur National Forest, P.O. Box 909, John Day, OR 97845.

Cover photo: Aspen stand with buck-and-pole fence constructed of local thinning slash 8 years prior to photo. Regeneration is lacking around the mature trees outside of the fenced area on the right. Blue Mountain Ranger District of the Malheur National Forest, in the vicinity of Camp Creek and Starr Ridge. Photo by Michael Tatum, Malheur National Forest.

Abstract

Swanson, David K.; Schmitt, Craig L.; Shirley, Diane M.; Erickson, Vicky; Schuetz, Kenneth J.; Tatum, Michael L.; Powell, David C. 2010. Aspen biology, community classification, and management in the Blue Mountains. Gen. Tech. Rep. PNW-GTR-806. Portland, OR: U.S. Department of Agriculture, Forest Service, Pacific Northwest Research Station. 117 p.

Quaking aspen (*Populus tremuloides* Michx.) is a valuable species that is declining in the Blue Mountains of northeastern Oregon. This publication is a compilation of over 20 years of aspen management experience by USDA Forest Service workers in the Blue Mountains. It includes a summary of aspen biology and occurrence in the Blue Mountains, and a discussion of aspen conservation and management techniques such as fencing, conifer removal, and artificial propagation. Local data on bird use of aspen stands, insects and diseases in aspen, and genetic studies of aspen are also included. An aspen community classification developed from over 200 sample plots is presented, with plant species composition and cover, environment and soils, and management considerations.

Keywords: *Populus tremuloides,* forest management, forest ecology, plant community classification.

Preface

This publication is a collaboration that draws on the efforts of many people who have worked with aspen in the Blue Mountains. Primary authorship of the various sections is as follows:

- Aspen Biology and Ecology–David K. Swanson, Kenneth J. Schuetz (Bird use of aspen on the Malheur National Forest), David C. Powell, and Michael L. Tatum
- Genetic Diversity and Structure of Aspen Stands in the Blue Mountains–Vicky Erickson
- Insects and Diseases of Aspen in the Blue Mountains–Craig L. Schmitt
- Aspen Management in the Blue Mountains–David K. Swanson, Diane M. Shirley, Michael L. Tatum, and Vicky Ericson with contributions from most of the collaborators
- Aspen Community Classification in the Blue Mountains–David K. Swanson

Aspen Biology, Community Classification, and Management in the Blue Mountains

David K. Swanson, Craig L. Schmitt, Diane M. Shirley, Vicky Erickson, Kenneth J. Schuetz, Michael L. Tatum, and David C. Powell

With contributions from (listed alphabetically): Roderick R. Clausnitzer, Lynda Cobb, Bill J. Collar, Elizabeth A. Crowe, Terry Hicks, Jerold Hustafa, Charles G. Johnson, Jr., Betsy H. Kaiser, Cynthia L. Kranich, Mark A. Penniger, Roy Schwenke, Joseph M. Sciarrino, Paul W. Survis, and Martin Vavra.

United States Department of Agriculture, Forest Service,
Pacific Northwest Research Station
General Technical Report PNW-GTR-806
May 2010

Contents

Introduction

Stands of quaking aspen (*Populus tremuloides* Michx.) are an uncommon and unique habitat type in the Blue Mountains (fig. 1). As one of very few broadleaf deciduous trees in a region dominated by conifers and semi-desert grassland and scrub, aspen brings important diversity to the landscape. Aspen's palatable twigs and foliage, and tendency to develop cavities, make it valuable habitat for wildlife such as deer (*Odocoileus* sp.), elk (*Cervus elephas*), woodpeckers, and songbirds. Aspen often grow in riparian areas, providing shade, streambank stability, and nutrients from leaf-fall to streams. Aspen are also appreciated for their scenic value, especially their golden colors in the fall.

With very few exceptions, aspen stands in the Blue Mountains have been declining in number, area, and stocking. This unfortunate situation has prompted action by managers of both public and private lands to protect, restore, and propagate aspen. United States Department of Agriculture (USDA) Forest Service land managers have gained considerable experience in aspen management over the past 25 years. The purpose of the present publication is to summarize the state of our knowledge about the biology, ecology, and management of aspen, especially as it pertains to the Blue Mountains area. The local experience with aspen described here was obtained mainly on lands of the Malheur, Umatilla, and Wallowa-Whitman National Forests of northeastern Oregon and adjacent Washington and Idaho (fig. 1). Our results will apply most closely to this ecological region, but they should also be pertinent to other parts of the semiarid Western United States.

Aspen Biology and Ecology

Aspen Clones and Root System

Aspen trees have the unique ability to spread laterally by roots and produce new stems (traditionally called suckers) that develop into trees. As a result, a grove of genetically identical aspen trees can develop from a single seedling that germinated some time in the past (Barnes 1966). Although individual aspen stems are relatively short-lived (roughly 100 years), the clone itself may have existed for thousands of years. An aspen clone has existed for perhaps thousands of years in the Morsay Creek drainage of the North Fork John Day Ranger District (Shirley and Erickson 2001). One clone in Utah covers 107 acres, and its growth to this size must have taken thousands of years (Kemperman and Barnes 1976).

Many tree characteristics, such as leaf shape and size, bark color, branching habit, autumn leaf color, and disease resistance, are remarkably uniform within a clone but differ from one clone to another; in other words, clones are phenotypically diverse (Barnes 1975). Where clones grow together, variations in one or more of these characteristics can sometimes be used to identify different clones in the field without the cost of genetic testing.

Aspen roots can grow laterally far from their parent trees and produce suckers. Excavations of aspen root systems in the Great Lakes region revealed root growth rates of 2.5 ft/year (Day 1944) to 4.5 ft/year (Buell and Buell 1959) in good soils without competing trees. Some managers believe that aspen clones grow preferentially in the south and southwesterly direction from the parent tree, presumably in response to increased light and higher soil temperatures. Root connections between developing trees persist even as some of the stems along a root die owing to natural self-thinning (DesRochers and Lieffers 2001a).

Although the large interconnected root system in aspen supports new suckers, the suckers also support the root system, both in laterally expanding clones and clones regenerating after disturbance. Root segments distal to a sucker (farther from the older trees) are enlarged for several feet (fig. 2) (Barnes 1966, Gifford 1966). In other words, the parent root has faster radial growth on the distal side of the sucker, suggesting that most of the photosynthates are directed toward the distal side of the parent root. Thus suckers contribute to the health and vigor of the root system and promote its continued spread. After the aboveground portion of an aspen clone is killed by disturbance (e.g., fire or clearcutting), an abundant crop of suckers can produce enough photosynthate to maintain much of the preexisting root system, such that only large roots at the bases of former trees may die (DesRochers and Lieffers 2001b). The regenerating stand can thus benefit from the nutrient- and water-gathering ability of an extensive established root system.

Reproduction

Aspen are unique among the major western tree species in that they reproduce almost exclusively by vegetative means. The ability to regenerate vegetatively allows aspen to thrive after disturbance such as fire. Periodic disturbance is necessary to maintain clone vigor. Root suckers benefit from stored carbohydrate reserves and an established root system, allowing them to grow rapidly and initially outcompete other tree species that must regenerate from seed. Aspen's ability to sprout from roots aids it in colonizing sites such as moist meadows with dense herbaceous vegetation where seedling establishment is difficult.

Sucker production in aspen is strongly influenced by the interplay of plant growth hormones. Suckering is suppressed by a plant growth hormone called auxin (Schier 1973). Auxin is produced by the aerial parts of the tree, including the stem, and moves downward along with carbohydrates in the phloem. The hormonal control exerted by a stem over the root system is called "apical dominance" (Schier et al. 1985a).

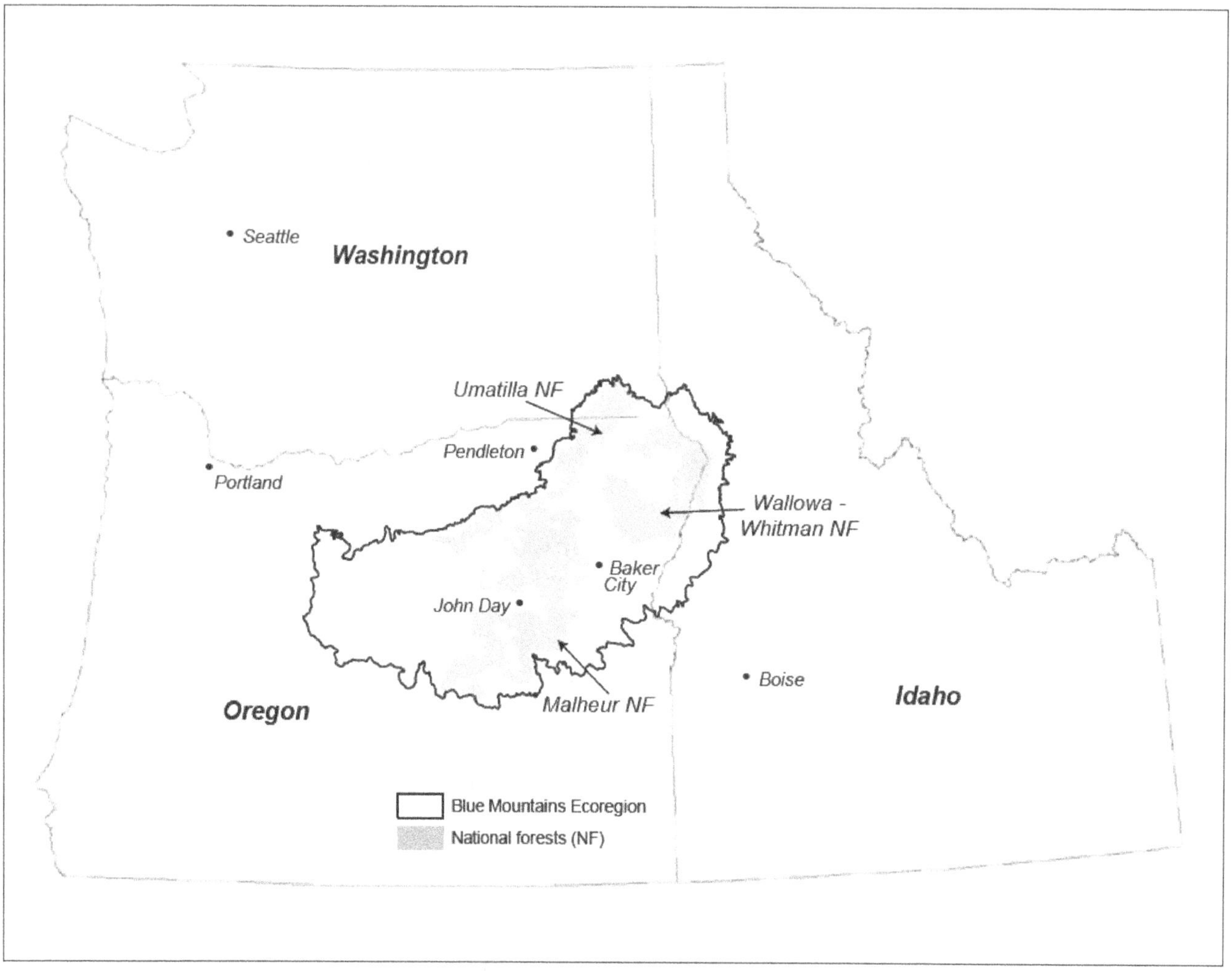

Figure 1–Blue Mountains aspen study area. Most of the data and experience that went into this publication was gained from the national forest lands within the Blue Mountains Ecoregion (boundaries from USEPA 2007).

Alicia Ritner

Figure 2–A 20-ft-long root excavated from a sod-covered meadow. This root yielded several hundred plantable trees. The parent tree of this root was located to the left side of the photo, and the significant enlargement of the root can be seen particularly near the left hand of the person on the left and in front of the person second from right; in both cases the swelling is distal to a sucker.

When auxin movement into roots is halted or reduced by cutting, burning, girdling, killing, or defoliating the stems, auxin levels in the roots decline rapidly. Whereas auxin acts to suppress sucker production, another group of growth hormones–cytokinins–are produced by the root system and promote sucker initiation and development. Cytokinins and water move upward toward the crown through a tree's xylem. High ratios of cytokinin to auxin favor sucker initiation, but low ratios inhibit it (Schier 1973, 1975; Schier et al. 1985a). Cytokinin production apparently may also be stimulated by increasing soil temperatures alone (Williams 1972), for example, after removal of conifers shading a sparse aspen stand. However, if the aspen overstory layer is continuous, conifer removal is likely to stimulate overstory tree growth and suckering will continue to be suppressed.

It is common in the Blue Mountains to see two-storied aspen stands with an open cohort of mature and overmature aspen (often overtopped by conifers), and a relatively sparse cohort of aspen suckers or saplings. As overstory mortality causes reduced auxin production, limited amounts of aspen suckering occur. The age of a lower layer–if present at all–typically coincides with the date at which fencing was constructed, allowing the aspen suckers to escape herbivory.

After a change in hormone balance triggers a new aspen cohort, carbohydrate reserves stored in the root system supply the energy needed for sucker initiation and early development. An elongating sucker is entirely dependent upon the parent root system until it emerges from the soil and can begin photosynthesizing on its own (Schier and Zasada 1973, Tew 1970). Low carbohydrate reserves allow fewer root buds to initiate into suckers, or it results in some of the elongating suckers not being able to reach the soil surface, and either condition contributes to reduced aspen regeneration (Schier et al. 1985a).

A land manager can actively intervene to promote a new cohort of young aspen stems by killing the overstory aspen trees, thus reducing or eliminating auxin production and its inhibitory effect on sucker production. This tactic involves risk, however, because carbohydrates produced by overstory trees nourish the root system; if killing the overstory aspen trees does not result in suckering, both the root system and the clone might be lost.

A healthy aspen clone that has received strong hormonal stimulation by overstory removal will produce stem densities far in excess of what can be supported in a mature stand; densities as high as 30,000 stems/acre have been reported in the Rocky Mountain region (Schier et al. 1985a). In contrast to conifer stands, where very high seedling densities result in stunted growth owing to competition, dense stands of aspen suckers are thought to be beneficial to the future of the clone: high initial densities are able to maintain the clonal root biomass of the predisturbance

stand so that it will be available in the future, and they limit competing vegetation (DesRochers and Lieffers 2001b, Frey et al. 2003). Sucker densities are highest where predisturbance aspen stocking is high. Removal of the aboveground stems in the dormant season results in more suckers than does stem removal in June or July, because carbohydrate reserves are low at the latter time and peak hormone production is past (Schier 1976, Schier et al. 1985b, Webber 1990). In dense stands that form after fire or clearcutting, sucker numbers peak in the first or second growing season after the disturbance and decline rapidly by self-thinning in the first few years thereafter (Shepperd 1993). After conifer removal, the suckering response is more prolonged, and new suckers may appear for 4 or more years (Jones et al. 2005).

Sucker growth rate and survival is strongly dependent on light availability (Farmer 1963, Sandberg and Schneider 1953). Under well-stocked overstories, some aspen suckers appear but most die within a few years (Baker 1925). Under more open canopies, more suckers survive and they grow faster, which increases their chance of escaping herbivores. The suckers in a two-layer stand generally have low vigor as a result of ungulate browsing, shading by overstory aspen or encroaching conifers, and continuing influence from auxin produced by overstory aspen trees. However, satisfactory aspen regeneration can occur with a residual overstory basal area of about 50 ft^2/ac on good sites in New Mexico and Colorado (Walters et al. 1982).

High soil temperatures are considered by many to be important in stimulating suckering and enhancing sucker growth rates (Maine and Horton 1966, Zasada and Schier 1973). High temperatures are thought to favor suckering by affecting the cytokinin production as mentioned above, and by allowing faster physiological growth processes (Frey et al. 2003). Cold soils result in less leaf area for photosynthesis and reduced photosynthetic rates (Jackson 1993, Lawrence and Oechel 1983). Soil temperatures in the 70s and 80s °F appear to be optimal (Maine and Horton 1966). Soil temperatures under Douglas-fir (*Pseudotsuga menziesii*) (see app. B for plant names and authorities) were found to be distinctly lower than under aspen in northern New Mexico, especially on south-facing slopes (Gary 1968). Soil temperatures increase when the overstory is removed and more sunlight reaches the soil surface. The same is observed after fires, when the insulating litter is removed and the blackened soil surface absorbs sunlight (Hungerford 1988). Large amounts of slash or chipped residue can retard suckering by reducing soil temperatures (Frey et al. 2003, Schier et al. 1985b), as can a dense herbaceous vegetation layer (Landhäusser and Lieffers 1998).

Existing aspen clones can also expand laterally by root growth and suckering beyond the existing perimeter of

David Swanson

Figure 3–Aspen established naturally from seed inside of a ponderosa pine seed tree exclosure after the 1989 Dooley Mountain wildfire. The photo was taken in 2003.

roots. Most suckers develop within about 30 ft of an existing stem, although in patches of severely hedged suckers, they can appear much farther from any normally developed stems. Suckers generally develop from horizontal roots that are 1 to 6 in below the surface and less than 2 inches in diameter (Schier and Campbell 1978).

Aspen are dioecious (male and female flowers are borne on separate plants). They produce numerous, small, wind-borne seeds. Seed reproduction by aspen is limited by short seed viability and exacting seedbed requirements (McDonough 1985). Aspen seed viability declines quickly under natural conditions to negligible levels within 2 months, and seedlings require a moist mineral seedbed for germination and early growth. Seed production in our area may be limited by the scarcity of female clones growing in proximity to a male clone for pollination.

Although aspen reproduce predominantly by vegetative means, we have observed reproduction by seed after fires in the Blue Mountains. Our best-documented example is a group of aspen in a seed tree exclosure established after

the 1989 Dooley Mountain Fire in T11S, R40E, section 24, south of Baker City (fig. 3) (see also the genetics section below). There were no aspen stems in this area prior to the fire, and the nearest seed source is several miles away. As discussed further below, dry summers in the Blue Mountains make seedling establishment very difficult, and present herbivore levels in the Blue Mountains make survival of any seedlings unlikely.

Ecological Range

Quaking aspen is the most widespread tree in North America (Perala 1990). It grows in a wide variety of environments, such as temperate hardwood forests of eastern North America, as scattered groves in Great Plains grasslands, in riparian zones of semidesert shrub-steppes in the intermountain West, and in cold boreal forests of high elevation and in the far north near arctic treeline. It is shade intolerant and occurs as an early seral species in most environments. In the Blue Mountains, it is mostly restricted to riparian communities and moist areas, but occasionally occurs in upland areas and talus slopes. More information on aspen communities is given in the aspen community classification chapter of this publication.

Temperature–
Aspen are highly tolerant of cold winter temperatures. Experiments with dormant twigs show that aspen can survive winter temperatures below -112 °F (-80 °C) (Sakai and Weiser 1973), which is considerably lower than any temperature ever recorded in the Blue Mountains. Among aspen's conifer competitors, lodgepole pine (*Pinus contorta*), Engelmann spruce (*Picea engelmannii*), and subalpine fir (*Abies lasiocarpa*) are also resistant to extremely low temperatures when dormant, but grand fir (*Abies grandis*), ponderosa pine (*Pinus ponderosa*), Douglas-fir, and western larch (*Larix occidentalis*) show damage at temperatures in the -22 °F to -40 °F (-30 °C to -40 °C) range (Sakai and Weiser 1973). Only a few localities in the Blue Mountains (Seneca and Ukiah, Oregon) (Western Regional Climate Center 2007) have recorded temperatures below -40 °F, and the less cold-tolerant tree species are ubiquitous in the Blue Mountains. Thus the relatively mild winters in the Blue Mountains allow more competing conifers to grow here than in colder environments.

Summer frosts of 26.6 °F (-3 °C) do not harm aspen leaves, but most leaves are killed by temperatures of 21.2 °F (-6 °C) (Lamontagne et al. 1998). Aspen can escape spring frosts by leafing out late (Strain 1966), but this strategy may not be effective where lethal frosts occur throughout the summer. Climatic data for our area (Western Regional Climate Center 2007) show that some locations such as Austin, Seneca, and Ukiah, Oregon, have recorded temperatures in the low 20s °F in June, early July, and late August, which could prevent aspen growth. Meanwhile, ponderosa pine and lodgepole pine can tolerate summer freezes down to about 15 °F (-10 °C) (Cochran and Berntsen 1973, Korstian 1921, Parker 1955).

Soils–
Aspen grow on a wide variety of soil types. Aspen in the Blue Mountains have been documented growing on essentially the full range of soil textures that occur here. These are mostly clay loam, loam, and sandy loam; coarse fragments content ranges from none to so high that the loamy material occurs only in spaces between large rocks of a boulder field. Soils under stable (as opposed to seral) aspen communities in the Western United States are known for their thick, nutrient-rich surface A horizons that are produced by the rich litter of the aspen and associated herbaceous species (Jones and DeByle 1985c). In the Blue Mountains, riparian and meadow aspen usually occur on soils with thick A horizons, although there are factors in addition to the aspen themselves that act to increase soil fer-

tility, including dense herbaceous vegetation, abundant soil moisture, and slow sedimentation by alluviation or slope-wash. For more information on the morphology of soils in Blue Mountains aspen stands, see the aspen community classification section of this publication.

Aspen grow best in near-neutral soils. Aspen are sensitive to aluminum toxicity, and thus in acid soils, aspen growth rates increase with increasing soil pH (Chen et al. 1998, Lu and Sucoff 2003). Poor growth form of aspen saplings that could be attributed to soil pH limitations has been observed in the Blue Mountains on soils with pH readings of about 5.6. Unpublished soils data from the Ecological Unit Inventory of the Blue Mountains (available from the USDA-NRCS National Soils Information System, http://soils.usda.gov/technical/nasis [29 May 2009]) shows that soils with pH less than 6 formed in volcanic ash material are rather common in the grand and subalpine fir zones, and this could limit aspen occurrence there. Aspen regeneration after fires is probably enhanced by the release of bases from burned material that reduce soil acidity.

Soils with an alkaline, calcareous horizon within 2 ft of the surface have been reported to produce poor aspen growth (Jones and DeByle 1985c). Only one of 128 plots with pH data used in the community classification section of this publication had calcareous subsoil, in this case below 14 in deep. Unpublished soils data from the Ecological Unit Inventory of the Blue Mountains show that calcareous soils with pH greater than 8 are quite rare on national forest lands in the Blue Mountains, but they are common at lower elevations in the area (e.g., Laird 1997).

Moisture–
Soil moisture is more important to aspen than soil texture per se, because aspen are not well adapted to extremes of either wetness or dryness (Jones and DeByle 1985c). Aspen occur on some of the wettest sites in our area, giving the impression that they require saturated soils. In fact, aspen's coincidence with wetland habitats in the Blue Mountains is unusual from the perspective of aspen habitats across its whole range, where it is a typical mesic-site species. Aspen roots die in water-saturated, anaerobic soils (Bates et al. 1998), and we must assume that the aspen we see in wetlands of the Blue Mountains are finding rooting space in the aerated soil above the water table. Aspen's ability to sprout from roots is probably an important factor in its survival in wetlands in our area. An episode of high water table could kill most of the roots and tops of an aspen clone, but as long as some roots survive in a better-aerated part of the wetland, the clone can resprout and survive. Aspen can spread by root sprouts from these refugia in a subsequent dry climatic cycle and have a competitive advantage over conifers, which are also killed in anaerobic wet soils but must regenerate by seed in the dense sod of meadow vegetation.

Moist sites suitable for aspen may have been more widespread in the past when beavers (*Castor canadensis*) were common in the Blue Mountains. Beaver dams increase water storage in headwater streams, raise the water table in riparian zones, and increase the area of moist riparian habitat (Kay 1994). Aspen are well adapted to propagate around beaver ponds. Aspen can spread by root growth around and into lush meadows such as those that form along beaver ponds. The moist mud exposed after beaver dams breach is a good seed environment for willows (*Salix* sp.) and cottonwood (*Populus trichocarpa*) (Demmer and Beschta 2008). The seed physiology and ecology of these plants are similar to aspen, and we can surmise that beavers increase the opportunity for aspen seedling establishment. Aspen is a preferred food of beaver, but beaver use tends to be episodic, allowing plants to resprout after cutting (Demmer and Beschta 2008).

Aspen are moderately drought-tolerant and occupy the grassland-forest ecotone in cold climates (Lieffers et al. 2001). The leaf fluttering that gives quaking aspen its name is widely thought to be an adaptation that cools leaf temperatures and allows aspen to tolerate drought better than most other temperate-zone broadleaf deciduous trees. However, in our area, several other tree species (western juniper, ponderosa pine, and probably Douglas-fir) are more drought-tolerant than aspen. At low elevations in the Blue Mountains, where vegetation is mostly ponderosa pine forest, juniper woodland, sagebrush steppe, or grassland, aspen are limited by dryness to spatially very restricted sites with abundant soil moisture, such as wetlands and riparian areas. In environments with more precipitation—those that support grand and subalpine fir–aspen have been documented in the Blue Mountains on a wide variety of upland habitats (see the community classification portion of this publication), although they are still uncommon and most frequent on relatively moist sites.

In the Intermountain Region, aspen are most common where mean annual precipitation is at least 20 in, although on moist sites they are common where precipitation is as low as 15 in (Jones and DeByle 1985a). The 20-in minimum for aspen to occur on upland sites is met over much of the Blue Mountains where grand fir is present, as shown by data for weather stations at Meacham, Granite, and Austin, Oregon (Western Regional Climate Center 2007), and USDA-NRCS SNOTEL precipitation monitoring stations (USDA NRCS 2007). However, nowhere in the portions of the West where aspen are prominent (i.e., Utah and Colorado) are routine summer droughts as severe as in the Blue Mountains. In the Blue Mountains, most stations with annual precipitation of 20 to 40 in (i.e., locations with annual precipitation totals adequate for aspen) average less than 2 in total for July and August. Summers are also dry

in central Utah where aspen are widespread, but there most sites with aspen average at least 3 in total precipitation for July and August (Jones and DeByle 1985a, USDA NRCS 2007).

Competition and Succession

Aspen is a shade-intolerant, early-seral species (Perala 1990). Even our least shade-tolerant conifer, western juniper (*Juniperus occidentalis*) (Minore 1979), can outcompete aspen (Wall et al. 2001). Aspen's ability to reproduce by root suckers and grow rapidly allow it to thrive as a seral species when conifers are removed by disturbance such as fire. Succession of aspen to conifers in our area is driven by both the greater shade tolerance of the conifers, and by competition for moisture. Conifers intercept more moisture than aspen, especially snow (DeByle 1985c). In the Blue Mountains, where most of the precipitation occurs as snow and summer moisture is very limited, this probably results in considerably less available soil moisture under conifers. As most of our conifers are more drought-tolerant than aspen, their presence probably provides a positive feedback mediated by soil moisture that promotes continued replacement of aspen by conifers.

Most aspen stands in the Blue Mountains are seral to conifers. Extensive stands of aspen forests that are stable or succeeding very slowly to conifers, such as those in the Intermountain Region (Mueggler 1988), are not present in the Blue Mountains. Only in rare microsites do aspen appear to be stable in our area. Aspen sometimes occur in narrow stands fringing wetlands that are not obviously succeeding to conifers. Here, aspen's ability to tolerate fluctuating wetness conditions and reproduce by suckering in dense meadow sod may allow it to locally outcompete conifers. Aspen also occasionally occur in rubble or talus fields where conifer seedling establishment is rare but aspen can spread successfully by root suckering. These rubble and talus environments also serve as refugia from browsing ungulates, which typically avoid extremely rocky areas or talus slopes.

Fire Effects

Aspen is well known as a postfire seral species. After stand-replacing fires, it regenerates abundantly by suckering and grows rapidly. Fire stimulates suckering by removal of the aspen overstory (which alters the hormone balance) and by postfire warming of the soil associated with reduced crown shading. Suckers thrive in the abundance of light and generally outgrow other trees species that regenerate by seed (Jones and DeByle 1985b). Aspen establishment by seed, although rare in comparison to vegetative regeneration, is more likely to occur on bare soil after fire than in a densely vegetated community. The reduced frequency of wildfires starting around 1900 in the Blue Mountains (Heyerdahl et al. 2001) is widely believed to be an important factor in the decline of aspen here.

Aspen are highly fire-adapted, but aspen-dominated communities do not burn readily (Jones and Debyle 1985b). Aspen foliage is not highly flammable, and the moist herbaceous vegetation that typically forms the understory often will support only light ground fires or no fire at all. Severe fires in aspen are much more likely when there is a dense understory of shrubs or conifers (Jones and Debyle 1985b). Under the historical fire regime of the Blue Mountains, with its severe late-summer droughts that spawned frequent fires, invasion of aspen stands by conifers probably set the stage for stand-replacing fires that would kill the conifers and allow aspen to regenerate.

The numerous accounts in the literature of aspen fire ecology deal primarily with stand-replacing fires. Little has been written about the effect of low-severity fires in mixed aspen-conifer stands. This topic is especially pertinent because frequent low-severity underburns were the historical fire regime of most low-elevation forests in the Blue Mountains (Heyerdahl et al. 2001), and aspen occur here in small stands mixed with conifers. Prescribed fires in our area are also typically low-severity underburns, because the goal is usually to reduce fuels and thin small trees while retaining most large conifers. Several of aspen's serious conifer competitors–ponderosa pine, Douglas-fir, western larch, and grand fir–are distinctly more tolerant of fires than aspen once they have achieved a diameter of 1 to 2 in. Thus, light fire in forests of aspen mixed with these species could kill most of the aspen while leaving intact a conifer overstory that will shade out and kill any aspen regeneration. Keyser et al. (2005) studied light and moderate-severity fires in small aspen clones with conifer invasion in the Black Hills of South Dakota. They found that with both types of fires, more aspen died than ponderosa pine; suckering was not significantly stimulated by light fires, and light fires hasten the succession of aspen to conifers by preferentially killing overstory aspen. The implication is that low-severity fires in stands of aspen mixed with mature fire-tolerant conifers will not favor aspen.

Herbivores and Aspen

Aspen communities provide important wildlife habitat in the Western United States used by a wide variety of ungulates, small mammals, and birds (DeByle 1985b). Aspen is a highly preferred forage species for domestic cattle (*Bos taurus*), deer, and elk in the Blue Mountains; this is a major factor contributing to poor aspen regeneration (Shirley and Erickson 2001). Most aspen in our area are either mature trees well beyond the reach of ungulate herbivores, or suckers with arrested-type growth form indicative of continu-

ous intense browsing (Keigly and Frisina 1998, Keigley et al. 2002). An unbrowsed aspen sapling is a rare sight in the Blue Mountains outside of an exclosure. Moose (*Alces alces*), which have recently become established in the northern Umatilla National Forest, may add to aspen regeneration problems if they become common. Our observations suggest that wild and domestic ungulates impact aspen most in the late summer and fall when herbaceous vegetation has senesced and aspen leaves are still green. At this time, browsers strip leaves and trim fine green stems (fig. 4). When elk and moose winter among aspen, they also consume larger twigs. Elk are well known for eating the bark off larger trees in the winter (DeByle 1985a). This provides entry for diseases and occasionally causes tree death by girdling (fig. 5).

Aspen's relative scarcity in our area, combined with high palatability, make it highly vulnerable to browsing. Browsing pressure on aspen is greatest when sucker densities are low (Shepperd 1993) and where size classes of aspen susceptible to browsing occur in small patches of less than 12 ac (Mueggler and Bartos 1977). Nearly all of the aspen stands in the Blue Mountains occur in small patches, and nearly all unfenced stands have low sucker density, making them particularly susceptible to browsing.

Aspen Occurrence in the Blue Mountains

Aspen is a widespread yet uncommon species in the Blue Mountains. Detailed inventories performed on some ranger districts have located hundreds of stands, broadly distributed over our entire area (fig. 6). Although these aspen stands are numerous, they are invariably small. An inventory of approximately 25 percent of the 1.7-million-ac Malheur National Forest has revealed 1,327 stands, with a median area of less than 1 ac; only 5 percent of the stands are greater than 10 ac. The Umatilla National Forest's inventory (514 stands) also shows a median area of less than 1 ac and only 1 percent of the stands larger than 10 ac. The total basal area of aspen is also quite low, less even than the very locally distributed species western white pine (*Pinus monticola*), mountain hemlock (*Tsuga mertensiana*), and black cottonwood, according to Current Vegetation Survey (CVS) data (Johnson 2001) from the three national forests in the Blue Mountains.

As described below, aspen are currently in decline in the Blue Mountains, but historical photography (Skovlin and Thomas 1992) and early accounts (Bright 1994) indicate that aspen forests were never as widespread here as in other parts of the West such as Colorado (Manier and Laven 2002) and Utah (Mueggler 1988). The historical rarity of aspen in the Blue Mountains, even where mean annual precipitation is apparently adequate (over 20 in), is puzzling. Herbivory is obviously responsible for much of the decline

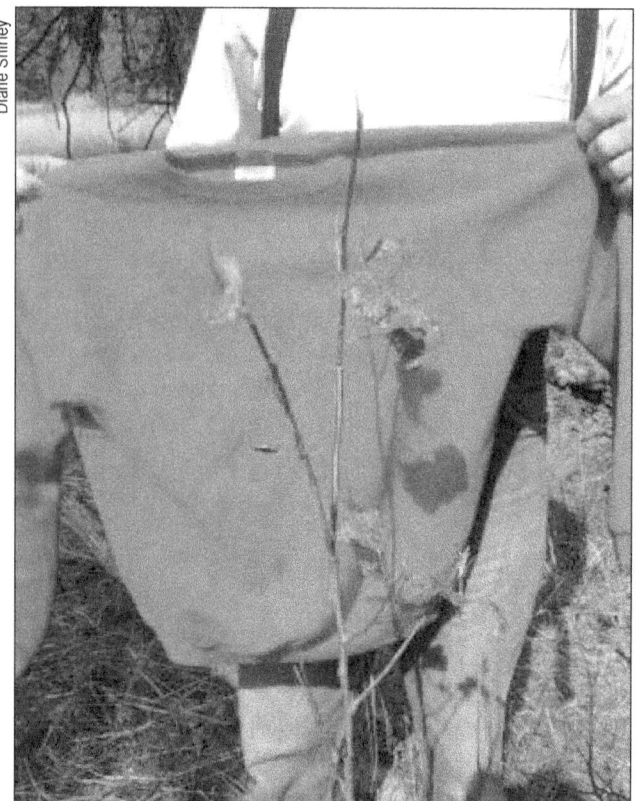

Figure 4–Example of aspen browsing by elk.

Figure 5–Bark damage by elk tooth scraping has girdled and killed this tree.

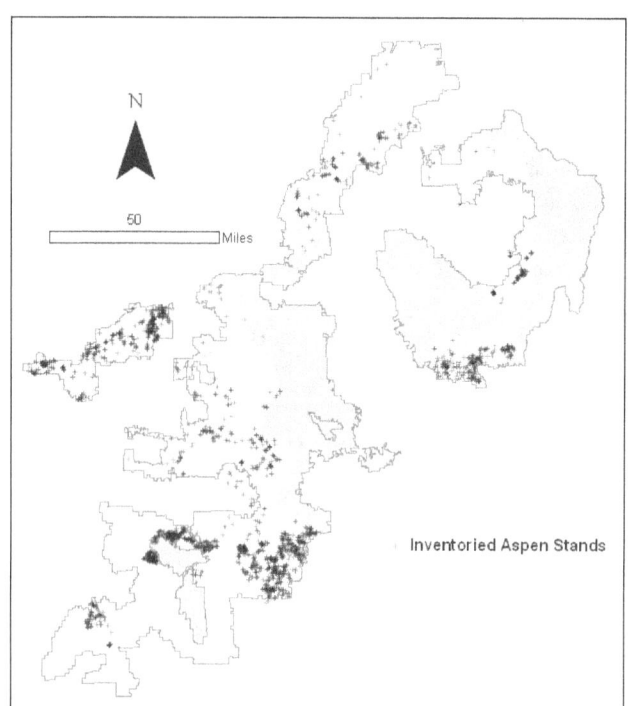

Figure 6–Locations of inventoried aspen stands in the Malheur, Umatilla, and Wallowa-Whitman National Forests. Shaded administrative units have no data. Areas with many overlapping label points appear black. Sampling effort is uneven, which is responsible for some of the patchiness apparent in aspen occurrence.

in recent decades, but it alone cannot explain the historical low abundance of aspen here, because historically aspen were eaten by the same herbivores in the Blue Mountains as they were elsewhere in the West.

Our current working hypothesis is that, historically, climate and conifer competition interacted in the Blue Mountains to keep aspen abundance lower than in many other parts of the West; this low abundance has in turn made aspen more vulnerable here to modern negative factors such as increased herbivory and fire suppression. Eight species of coniferous trees are common across the Blue Mountains, and all are more shade tolerant than aspen. Two of the conifers (western larch and lodgepole pine) are fast-growing disturbance-adapted species like aspen, and two others (western juniper and ponderosa pine) are clearly more drought tolerant than aspen. The environmental factors that give conifers a competitive edge in the Blue Mountains were discussed above and are summarized as follows. First, the relatively mild winters of the Blue Mountains allow the growth of several temperate-zone conifer species that cannot survive over most of aspen's range. Second, although winters in the Blue Mountains are relatively mild, summer frosts can be severe and are more lethal to aspen than at least some of the conifers. Third, extreme precipitation seasonality is a factor, perhaps the most important. The severe summer droughts in the Blue Mountains present challenges for establishment of trees of any species, but especially for aspen with their tiny, short-lived seeds. Finally, soils with pH less than 6 formed in volcanic ash are fairly common in moist grand fir and sub-alpine fir forests of the Blue Mountains; this gives the more acid-tolerant conifers a competitive advantage even in areas where aspen are less limited by drought.

The hypothesis that conifer competition is the critical factor that has historically limited aspen's overall abundance in our area is supported by aspen's abundance on certain isolated mountains in eastern Oregon where the assortment of competing conifers is restricted. On Steens Mountain in east-central Oregon, where western juniper is the only widespread conifer, aspen form extensive pure stands in the 7,000- to 7,500-ft elevation range above a zone dominated by juniper. In the Trout Creek Mountains of southeastern Oregon, even junipers are rare, and aspen forms large groves at about 7,500-ft elevation in a landscape otherwise dominated by sagebrush. On Big and Little Lookout Mountains in northeastern Oregon (Baker County), aspen is widespread in mixed stands with juniper and Douglas-fir (fig. 7). Here lodgepole pine is absent, ponderosa pine is restricted to one small occurrence, and grand fir and larch occur only on restricted sites with favorable north aspects.

Decline of Aspen in the Blue Mountains

There is consensus among Forest Service land managers that aspen are seriously declining in the Blue Mountains (Shirley and Erickson 2001). A decline in the area occupied by aspen can be inferred from observations of dead aspen representing former groves with no survivors, the predominance of clones where many individuals are decadent or dead (fig. 8), and the rarity of unbrowsed aspen suckers or young age cohorts. The amount of decline in area of aspen since the arrival of Europeans is not known. The two main factors believed to be responsible for the decline of aspen in the Blue Mountains are herbivory and shading by conifers (Shirley and Erickson 2001). In most aspen stands, regeneration has been suppressed to some degree by both processes.

Herbivory–
Although many herbivores use aspen, those most often mentioned as responsible for aspen decline in the Blue Mountains are domestic cattle, elk, and deer (mainly mule deer, *Odocoileus hemionus*). Exclosures erected in the Blue Mountains to protect aspen have clearly demonstrated that these herbivores strongly suppress aspen regeneration in our area.

The most obvious reason for increased herbivore pressure on aspens in historical times is the introduction of domestic

David Swanson

Figure 7–Aspen and Douglas-fir mosaic with steppe on Big Lookout Mountains, Baker County, Oregon. Shallow soils are steppe or steppe with scattered juniper (*Juniperus occidentalis*). Deeper soils have mixed aspen and Douglas-fir forest with shrub understory. This scene illustrates how aspen occupies a wide variety of upland sites when these two conifer species are its only competitors. Western larch (*Larix occidentalis*) is also present in the vicinity, but only on north-facing aspects not visible in this photograph.

Michael Tatum

Figure 8–This aspen clone near Crane Crossing on the Malheur National Forest suffered severe encroachment by ponderosa pine and is completely dead. The numerous white downed aspen trunks are evidence of a former dense aspen stand.

livestock (cattle, sheep, and horses). Livestock represent a negative effect that was entirely absent prior to the arrival of Europeans. Today cattle are the most important species of livestock, and they alone appear capable of preventing aspen regeneration in many areas. Livestock populations were much higher in the early 1900s than they are today, owing primarily to large numbers of sheep (Galbraith and Anderson 1971, Irwin et al. 1994, Powell 2008); this suggests that livestock have inhibited aspen regeneration here for over a century.

The population densities of native browsers in the Blue Mountains prior to European settlement remain unknown, although elk populations have increased substantially in the Blue Mountains since their near extirpation in the late 1800s (Irwin et al. 1994). Several factors combine to make native herbivore browsing effects significant today, regardless of whether numbers are actually greater now than historically. First, there is probably lower overall diversity and quantity of browse plants available to herbivores today than in the past, which concentrates browsing pressure on remaining palatable plants such as aspen. We suspect that the abundance of many palatable species decreased during the peak of livestock numbers in the early 1900s. Continued heavy use today suggests a long-term decline of many palatable species, including western serviceberry (*Amelanchier alnifolia*), common chokecherry and bitter cherry (*Prunus virginiana* and *P. emarginata*), yew (*Taxus brevifolia*), curlleaf mountain mahogany (*Cercocarpus ledifolius*), bitterbrush (*Purshia tridentata*), Rocky Mountain maple (*Acer glabrum*), Cascade mountain ash (*Sorbus scopulina*), willow, cottonwood, and elderberry (*Sambucus cerulea* and *S. racemosa*). Exclosure studies in the Blue Mountains show that ungulates are indeed limiting shrub biomass at the present (Riggs et al. 2000). Because most of these browse plants are shade-intolerant early-seral species, fire suppression has also probably led to their decline. In addition, many low-elevation areas that once served as winter range for deer and elk are now occupied by farms and cities. Decline in all palatable browse species (including aspen), without a corresponding decline in herbivore numbers, concentrates continued use on remaining plants and is a positive feedback on their decline.

Finally, the behavior of native browsers has probably changed in the absence of their main historical predator–the gray wolf (*Canis lupus*). Studies in Yellowstone National Park have shown that aspen regeneration has improved since the reintroduction of wolves, and that both reduction in elk density and changes in elk behavior are responsible (Fortin et al. 2005, Halofsky and Ripple 2008, Ripple and Beschta 2007, Ripple et al. 2001). Damage of aspen by elk is particularly severe where elk are sedentary in aspen stands, a behavior that was presumably less common in our area when wolves were present. Also, postfire recruitment of aspen is probably more successful in the presence of wolves, because the thickets of aspen regeneration (which restrict visibility) and fire-killed dead-fallen trees (which are potential obstacles to elk escape) create a risky environment that elk may avoid (Halofsky et al. 2008).

Shading by conifers–
Loss of aspen owing to competition from more shade-tolerant species is a natural process that on a landscape scale was historically balanced by disturbance, primarily by fire, and to a lesser degree by other processes such as windthrow, insect outbreaks, and snow avalanches. Fire frequency in the Blue Mountains decreased abruptly about 1900 (Heyerdahl et al. 2001) owing to livestock grazing and fire suppression, and it is widely believed that this has allowed the more long-lived and shade-tolerant conifers to replace aspen.

Other factors–
The decline of aspen in the Blue Mountains may have also been furthered by reduction of soil moisture in some habitats. Soil moisture has been reduced by conifer encroachment (both in the aspen stands themselves and in the surrounding watersheds) and by lowered water tables resulting from downcutting of streams after extirpation of beavers (Finley 1937) and introduction of livestock. Beavers were historically present throughout the Blue Mountains before being extirpated by trappers in the early 1800s (Ontko 1993, Robbins 1997). They are still only locally present in our area and functioning dams are rare. As discussed above in connection with the effect of moisture on aspen, beavers increase the area of moist riparian habitat favorable to aspen, and the near extirpation of beavers over 150 years ago was probably the first step in the long-term decline of aspen in the Blue Mountains.

Invasive Plants and Aspen

Our sample of 220 plots in aspen stands, which was taken for the aspen community classification section of this report and is described in detail there, includes five species currently listed on the Oregon State Noxious Weeds list (table 1). This sample is neither exhaustive nor statistically representative, but nonetheless provides a picture of the typical weed problems in aspen stands. Three of the weed species are rather common (were recorded on over 5 percent of all plots), but canopy cover is low. The moist soils of aspen stands tend to produce a dense sod that inhibits the development of a high weed cover, although this sod often consists of nonnative species such as Kentucky bluegrass (*Poa pratensis*). Livestock grazing is often responsible for the surface disturbance that allows weed establishment and can also lead to the formation of a sod of introduced pasture grasses with low diversity of native forbs. More information on grazing effects on aspen communities is found in the aspen community classification section of this publication.

Bird Use of Aspen Habitats in the Blue Mountains

Scant information is available for avian species composition in aspen communities in the Blue Mountains.

Table 1—Oregon state listed noxious weeds[a] recorded in plots on aspen stands

Latin name	Common name	Average cover where present	Constancy[b]
		------------Percent------------	
Agropyron repens	Quackgrass	3	1
Cirsium arvense	Canada thistle	1	6
Cirsium vulgare	Bull thistle	1	18
Cynoglossum officinale	Houndstongue	3	7
Hypericum perforatum	St. Johnswort	1	2

[a] Oregon Department of Agriculture (2008).

[b] Constancy is the percentage of plots where the species was recorded (N = 220).

Consequentially most avian information is extrapolated from studies that cover larger expanses of aspen's range throughout the West, derived from studies unique to a single avian species, or locally observed but anecdotal in nature.

One of the most comprehensive compilations of information on aspen and wildlife in the interior Western United States is Debyle (1985b). Despite the omission of Oregon in its discussion on aspen range, much of the underlying avian information is applicable to the Blue Mountains. A wide variety of avian species are known to use aspen stands (Debyle 1985b). Aspen communities can provide nesting, foraging, and cover habitat. Some species appear tied almost exclusively to aspen habitats, whereas other species may use a variety of habitats. Bird species in aspen can be grouped by their nesting and feeding habits into a series of guilds (Debyle 1985b). Nesting guilds include canopy nesters, shrub or understory nesters, ground nesters, and cavity nesters. Feeding guilds include ground-insect, ground-seed, foliage-insect, air-perching, and air-soaring guilds. As examples, the tree swallow (*Tachycineta bicolor*) is a cavity-nesting, air-soaring, insectivorous species; the warbling vireo (*Vireo gilvus*) is a canopy-nesting, foliage-insect feeder; and the dark-eyed junco (*Junco hyemalis*) is a ground-nesting, ground-seed eater.

Several studies throughout the West have concluded that bird species richness may be greater in more mature aspen stands versus younger stands and in aspen stands as a habitat type versus pure or mixed-conifer-aspen stands (Shepperd et al. 2006). In the Sierra Nevada Mountains, features of aspen stands that appear to increase bird species richness include a thick herbaceous layer for forage and cover; aspen's susceptibility to heart rot, which provides habitat for primary and secondary cavity nesters; and the abundance and diversity of insects in aspen communities (Shepperd et al. 2006). In the Blue Mountains, these correlations may not be as strong given the drier climate and site conditions of local aspen habitats.

Richardson and Heath (2004) studied bird-habitat relationships within and across a range of aspen habitats in eastern Sierra Nevada Mountains of California and Nevada. Bird species richness and abundance were positively correlated with lower percentage of conifer cover, increased herbaceous cover, and lower shrub-class aspen cover. The results suggest that mature aspen stands with healthy herbaceous communities and limited or no conifer intrusion are optimal habitats for aspen-breeding birds in the eastern Sierra Nevada. These researchers suggest that to maximize bird species richness and bird abundance, management actions in aspen stands should concentrate on conifer removal, where conditions warrant, and the promotion of a healthy herbaceous layer. Again, given the wide ecological amplitude of quaking aspen, such correlations should be tested locally in the Blue Mountains before making similar conclusions about bird richness and abundance. Nevertheless, as discussed elsewhere in this publication, the removal of encroaching conifers can be justified for several reasons to ensure aspen persistence.

Two recent studies in the Blue Mountains have monitored avian species in aspen communities: *Diurnal Breeding Birds in Aspen* (Populus tremuloides) *Communities on the Malheur National Forest, 1997* (Cobb 1997) and *Restoring High Priority Habitats for Birds: Aspen and Pine in the Interior West* (Sallabanks et al. 2005).

In the Malheur study, Lynda Cobb of the Grant County Bird Club monitored 34 aspen stands using point counts of 10 minutes duration (table 2) (Cobb 1997). A total of 71 bird species were detected. The top five most frequently detected species were American robin (*Turdus migratorius*), warbling vireo, mountain chickadee (*Poecile gambeli*), northern flicker (*Colaptes auratus*), and western tanager (*Piranga ludoviciana*). A total of 101 active nests were located. Sixty-four cavity nests representing 10 species and 37 open-cup nests representing 8 species made up the total. The top five cavity nesters were red-naped sapsucker (*Sphyrapicus nuchalis*), northern flicker, Williamson's sapsucker (*Sphyrapicus thyroideus*), hairy woodpecker (*Picoides villosus*), and house wren (*Troglodytes aedon*). The top five open-cup nesters were American robin, Hammond's flycatcher (*Empidonax hammondii*), western-wood pewee

(*Contopus sordidulus*), warbling vireo, and dusky flycatcher (*Empidonax oberholseri*).

In the Wallowa Mountains, Sallabanks et al. (2005) are participating in a long-term habitat restoration study, which includes six aspen stands and six ponderosa pine stands. All six aspen stands are fenced to minimize or eliminate herbivory. Initial avian data were collected in 2000 and 2001. Bird count data detected 71 species in the aspen stands (table 3). Species closely associated with aspen included red-naped sapsucker, downy woodpecker (*Picoides pubescens*), dusky flycatcher, common raven (*Corvus corax*), red-winged blackbird (*Agelaius phoeniceus*), house wren, mountain bluebird (*Sialia currucoides*), western bluebird (*Sialia mexicana*), tree swallow, and Williamson's sapsucker. In the aspen stands, a total of 637 nests representing 39 species were identified. Many of the species Sallabanks et al. (2005) found nesting in abundance match those observed by Cobb (1997). In addition, Sallabanks et al. identified chipping sparrow (*Spizella passerina*), dark-eyed junco, mountain chickadee, pygmy nuthatch (*Sitta pygmaea*), red-winged blackbird, tree swallow, western bluebird, and yellow-rumped warbler (*Dendroica coronata*) as relatively abundant nesters in aspen. Multiple species were found nesting exclusively in the aspen stands, with few to no nests in the pine stands.

The Wallowa study (Sallabanks et al. 2005) suggested that aspen communities support a richer breeding bird community than ponderosa pine. This finding agrees with other bird richness studies discussed previously, but contrasts with Sallabanks et al. (2001) who analyzed species habitat associations in forests of eastern Oregon and Washington. In that review, 77 bird species were associated with upland aspen and 131 species were associated with ponderosa pine versus 71 species in aspen and 60 species in pine in the Wallowa study. Sallabanks et al. (2005) suggested that one possible reason for the relatively high number of species detected in the Wallowa study is that the aspen studied did not occur in pure stands of climax forest but rather as mixed seral forest including ponderosa pine, grand fir, lodgepole pine, and western larch. Increased habitat heterogeneity would presumably support a more diverse bird community. As a result, bird species that are not typically considered aspen associates were abundant in the aspen sites (e.g., chipping sparrow and pine siskin *Carduelis pinus*). Consequently, birds considered to be aspen specialists (e.g., red-naped and Williamson's sapsuckers) may suffer negatively from increased competition with other species for resources.

The Oregon/Washington Partners in Flight Northern Rocky Mountains Conservation Plan (Altman 2000) identified aspen as a high-priority habitat for protection and restoration. The plan identifies red-naped sapsucker as the focal

species for this habitat. Data from both the Malheur and Wallowa studies, as well as other bird-aspen habitat studies throughout the West, confirm the importance of aspen to birds and justify its classification by Partners in Flight as a high-priority habitat. Information in the studies reiterates the need for restoration efforts.

Genetic Diversity and Structure of Aspen Stands in the Blue Mountains

Information on genetic variability and clonal structure can aid in the development of efficient restoration strategies for aspen, and in prioritizing stands for treatment and protection. This information is also crucial for preserving aspen genetic resources, an important goal in conservation of "at-risk" species. If an aspen stand is a single clone, for example, protecting a small part of it will preserve existing diversity. If each stand contains many clones, more extensive efforts may be required to conserve genetic diversity. Genetic inventories also provide baseline information for monitoring regeneration and demographic trends, and for determining the effects of management practices and disturbances such as climate change on biodiversity.

In 1997, a genetic survey of aspen stands was initiated in the Blue Mountains. Leaf tissue from root suckers and young saplings was sampled from a total of 92 aspen stands in 7 geographic subregions (fig. 9). The purpose of the project was to (1) determine the number and uniqueness of clones in each stand, (2) determine whether stands are similar or genetically distinct from nearby stands, and (3) assess genetic diversity within and among individual stands and geographic areas within the Blue Mountains.

Samples were collected along transects made through the long axis of each stand. Characteristics such as bark and leaf color, angle between lateral branches and the main bole, degree of straightness of recent shoot extension growth, rust infection, and overall vigor were used to classify shoots as belonging to unique phenotypic groups (putative clones). Only one plant was sampled from each phenotypic group, except in stands comprising one or a very low number of overstory trees, where leaves were collected from at least two trees. Samples were taken at roughly even intervals along each transect, but each putative clone was sampled as well as isolated trees growing within the boundary or on the periphery of the main stand. Therefore, sampling was denser where two or more clones grew together and where tree spacing was uneven. The total number of plants sampled per stand ranged from 2 to 43 (app. A).

Sample/stand location maps were drawn for each site (fig. 10). Clone maps, as well as other study results, are available upon request from V. Erickson. Sampled leaf tissue was transported on ice to the National Forest

Table 2–Diurnal breeding birds in aspen communities on the Malheur National Forest[a]

English name	Latin name	Detections	Detection ranking	Nests found	Nest ranking
American robin	*Turdus migratorius*	102	1	13	2
Warbling vireo	*Vireo gilvus*	81	2	4	6
Mountain chickadee	*Poecile gambeli*	81	2	4	6
Northern flicker	*Colaptes auratus*	66	3	11	3
Western tanager	*Piranga ludoviciana*	65	4		
Hammond's flycatcher	*Empidonax hammondii*	60	5	9	4
Yellow-rumped warbler	*Dendroica coronata*	58	6		
Dark-eyed junco	*Junco hyemalis*	52	7	1	8
Red-naped sapsucker	*Sphyrapicus nuchalis*	50	8	15	1
Western wood-pewee	*Contopus sordidulus*	41	9	4	6
Dusky flycatcher	*Empidonax oberholseri*	41	9	4	6
Cassin's finch	*Carpodacus cassinii*	39	10		
Williamson's sapsucker	*Sphyrapicus thyroideus*	37	11	11	3
Hairy woodpecker	*Picoides villosus*	36	12	9	4
Red-breasted nuthatch	*Sitta canadensis*	36	12		
House wren	*Troglodytes aedon*	33	13	5	5
Chipping sparrow	*Spizella passerina*	32	14	1	8
Lincoln's sparrow	*Melospiza lincolnii*	30	15		
Pine siskin	*Carduelis pinus*	29	16		
Brown-headed cowbird	*Molothrus ater*	29	16		
White-breasted nuthatch	*Sitta carolinensis*	25	17	4	6
Steller's jay	*Cyanocitta stelleri*	17	18		
Hermit thrush	*Catharus guttatus*	15	19		
Wilson's snipe	*Gallinago delicata*	13	20		
Red-winged blackbird	*Agelaius phoeniceus*	12	21		
Downy woodpecker	*Picoides pubescens*	12	21		
Solitary vireo	*Vireo solitarius*	12	21		
Western bluebird	*Sialia mexicana*	12	21	1	8
Red crossbill	*Loxia curvirostra*	11	22		
Western meadowlark	*Sturnella neglecta*	11	22		
Brewer's blackbird	*Euphagus cyanocephalus*	10	23	1	8
Macgillivray's warbler	*Oporornis tolmiei*	10	23		
Ruby-crowned kinglet	*Regulus calendula*	10	23		
Common raven	*Corvus corax*	7	24		
Red-tailed hawk	*Buteo jamaicensis*	7	24		
Black-headed grosbeak	*Pheucticus melanocephalus*	6	25		
Brown creeper	*Certhia americana*	6	25		
Pileated woodpecker	*Dryocopus pileatus*	5	26	2	7
Yellow warbler	*Dendroica petechia*	5	26		
Clark's nutcracker	*Nucifraga columbiana*	4	27		
Hammond's or dusky flycatcher (unknown)	*Empidonax hammondii or oberholseri*	4	27		
Sandhill crane	*Grus canadensis*	4	27		
Townsend's solitaire	*Myadestes townsendi*	4	27		
American crow	*Corvus brachyrhynchos*	3	28		
American kestrel	*Falco sparverius*	3	28		
Lazuli bunting	*Passerina amoena*	3	28		
European starling	*Sturnus vulgaris*	2	29		
Gray jay	*Perisoreus canadensis*	2	29		
Long-billed curlew	*Numenius americanus*	2	29		
Mountain bluebird	*Sialia currucoides*	2	29		

(continued)

Table 2—Diurnal breeding birds in aspen communities on the Malheur National Forest[a] (continued)

English name	Latin name	Detections	Detection ranking	Nests found	Nest ranking
Mourning dove	Zenaida macroura	2	29		
Tree swallow	Tachycineta bicolor	2	29	2	7
Vesper sparrow	Pooecetes gramineus	2	29		
White-headed woodpecker	Picoides albolarvatus	2	29		
Black-backed woodpecker	Picoides arcticus	1	30		
Broad-tailed hummingbird	Selasphorus platycercus	1	30		
Canada goose	Branta canadensis	1	30		
Common nighthawk	Chordeiles minor	1	30		
Evening grosbeak	Coccothraustes vespertinus	1	30		
Golden-crowned kinglet	Regulus satrapa	1	30		
Killdeer	Charadrius vociferus	1	30		
Orange-crowned warbler	Vermivora celata	1	30		
Olive-sided flycatcher	Contopus cooperi	1	30		
Spotted towhee	Pipilo maculatus	1	30		
Rufous hummingbird	Selasphorus rufus	1	30		
Song sparrow	Melospiza melodia	1	30		
Townsend's warbler	Dendroica townsendi	1	30		
Vaux's swift	Chaetura vauxi	1	30		
Willow flycatcher	Empidonax traillii	1	30		

[a] Sampling from 34 aspen stands in 1997. Stands range in size from 1 to 20 ac. Counts of individuals are from a single 10-minute point count at the center of each stand, or multiple points 200 m apart if the stands were large enough. Nest searches were conducted casually in all stands and systematically in seven stands.
Source: Cobb 1997.

Table 3—Breeding birds in aspen in the Wallowa Mountains, 2000 and 2001[a]

English name	Latin name	Detections	Detection ranking	Nests found	Nest ranking
House wren	Troglodytes aedon	248	1	63	1
American robin	Turdus migratorius	236	2	46	3
Warbling vireo	Vireo gilvus	186	3	42	4
Dark-eyed junco	Junco hyemalis	175	4	28	8
Chipping sparrow	Spizella passerina	167	5	32	6
Dusky flycatcher	Empidonax oberholseri	165	6	59	2
European starling	Sturnus vulgaris	162	7	37	5
Pine siskin	Carduelis pinus	158	8	2	23
Mountain chickadee	Poecile gambeli	140	9	30	7
Yellow-rumped warbler	Dendroica coronata	137	10	13	16
Western wood-pewee	Contopus sordidulus	123	11	24	10
Cassin's finch	Carpodacus cassinii	98	12	7	18
Western bluebird	Sialia mexicana	91	13	46	3
Northern flicker	Colaptes auratus	89	14	27	9
Red-breasted nuthatch	Sitta canadensis	81	15	11	17
Ruby-crowned kinglet	Regulus calendula	66	16	2	23
Red-winged blackbird	Agelaius phoeniceus	65	17	23	11
Red crossbill	Loxia curvirostra	62	18		
Hairy woodpecker	Picoides villosus	61	19	15	14
Western meadowlark	Sturnella neglecta	58	20		
Common raven	Corvus corax	57	21		
Brown-headed cowbird	Molothrus ater	51	22		
Tree swallow	Tachycineta bicolor	50	23	20	12
Red-naped sapsucker	Sphyrapicus nuchalis	47	24	24	10

(continued)

Table 3—Breeding birds in aspen in the Wallowa Mountains, 2000 and 2001[a] *(continued)*

English name	Latin name	Detections	Detection ranking	Nests found	Nest ranking
Macgillivray's warbler	*Oporornis tolmiei*	46	25	5	21
Pygmy nuthatch	*Sitta pygmaea*	44	26	18	13
Western tanager	*Piranga ludoviciana*	42	27	3	22
Lincoln's sparrow	*Melospiza lincolnii*	32	28	6	20
Orange-crowned warbler	*Vermivora celata*	27	29		
Hermit thrush	*Catharus guttatus*	27	29		
Mountain bluebird	*Sialia currucoides*	26	30	14	15
White-breasted nuthatch	*Sitta carolinensis*	21	31	8	18
Hammond's flycatcher	*Empidonax hammondii*	19	32	1	
Downy woodpecker	*Picoides pubescens*	17	33	7	19
Williamson's sapsucker	*Sphyrapicus thyroideus*	15	34	8	18
Brewer's sparrow	*Spizella breweri*	12	35		
Golden-crowned kinglet	*Regulus satrapa*	11	36		
Steller's jay	*Cyanocitta stelleri*	11	36		
Western meadowlark	*Sturnella neglecta*	11	36		
Calliope hummingbird	*Stellula calliope*	9	37	1	24
Mountain quail	*Oreortyx pictus*	8	38		
Pileated woodpecker	*Dryocopus pileatus*	8	38	2	23
Clark's nutcracker	*Nucifraga columbiana*	7	39		
Gray jay	*Perisoreus canadensis*	6	40		
Red-tailed hawk	*Buteo jamaicensis*	6	40		
White-crowned sparrow	*Zonotrichia leucophrys*	6	40		
Cassin's vireo	*Vireo cassinii*	6	40		
Rufous hummingbird	*Selasphorus rufus*	5	41		
Brown creeper	*Certhia americana*	4	42	1	24
California quail	*Callipepla californica*	4	42		
Wilson's warbler	*Wilsonia pusilla*	4	42		
Killdeer	*Charadrius vociferus*	3	43		
Lazuli bunting	*Passerina amoena*	3	43		
Spotted towhee	*Pipilo maculatus*	3	43		
Townsend's warbler	*Dendroica townsendi*	3	43		
White-headed woodpecker	*Picoides albolarvatus*	3	43	5	21
American goldfinch	*Carduelis tristis*	2	44		
Black-headed grosbeak	*Pheucticus melanocephalus*	2	44		
Brewer's blackbird	*Euphagus cyanocephalus*	2	44	1	24
Wilson's snipe	*Gallinago delicata*	2	44	1	24
Northern pygmy-owl	*Glaucidium gnoma*	2	44		
Olive-sided flycatcher	*Contopus cooperi*	2	44		
Yellow warbler	*Dendroica petechia*	2	44		
Cedar waxwing	*Bombycilla cedrorum*	1	45		
Common nighthawk	*Chordeiles minor*	1	45		
Prairie falcon	*Falco mexicanus*	1	45		
Ruffed grouse	*Bonasa umbellus*	1	45		
Sharp-shinned hawk	*Accipiter striatus*	1	45		
Song sparrow	*Melospiza melodia*	1	45		
Swainson's thrush	*Catharus ustulatus*	1	45		
Townsend's solitaire	*Myadestes townsendi*	1	45		
Vaux's swift	*Chaetura vauxi*	1	45		

[a] Detections of individuals at 35 fixed-area (50-m-radius) plots in six aspen stands visited multiple times in May-June 2000 and 2001, for a total of 125 point counts. Nest detections were made by comprehensive search of five of the stands, with an average plot area of 43 ac; 2 years of data are combined. Source: Sallabanks 2005.

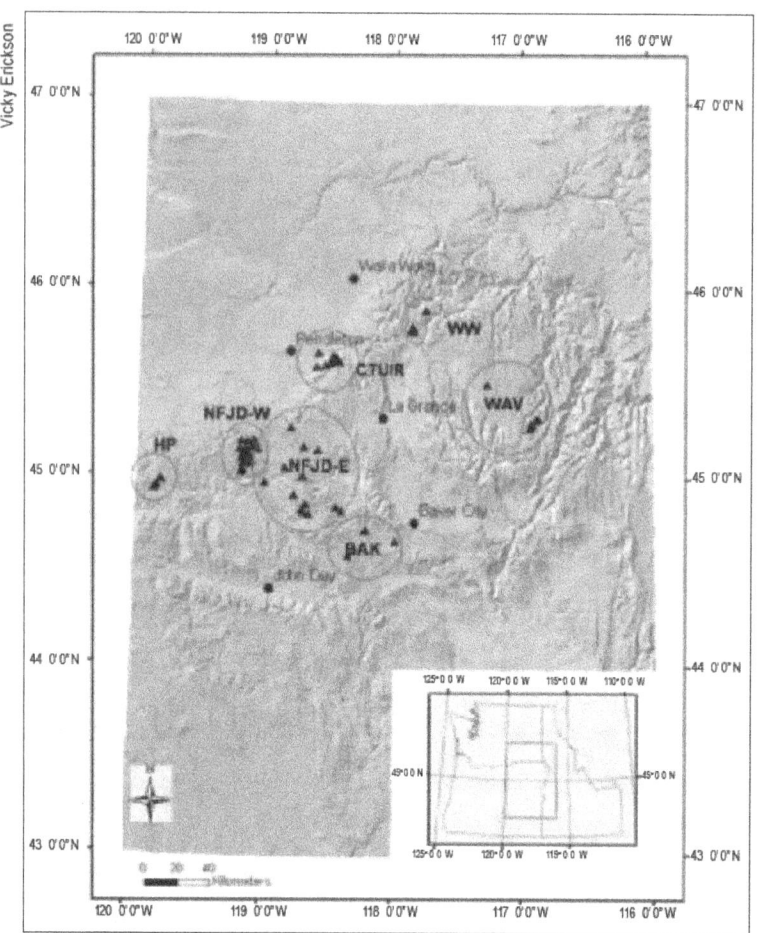

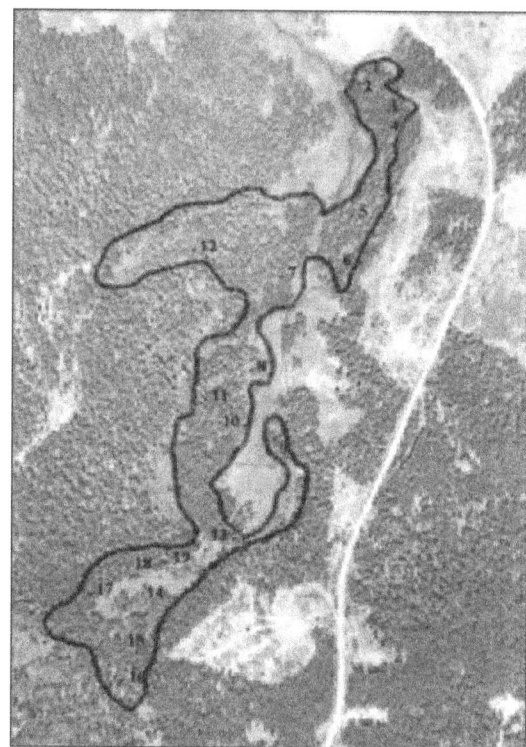

Figure 9–Location of the 91 aspen stands sampled for genetic study in seven subregions of the Blue Mountains in northeastern Oregon. Subregions: BAK = Baker Ranger District, CTUIR = Confederated Tribes of the Umatilla Indian Reservation, HP = Heppner Ranger District, NFJD = North Fork John Day (east and west), WW = Walla Walla Ranger District, and WAV = Wallowa Valley Ranger District.

Figure 10–Sampling map of Elk Flat aspen stand (POTR0001, Walla Walla Ranger District). Nineteen aspen individuals were sampled for genetic analysis (1-19). Genetic analysis revealed four clones, as indicated by the red polygons. Maps of the additional 90 sampled stands are available upon request from V. Erickson.

Genetic Electrophoresis Laboratory (NFGEL, Placerville, California) for analysis. A total of 19 allozyme loci were resolved using standard electrophoresis methodology.

Genetic Variation at the Stand Level

Over all sampled stands, the number of clones per stand ranged from 1 to 14 (mean = 2.5). Nearly half (41 of 92) of the stands were monoclonal, indicating that the genetic structure of aspen stands in the Blue Mountains is strongly influenced by clonal spread and persistence via root suckering. Exceptions to this overall pattern were observed in two young seedling stands growing in recent wildfire areas (Dooley Mountain, Baker Ranger District and Oriental Basin, North Fork John Day Ranger District). Here, nearly every sprout sampled represented a unique genotype. Similar effects of fire on aspen population structure have been reported in other geographic regions (Stevens et al. 1999, Tuskan et al. 1996). We suspect that the high diversity observed in the more established Target Springs stand (Wallowa Valley Ranger District) also reflects

seedling establishment after fire (14 unique genotypes out of 14 samples).

Geographic Variation in Genetic Structure

The extent and diversity of clones varied within and among subregions owing to differences in stand size, the degree of spatial separation among stands, and possibly also fire history. For example, in the eastern portion of the North Fork John Day subregion (NFJD-E, fig. 9) where stands are extremely small and geographically isolated, 73 percent of the stands were monoclonal and no stand consisted of more than two clones. Stands in this subregion were also highly differentiated and had low genetic similarity. The data indicate that the stands are in a self-reinforcing cycle of rarity, being isolated and predominantly single sex, with limited opportunity for new recruitment or stand expansion via sexual reproduction. In contrast, stand structure and corresponding genetic patterns in the western portion of the subregion (NFJD-W, fig. 9) were very different, possibly owing to presettlement wildfire history. Aspen stands in this area are more abundant and expansive, with shorter distances between them. They exhibited exceptionally high within-stand diversity (as many as 14 clones per stand), and tended to form tight genetic clusters based on geographic proximity within a given drainage. Stands that showed strong genetic similarity may have seeded in during the same establishment event. Aspen in the NFJD-W subregion have much greater evolutionary potential as compared to those in the eastern portion of the district because they are generally multiclonal and likely contain more female clones. As a consequence, there are greater opportunities for sexual reproduction and increased seed availability when episodic disturbances (e.g., wildfires) create conditions conducive for seedling establishment.

Genetic Evidence for Decline of Aspen Clones

Among the surveyed stands, we found three clones that appear to represent the fragments of large relict stands (Jarboe Meadows, Walla Walla Ranger District; Morsay Creek, NFJD-W; and Taylor Creek, NFJD-W). Ramets of each of these three clones grow in what are now unconnected stands that are separated by over 770 ft (200 m). The Morsay clone was especially impressive, with some of the remnant segments separated by nearly 3,000 ft (M01 and M02) (Shirley and Erickson 2001). Apparently a single aspen clone became established and spread along Morsay Creek, but died out in the middle section. The size of the original Morsay clone could rival that of the Fish Lake Basin aspen stand in Utah, which has been characterized as the most massive living organism on earth (Grant 1993).

Management Implications

Results from the genetic inventory can be used in conjunction with other survey information to help guide conservation and restoration activities and to identify priority stands for protection. Because most aspen stands contained clones with unique genotypes, we recommend that management strategies emphasize the protection and treatment of a large number of stands rather than many clones within each stand. From a genetic perspective, priority stands for restoration and protection include those that contain large amounts of genetic variation, are highly differentiated, or have rare or unusual genes. Individual stand clone maps (e.g., fig. 10) can assist in making more fine-scale management decisions, such as fence placement or the number and location of root collections to help ensure genetic diversity of planting stock.

Restoration activities that stimulate/protect vegetative regeneration and provide enhanced opportunities for sexual reproduction will play a vital role in preserving aspen

genetic resources in the Blue Mountains. Without management actions such as fencing, removal of conifer encroachment, and planting, many aspen stands will continue to decline and will not replace themselves except through rare, episodic disturbance events such as wildfire. Isolated monoclonal stands with high herbivory pressure are at greatest risk of extirpation. When artificial regeneration is used to enhance genetic diversity or stand size, or to create new aspen stands, plantings should include both male and female individuals to help promote sexual reproduction in this dioecious species.

Insects and Diseases of Aspen in the Blue Mountains

Aspen is host to a relatively long list of insects and diseases that result in mortality and various types of damage and injury. Thin, living bark, characteristic of aspen, is easily damaged by man, animals, and birds. Feeding on bark is done by a variety of small and large mammals from voles to elk. Big game will often damage saplings and larger trees by rubbing their antlers against the stems. Even birds, sapsuckers for example, will scar trees when they drill holes. Wounding of the stem bark predisposes trees to attack or entry by damaging diseases and insects.

Aspen are damaged and killed by insects and diseases throughout their life history. Some blights and cankers will effectively kill small-diameter young stems, whereas those same agents on older larger trees are not lethal. However, the diversity of damaging agents and types and severity of damage generally increase as stems mature, and overmature aspen often decline and succumb to one or more disease or insect agents.

Because aspen has never been a commercial timber species in the Blue Mountains, the traditional goal of producing large straight and sound boles has never been an important management objective. Similarly, because of low economic value and minor utilization, documented history and even current information regarding insect and disease incidence and associated impacts are largely lacking for aspen in the Blue Mountains.

Ecological values, especially for wildlife, and its contributions to landscape diversity and aesthetic enjoyment, are generally considered the greatest importance of aspen in the Blue Mountains. Aspen health management strategies focus on restoring, maintaining, or expanding clone dimensions, and increasing stand vigor, reproduction, and resilience; however, these strategies do not strive to promote stands of insect- and disease-free trees. Defective trees, those with stem decay and dead tops and forks, especially the larger and older trees, create habitat and are valuable for a variety of wildlife.

Healthy stands of aspen can be characterized as being well represented by different age classes of stems, from sucker sprouts to large old trees. Often the oldest stems will be in poor condition, with breakage, decay, and cankering, which can result in dead branches, tops, or entire trees. However, healthy clones will have existing young and periodic recruitment of young stems to replace those that die. Healthy clones also maintain or fully occupy their community type, and especially where restorative action has occurred, may be expanding their colonized area. Healthy clones will be sufficiently large and with enough healthy stems and a vigorous root system that there is no danger of individual clones dying out in the short term because of disturbance, lack of disturbance, browsing and wounding by ungulates, competition by conifers, or pest-caused mortality. Healthy stands will retain the genetic diversity of existing different clones if they are present. Unfortunately, there are substantially fewer healthy aspen clones than those that are in poor condition, declining in size and number of stems.

Insects and diseases greatly increase diversity in stands of aspen, creating snags, downed stems, live trees with decay and broken tops, and generally resulting in the demise of overmature individuals. This provides habitat for a variety of birds and mammals.

The following descriptions are of insects and diseases of aspen confirmed or believed to occur in the Blue Mountains. With the exception of very recent mapping of defoliated aspen in the annual Aerial Insect and Disease Detection Survey (http://www.fs.fed.us/r6/nr/fid/data.shtml), there are virtually no quantitative or distribution data on insects and diseases of aspen for this area; thus this information is observational.

Stem Decays

White trunk rot, also called aspen trunk rot–
The most common stem decay of aspen is white trunk rot, caused by *Phellinus tremulae* (fig. 11). This trunk rot is very common in aspen stands throughout the Blue Mountains. Only aspen is affected by *P. tremulae*, and some other species of hardwoods, exclusive of aspen, will host a very similar white trunk rot, caused by closely-related *Phellinus igniarius*, which is only distinguishable from *P. tremulae* based on its host. Most Blue Mountain aspen communities have at least a minor amount of infection, as confirmed by conks or other indicators. Some clones have numerous decadent trees. No comprehensive survey has been done on the occurrence of white trunk rot, and in casual observations, no trends or patterns have been noticed. Susceptibility to infection is probably at least partially influenced by the genotype of the clone. Thrifty vigorous trees are less likely to have decay, and less thrifty and wounded trees are more likely to have white trunk rot.

Trees are infected by airborne spores of the causal fungus that colonize branch stubs and wounds. Following infection, decay develops and progresses in the stem, often affecting most of the length of the bole. One or more conks are produced on some infected and decadent trees. Conks are distinctive hoof-shaped perennial hard woody fungal fruiting bodies with a gray to black vertically cracked and roughened upper surface and a pored brown undersurface. In addition to conks, other indicators of decay include sterile conks, blind conks, or punk knots, which are swellings packed with fungal tissue generally at branch stubs. Unfortunately, many infected and decadent trees have no conks or other signs or indicators to aid recognition. In some cases, bird excavations and nesting holes expose heart rot and confirm infection in the absence of conks or other fungal signs.

Wood decay caused by *P. tremulae* is a white rot that is irregular in outline when viewed in cross section. Advanced decay is soft uniform yellow to white, bordered with distinct brown-black zone lines that outline the decayed wood. A reddish stain may surround the decay column. Cavity-excavating birds require trees with stem decay; they prefer to excavate trees with substantial advanced decay and will enter the decadent wood where the sapwood is thin. Sound sapwood is usually thinnest on the south sides of aspen with white trunk rot (Losin et al. 2006). Aspen stems that have been damaged by wounding and stands that have had fire damage are most likely to have a high incidence of white trunk rot. Open or thinned stands also have a higher incidence of decay (Callan 1998). Stands with wood borer infestation may also be predisposed to white trunk rot.

Live stems with decay that are used by birds and mammals are relatively valuable trees. These trees generally will remain standing and can serve as habitat for a number of

Figure 11–Conk of *Phellinus tremulae*, cause of aspen trunk rot.

James S. Hadfield

years, whereas similar dead trees will not remain standing for long. White trunk rot will not cause tree mortality, that is, kill standing trees; however, trees with well-advanced decay may fail, especially at points where the sapwood is thin and bird excavation has weakened the bole.

Peniophora polygonia–

Decay and stain caused by *Peniophora polygonia* probably causes some level of damage to aspen in the Blue Mountains. However, incidence has not been confirmed and severity of infection is unknown. Hinds (1985) reported that Davidson et al. (1959) found *P. polygonia* to have a higher incidence in Colorado than white trunk rot caused by *Phellinus tremulae*. Although incidence was high, total damage was substantially less, suggesting it slowly decays infected trees. Because a conk is not formed, this disease will not be recognized on live trees. Nearly all information regarding decay associated with disease is from saw-log defect and loss-of-merchantability studies (Davidson et al. 1959).

Infection may be recognized in the broken boles of trees. Infected younger trees usually have an incipient brown stain with a reddish-brown margin. In older trees, infection may have had time to develop into a yellow-stringy rot.

Trunk Butt and Root Rots

White mottled trunk and butt rot–

White mottled trunk and butt rot is caused by *Ganoderma applanatum*. The fruiting body of this fungus is commonly known as the "artist's conk," because the white, very fine pore surface is easily and permanently bruised brown when touched, allowing intricate designs to be drawn. These shelf-like woody, perennial conks are most commonly encountered on the roots or root collar of failed trees and at the ground line of dead standing trees. They have concentric ridges on the upper surface usually with a thick dusting of reddish brown spores. Conks rarely appear on trees while they are alive (Callan 1998), but the fungus actively causes decay in live trees.

White mottled trunk and butt rot affects a number of hosts in the Blue Mountains, but is most commonly observed on hardwoods including *Populus, Betula, Prunus, and Salix*. Of these, it is most frequently encountered on aspen and black cottonwood. It is also found on conifers. No comprehensive survey has been done to determine the distribution or prevalence of *G. applanatum*, or aspen stands that are infected in the Blue Mountains. It is occasionally observed and is not considered common. Reports in Colorado indicate that it is as common as *Phellinus tremulae,* which is not believed to be the case in the Blue Mountains.

With no apparent indicators except conks on dead material, nearly all *G. applanatum*-caused defect and damage

to live trees is hidden. Moist sites and mature stands are most likely to host infection, decay, and occurrence of the recognizable conks (Ross 1976). Trees are infected through wounds and reportedly broken tops (Holsten et al. 2001). Infected trees will have decay that usually is most advanced in the roots and lower butt, and the decay column will extend well up the bole. Decay is white to cream-colored, soft and spongy, and a brown-colored zone of stain surrounds the decay column. Black zone lines commonly occur in the decayed wood. Infected trees may fail while alive and usually break at the root collar or lower butt. Once the tree is dead, decay will continue to spread in the bole.

Armillaria root disease–

Armillaria root disease of aspen is caused by one of at least two closely related species of *Armillaria–A. sinipina* and *A. nabsnona*–and possibly *A. ostoyae* (Callan 1998). These and several other species of *Armillaria* had been known collectively as *Armillaria mellea* until the 1970s and 1980s when enough differences were documented that taxonomists began breaking different species out of the *Armillaria* genus (Shaw and Kile 1991). Aspen and cottonwood have frequently been observed in the Blue Mountains with evidence of decay and root disease caused by one of the *Armillaria* species. Prominence by species is not known.

In some regions of the West, *Armillaria* root disease in aspen is recognizable as mortality pockets in infected stands. Large aspen mortality pockets caused by *Armillaria* are infrequently encountered in the Blue Mountains. When observed, most aspen *Armillaria* mortality is single trees or small groups of trees. Confirmation of infection is the prolific mushroom production in the fall, or abundant black "shoestring" rhizomorphs observed where the bark has sloughed off or on the exterior of exposed roots. Trees may be dead and down with exposed decay on the roots and in the lower butt. Decay will be a white or yellowish stringy rot often with numerous black zone lines. Other decays of aspen are similar, and decay is not diagnostic enough to identify cause of failure or mortality.

Canker Diseases

Stem cankers of aspen are very common throughout the range of aspen in the West, including the Blue Mountains. Aspen are especially susceptible to canker diseases owing to their thin soft living bark that is easily damaged. Wounds that penetrate the bark allow infection by spore-spread diseases, including canker diseases. There are several common canker diseases of aspen, and a number of less-common ones as well. Most Blue Mountain aspen stands have some incidence of cankers and some clones are especially susceptible to one or more of these diseases.

Craig L. Schmitt

Craig L. Schmitt

Figure 12 (left)–Sooty-bark canker caused by *Encoelia pruinosa* on a dead aspen snag.

Figure 13 (right)–Bulls-eye target-like form of black canker, caused by *Ceratocystis fimbriata*, on aspen stem.

Canker diseases can girdle the stem, causing the crown above the canker to die, and if the canker is below the live crown, the stem will be killed. Some cankers will often be associated with decay that is behind the canker face, and stem breakage can occur, both in live trees and trees that have been killed.

Sooty-bark canker–
Sooty-bark canker is caused by *Encoelia pruinosa*, a common disease of aspen throughout the West (fig. 12). This canker is especially lethal, and infected trees will generally be killed within 3 to 10 years (Hinds 1985). Cankers extend rapidly in length, and can be as long as 12 ft within 4 years. Wounds are the common and the most frequent predisposing factor for infection by *E. pruinosa*.

Because the canker progresses so rapidly, callus tissue is not formed. Cankers may appear slightly sunken. The bark over the canker is dead, and after several years it sloughs off and the exposed inner bark is black. When well advanced, the bark is in long stringy strips. The term "sooty-bark" comes from the soot-like or powdery residue left on your hands when the dead bark is handled. Decay is usually not associated with this canker as wood tends to dry out and remain solid behind the canker face; however, stem breakage at the canker is not uncommon.

Sooty-bark canker is common in stands of aspen in the Blue Mountains based on observation. No local information is available for incidence, distribution, or severity of sooty-bark canker.

Black canker, target canker or *Ceratocystis* canker–
Black canker, also known as target canker and ceratocystis canker, is caused by *Ceratocystis fimbriata* (fig. 13). This canker is initiated most often at wounds. The canker face is characterized by a series of annually enlarging ragged callus ridges that take the appearance of a target, hence one of the common names. The wood and dead bark that adheres

to the canker face are black, giving this canker its other common name. This canker enlarges faster vertically than horizontally, but growth is still relatively slow; slower than trees grow in circumference, so unless two or more cankers coalesce, girdling will not occur. Decay is usually not associated with this canker, and trees and stands can have a rather substantial amount of infection and not experience too much breakage or mortality. Impact to cankered trees is primarily stem deformity.

Black canker is common in Blue Mountain aspen, but no surveys have been done to document incidence and distribution.

Cryptosphaeria canker–
Cryptosphaeria canker, caused by *Cryptosphaeria populina*, is known to occur in the Blue Mountains; however, information involving distribution and prevalence is not available. It has been identified throughout the range of aspen from northern Mexico to Alaska. Cankers and wood decay are associated with this disease. Small trees or sprouts and saplings can be killed within 1 and 2 years, respectively. This can occur before they are completely girdled.

Trunk wounds most frequently predispose trees to infection. Cankers form that are long and narrow; usually only 2 to 4 in wide, and 10 or more ft long (Hinds 1985). Infected bark beyond the vertical extent of the canker is stained light brown to orange. Annual callus tissue is formed, and dead black bark adheres to the canker face. Sapwood staining will occur beyond the vertical extent of the canker and is associated with decay development. The asexual stage of the causal fungus, *Libertella*, will often cause wood decay associated with cankers. Cankered trees with decay are predisposed to breakage.

Secondary infection by *Cytospora chrysosperma* is common on cryptosphaeria cankers and may complicate diagnosis.

Cytospora canker–

Cytospora canker is caused by *Cytospora chrysosperma*, also known by the sexual stage of the fungus, *Valsa sordida*. Aspen and other species of *Populus* and species of *Salix, Alnus,* and *Prunus* are common hosts to Cytospora canker, although evidence suggests hardwoods other than *Populus* are probably attacked by a different species of *Cytospora*. Cytospora canker is commonly found on aspen in the Blue Mountains, although distribution and prevalence have not been determined by survey.

Cytospora canker infects trees that have been wounded, weakened by drought, or damaged by frost, sunscald, or predisposed by other agents and is generally an opportunistic disease. Cankered trees may have topkill, or the entire crown may be killed by cankering that girdles the stem. Decay can also be associated with older cankers.

Infested trees will have bark on the canker face that initially discolors to an orange to orange-brown and in time will darken to black. Slightly sunken cankers may be diffuse or have concise boundaries. Several years after infection, the bark will start to slough off the canker face. Cankers are easily identified by the long orange conidial tendrils that are extruded during high humidity from pycnidia (small pimple-like fruiting bodies embedded in the bark). These will dry when the humidity drops but remnant orange threads may be found. Rain will partially dissolve conidial tendrils, which will dry into hard, orange hemispherical masses.

Foliage Diseases

Foliage of aspen may be damaged by several common and even more less-common diseases, which can infect the leaf tissue from the juvenile stage through senescence. Damage is characterized as development of spots, dying of portions or all of the leaf tissue, blackening, and shriveling, which usually results in premature defoliation. Symptoms generally become more pronounced as the season progresses.

Foliage diseases are generally annual, and infected tissues are confined to the leaf and petiole, being removed when the leaves fall. A few diseases can move from the foliage onto the shoot. Occurrence and severity of nearly all of these foliage diseases varies dramatically from year to year, depending primarily on favorable weather conditions coinciding with critical periods of fungi maturation and spore dispersal from fruiting bodies on older host tissue or fallen leaves on the ground and host bud flush in the spring. Two or more severe infection years in a row are much more likely to damage trees than single-year events. Susceptibility of aspen clones can differ, at least partially because timing of bud flush may differ between clones. Unusually mild wet spring weather will intensify foliage disease spread, development, and resultant effects

during those years. Many aspen are in microsites that are high hazard for spore-spread diseases–those sites characterized as being sheltered, typically having high humidity and moderate temperatures. Such sites may have absent or minor occurrence of diseases during low incidence years, but are apt to have epidemics during years when conditions are favorable, and at levels higher than stands on lower risk sites.

At least three rust fungi cause foliage diseases of *Populus*, one of which is common on aspen. For successful completion of their life cycle, most rust fungi must alternate between different hosts. Conditions required for spread, infection, and development of foliar rust on aspen are likely to be different from other fungal foliage pathogens.

Ink spot–

Ink spot caused by *Ciborinia whetzelii* is a common leaf blight throughout most of the range of aspen in the West and is frequently observed in the Blue Mountains. No survey information is available that documents the frequency and severity of such infestations.

Following conditions early in the year that are favorable for infection, leaves turn brown in the spring, about a month after budburst. On trees with severe infestation, crowns will be mostly to almost entirely brown. When infestation is light to moderate, only a portion of foliage is browned. A diagnostic feature of this disease is that petioles on browned leaves remain mostly green. Circular to ellipsoid black sclerotia, which appear as "ink spots," develop about a month after leaves turn brown and remain on the browned leaves until mid to late summer when they start to fall from the leaves, which are still attached to the tree. After the sclerotia fall, leaves have characteristic "shot-holes," holes in the leaf where the sclerotia had been attached. Damaged leaves will start to prematurely drop from the tree starting midsummer. Foliage damage is highest close to the ground, small trees are affected more than larger trees, and the lower crowns of larger trees are more blighted than the upper crown.

Black leaf spot or marssonina leaf blight–

Black leaf spot of aspen is caused by *Marssonina populi* and also reportedly by *M. brunnea* (Callan 1998). This is the most commonly occurring leaf disease of aspen in the Western United States. It is commonly observed in the Blue Mountains during years when it is in outbreak. Favorable weather conditions for spore dispersal coinciding with aspen bud burst is most apt to result in infection. In midsummer, brown spots start appearing on infected foliage. Spots later enlarge and turn black. These irregular-shaped black spots will have a distinctive yellow to golden-yellow border, and affected leaves will be smaller than similar uninfected leaves. Single-year damage is unlikely to cause appreciable damage, but consecutive years with severe defoliation have been documented as causing mortality (Walters 1984).

Aspen shoot and leaf blight or shepherds crook–

Aspen leaf and shoot blight is caused by *Venturia macularis*, which is likely a complex of at least several closely related species (Callan 1998). This is a common disease throughout the West, including the Blue Mountains. There is no information available regarding the distribution and levels of severity that have occurred in the past. Endemic damage has been observed in most years in some stands, especially those on sites where a high incidence of spore-spread diseases can be expected.

These pathogens infect host material in the spring during bud break and as new leaves expand. Infection can occur both from spores released from mature fruiting bodies on fallen leaves, or from conidia produced on blighted twigs. Mild, wet weather in the spring is conducive for effective spread and development of extensive infection and a resulting epidemic. This can be a periodic event, and the disease may be nearly absent following poor conditions for infection.

After young succulent leaf tissue is infected, tissue wilts and turns black, and dead areas become coated with olive-green fungal growth. Infected areas will enlarge, and infection may spread from the leaf down the petiole to the young shoot. In such cases, the shoot tip will wilt, die, and turn black. Later in the spring, secondary infections will develop rapidly on susceptible tissue. During outbreak years, most terminals will be affected and new sucker sprouts may be killed. Usually there is just terminal or tip dieback that results in loss of height growth in those years. Shoot tip dieback often is shaped like the crook in a shepherd's staff, hence the common name "shepherd's crook."

Conifer-aspen rust, leaf rust of aspen–

Conifer-aspen rust, also called leaf rust of aspen, is caused by *Melampsora medusae* (fig. 14). This rust is very common in aspen throughout the Blue Mountains, and can be found in many clones at some level most years.

The causal fungus has a complex life cycle that requires spread between conifers and aspen. At least six conifer genera are known to host *M. medusae*. Spores are produced in the spring from dead infested aspen leaves that are on the ground. The fungus will spread to conifer needless that are rather close as these fragile spores do not remain viable for long. In the summer, relatively hardy aeciospores are produced on infected conifer needles, which can disperse and remain viable and infect aspen over rather long distances. Infection can intensify on aspen over the summer as urediospores produced on leaves will continue to spread the fungus within individuals and to additional aspen. Distinctive numerous small bright yellow tufts of fungal growth occur

on the underside of aspen leaves. Later the fungi and leaf turn black. Colonized leaves will die and drop prematurely owing to this rust, but infection does not spread to perennial woody tissue. Effects from premature leaf mortality and drop are negligible, and this disease, although very common, is not considered serious.

Insect Pests of Aspen

There are a large number of insects that may feed on or infest aspen, causing various levels of damage. Nearly all insect pests of aspen that have been documented in the West are likely to be present in the Blue Mountains. Several insects have been observed locally commonly causing significant damage to aspen, and other insects may occasionally be damaging.

Defoliating insects and other foliage-damaging insects–

Defoliating insects that cause significant damage include leaf-feeding larvae of Lepidoptera. Defoliating beetles and their larvae may also occasionally cause damage. Leaf-rollers and leaf tiers are common; significant damage has not been noted, but may result during rarely occurring outbreaks. Healthy aspen may have another flush of foliage in the summer if defoliated in the spring. Summer-flushed foliage will be sparser and leaves smaller. Consecutive years of defoliation will weaken trees and may cause dieback, direct mortality, or contribute to predisposition to other insect or disease pests. Several defoliating insects probably are responsible for most of the defoliation during outbreaks in the Blue Mountains, including the forest tent caterpillar, satin moth, and large aspen tortrix. Other insects may also cause damage less frequently, for shorter duration, or on a smaller scale.

Figure 14–Yellow-colored uredinia of conifer-aspen rust (*Melampsora medusae*), on the underside surface of an aspen leaf.

Forest tent caterpillar–

The forest tent caterpillar (*Malacosoma disstria*) has a wide host range, feeding on a variety of broadleaf hosts, although aspen is preferred. As with most insects, population levels cycle dramatically, and during outbreaks, heavy feeding occurs on a number of hosts, including aspen. The forest tent caterpillar has been observed defoliating aspen in the Blue Mountains, but distribution, periodicity, and severity of defoliation events have not been documented. Defoliation of aspen by the forest tent caterpillar has not been mapped in the annual Aerial Insect and Disease Detection Survey in the Blue Mountains.

The forest tent caterpillar overwinters as eggs. The young larvae begin to emerge prior to budburst and initially feed on expanding flower and leaf buds and then on leaves after budbreak. During outbreaks, trees may be completely defoliated by the end of June. Larvae mature in a month or more and pupate. They then soon emerge as moths in midsummer, mate, and the female lays eggs. The most effective means of spread is when weather fronts transport adults. Cold weather that occurs during larvae hatch is believed to be a significant factor in reducing populations. Parasites and predators also play a role, increasing in number along with their host or prey. In addition, a rather host-specific nucleo-polyhedrosis virus may control caterpillar outbreaks. This virus builds during population outbreaks, spreading when densities of insects are high enough, and eventually causes populations to dramatically crash. As a result, outbreaks last several years and are then abruptly over.

Satin moth–

The satin moth (*Leucoma salicis*) is an exotic insect that was introduced to the west coast from Eurasia in the early 1920s. The larvae of this insect feed on the foliage of aspen, as well as cottonwoods, other poplars, and willow. Damage is defoliation (fig. 15), and successive years of severe defoliation can cause branch dieback. Satin moths belong to the same family as tussock moths and the gypsy moth (Lymantriidae); of which the caterpillars are characterized as having elaborate and abundant setae (hair).

Defoliation by the satin moth is often striking and can be observed from the air. Satin moth defoliation has been sketchmapped only in recent years in the annual Aerial Insect and Disease Detection Survey. Substantial satin moth defoliation was sketchmapped in 2008, and in one polygon in 2000, in aspen communities in the Big Lookout Mountain area and vicinity southeast of Baker City. Lesser amounts were mapped elsewhere in 2008, including mapped polygons of defoliation in the Sugarbowl Creek area west of Ukiah, Oregon.

This insect overwinters as small larvae in silken cocoons, and they emerge when host buds burst and leaves elongate. Larvae feed through early summer, pupate and emerge as

adults (fig. 16) in July. Females lay eggs in July, and, after hatching, the next generation of larvae skeletonize leaves until fall and the first frost when larvae prepare for hibernation. Damage is most noticeable about the end of June following feeding by mature larvae.

Lymantriidae tend to be generalist feeders, and have received most attention as a pest of ornamental and shade trees. In Blue Mountain forested communities, satin moths are most commonly observed on aspen. Severe defoliation of aspen has been noted at Elk Flats on the Umatilla National Forest, on the Malheur National Forest, and in large stands of aspen on Big Lookout Mountain southeast of Baker City. Other areas undoubtedly have been defoliated as well. Visible damage has been noted every few years during outbreaks. Low endemic populations of satin moths persist between outbreaks without causing noticeable damage. Birds are important predators, and a variety of parasitic and predatory insects, both native and introduced, help control this insect. Evidence in Wyoming suggests that epidemic outbreaks of satin moth are increasing in incidence and severity, and that situation may be occurring in the Blue Mountains as well.

Large aspen tortrix–

The large aspen tortrix (*Choristoneura conflictana*) is a leaf tier. It is considered the second most damaging defoliator

Figure 15–Defoliation caused by the satin moth. Photo taken in early August.

of aspen in the West, behind the western forest caterpillar. The larvae overwinter as second instars in silken webs in the nooks and crannies of rough bark near the base of host trees. Upon emerging, larvae crawl up the tree and bore into swelling buds, which they then enter. As the leaves unfurl, the larvae webs several together and then feeds inside the resultant enclosure. By early June, the larvae are mature and most or all of webbed-together leaves have been consumed. Larvae pupate in silken cocoons attached to leaves and emerge as adults in late June, fly, and mate; the females then lay eggs on the upper surface of leaves. After hatching, the tiny larvae again web several leaves together and feed, which skeletonizes the leaves. By early August, they travel to the base of the tree in search of an overwintering site. Other insects can be associated with large aspen tortrix outbreaks, including the aspen leaftier (*Pseudosciaphila duplex*).

The large aspen tortrix is known to occur in the Blue Mountains, but no historical information is available on periodicity of epidemic defoliation or confirmed distribution.

Other leaf-damaging insects–
A number of other insects are commonly found on aspen leaves and probably infrequently or rarely cause appreciable damage at the stand level. These may include sawflies

Figure 16–Adult satin moth (female) in early August.

Craig L. Schmitt

(Tenthredinidae), leafminers, leafhoppers (Cicadellidae), scales, Chrysomelid beetles, and a variety of true bugs (Hemiptera).

Boring insects–
The most important boring insects of aspen in the Blue Mountains belong to the Buprestidae (flatheaded borers) and perhaps the Cerambycidae (roundheaded borers). Wood-boring insects most often attack trees that have been weakened or damaged. In turn, boring facilitates colonization by various wood decay fungi, *Phellinus tremulae*, for example, as well as introducing other diseases and predisposing the tree to attacks by other insects.

The poplar borer–
The poplar borer, *Saperda calcarata*, is the most destructive insect pest of poplars, including aspen, in the Rocky Mountain region. Evidence of the poplar borer and associated damage is observed in numerous Blue Mountains aspen stands. Documented incidence, severity, and distribution are not available. Evidence of infestation on individual trees includes shellac-like exudate oozing from borer holes in the bark. Coarse-grained boring frass may be apparent being excavated from these boring holes. The larvae of these borers will remain in and mine the wood for several years.

Where borer damage occurs, stems that are 2 inches in diameter and larger can be attacked. Trees in fully stocked dense stands are less apt to be attacked than thinned stands or open-grown stands. It is likely that stands having recent conifer removal treatments may be susceptible to attack, especially if conifers are large. As the result of borer tunnels through the wood of branches and stems, trees are weakened and bole and branch breakage will occur. Affected trees will have evidence of boring in the boles, exude frass, and have wet stained areas resulting from sap leakage (fig. 17). Breakage will show evidence of mining through the wood. Infested trees are susceptible to attack by other insects and diseases as a result of reduced vigor and bore holes providing entrance for disease organisms and spores.

The bronze poplar borer–
Evidence of the bronze poplar borer (*Agrilus granulatus liragus*) has been frequently observed on dead and declining aspen in the Blue Mountains, and is believed to be the most common wood-boring insect affecting aspen in this area. This insect creates distinctive zig-zag winding galleries beneath the bark on large branches and the main stem (fig. 18). The gallery pattern can frequently be observed as "lumpy bark," where the bark is still intact. Attacked trees may also have crown symptoms of abnormally small leaf size, and off-color foliage. This borer primarily attacks injured, weakened, or stressed trees. Stands with numerous

Craig L. Schmitt

Figure 17–Evidence of recent poplar borer attacks, including boring frass and exudate flow.

Craig L. Schmitt

Figure 18–Distinctive zig-zag larval galleries of the bronze poplar borer, *Agrilus granulatus liragus,* on dead aspen stem. Note the *Phellinus tremulae* conk in the upper right.

wounded trees, often from big game disturbance, will have active borer activity. Breakage and trees killed by a combination of factors will often have bronze poplar galleries.

This insect generally has a 2-year life cycle. The larvae overwinter in one of several larval instars. Those that overwinter as the forth instar will begin feeding in the spring when sap begins to flow and, after a period, will pupate just under the bark. The adults will chew a "D"-shaped hole in the bark and emerge from about the end of June through the middle of August. Adult flying, mating, and egg-laying concludes about the end of August.

Aspen Management in the Blue Mountains
Overview
Efforts to save and restore dwindling aspen stands in the Blue Mountains have been underway for the past 25 years. The primary management objectives for aspen in the Blue Mountains are (1) to maintain genetic diversity through preservation of existing clones, (2) to restore a diversity of age structure among existing clones, and (3) to reverse the decline in aspen forest area. Our first priority is rescue of clones that are in danger of dying out entirely. Some believe that half or more of our remaining aspen clones on national

forest lands could be lost in the next two decades if active measures are not taken. Managers are also working to facilitate a modest increase in aspen area, in an attempt to restore historical acreages. Aspen's rarity and exceptional habitat value in the Blue Mountains essentially preclude any harvest for wood products. The issues and strategies for aspen management in the Blue Mountains are similar to those in the Sierra Nevada of California, and a recent publication about aspen in that area by Shepperd et al. (2006) contains much that is applicable to our area.

A decision model for aspen management (fig. 19) has been compiled by Mueggler (1989). Vigorous stands of mature aspen without codominant competing conifers need no treatment; however, if the overstory is breaking up, then regeneration is important. Breakup of the aspen overstory occurs as mature trees die owing to age, diseases, and insects, competition from conifers, or a combination of factors. In the Blue Mountains, there is very little aspen that could be considered self-sustaining; removal of competing conifers by natural disturbance or management action is required to perpetuate aspen. Although conifers are the main competitor in our area, aspen regeneration is occasionally affected by competition from deciduous tall shrub

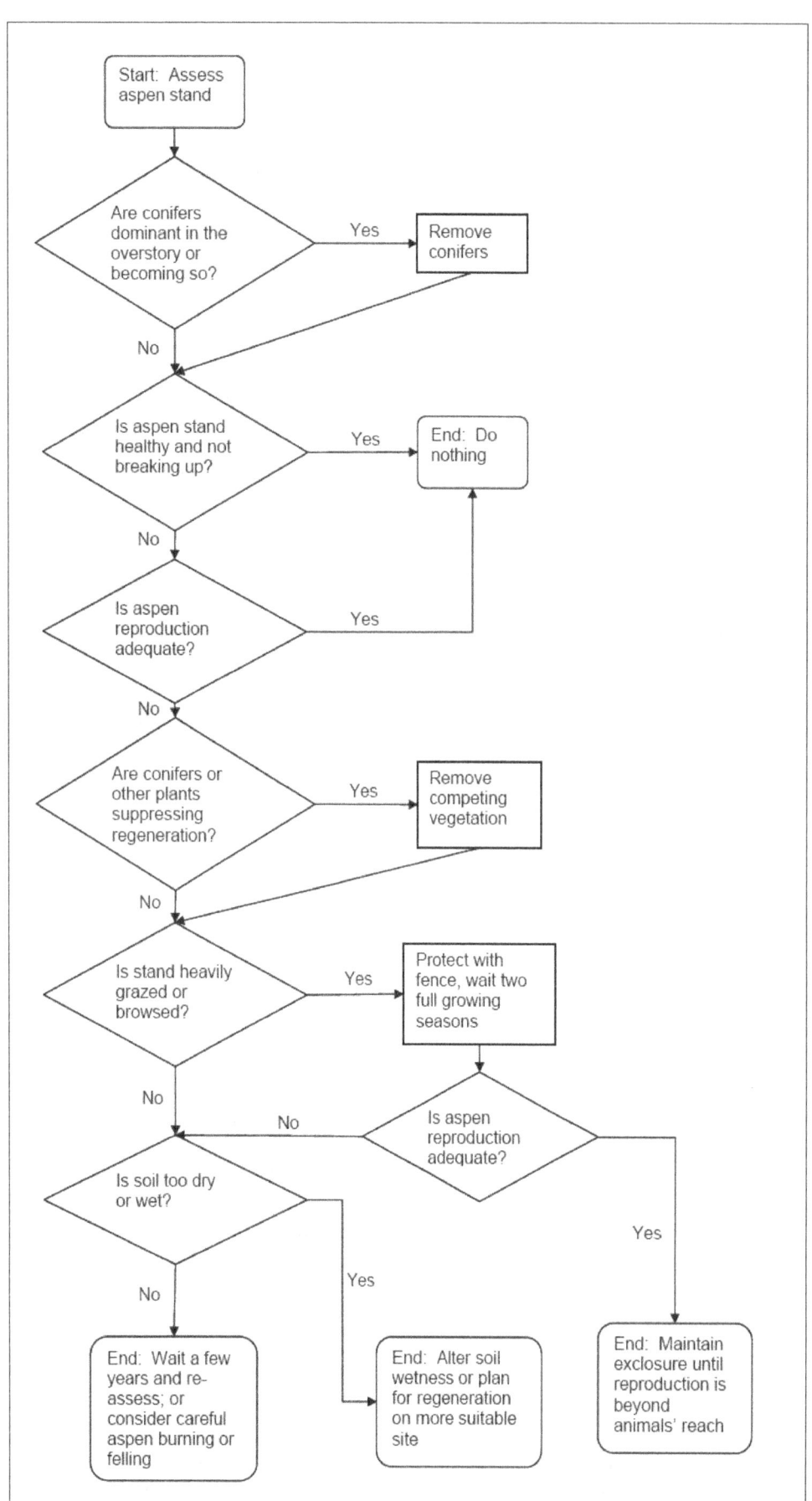

Figure 19—Aspen management decision flowchart for the Blue Mountains, modified from Mueggler (1989).

Diane Shirley

Figure 20–Successful aspen regeneration. The overstory is dying, but regeneration is present and large enough to withstand browsing pressure. Note the foliage trim line on young aspens from browsing. North Fork John Day Ranger District, Umatilla National Forest.

Michael Tatum

Figure 21–An aspen sucker subjected to many years of intense browsing pressure will develop into a thick woody stub.

species, notably hawthorn (*Crataegus* spp.). Regeneration of aspen can be considered successful when vigorous young trees numerous enough to restock the stand reach a size that makes them resistant to browsers (fig. 20).

Successful vegetative regeneration of aspen requires simultaneous hormonal stimulation, proper growth environment, and protection from herbivores (Shepperd 2001). Inadequate aspen regeneration under a decadent aspen overstory in our area is most often due to (1) competition from conifers, (2) herbivores killing suckers, or (3) continuing suppression of suckering by apical dominance of the remaining mature aspen. Management actions that treat these basic factors limiting aspen regeneration have a very high success rate in the Blue Mountains. As discussed below, removal of as many conifers as possible from all size classes will benefit aspen regeneration. While mature aspen are healthy, conifers can colonize the understory without adversely affecting the mature aspen; but when the aspen overstory begins to break up, even sapling conifers should be removed to allow aspen regeneration. Herbivory will prevent aspen regeneration over most of our area, and thus fencing is usually needed. Browsing of aspen suckers is often so intense that suckers are difficult to find among other vegetation. Many will die, and those that survive after several years of intense browsing will develop into a low shrub or a single thick woody stub just a few inches high (fig. 21).

Management action is triggered when aspen regeneration is considered "inadequate." How many aspen suckers are needed to regenerate a stand? The mortality rate of aspen suckers is very high in the first few years (Shepperd 1993), and thus initially high density of suckers is considered beneficial. Several suckers are typically clustered at each root node, of which only one will usually survive to maturity. Mueggler (1989) considered stands with fewer than 500 suckers per acre to have regeneration problems, and stands with over 1,000 suckers per acre to have a good chance of replacing themselves. Thus management action (i.e., conifer removal and fencing) should be considered if a stand appears unable to bring 1,000 trees per acre (about 6.5-ft spacing) to a size safe from herbivores. As discussed below, a safe size is diameter at breast height (d.b h.) of about 4 in. The number of sucker clumps per acre may be a better guide to regeneration success than individual suckers, because only one sucker in a clump will survive to maturity. Schier (1975) considered clones with less than 300 sucker clumps per acre to be deteriorating, whereas healthy clones had 750 to 1,500 clumps per acre.

In our area, aspen are often in wetlands or riparian areas where major changes in soil wetness are possible and may affect aspen regeneration; for this reason we have added a decision diamond about soil wetness to Mueggler's (1989) diagram (fig. 19). Aspen suckering among remnant trees on

Figure 22–Effect of a change in soil moisture on the success of postfire aspen regeneration. On the left is ecology plot MW2991 in 1995, 1 year after a wildfire. Note mature aspen trees that existed before the fire. On the right is the same view in the year 2000, 6 years after the fire. The depression once occupied by an aspen grove is now a cattail marsh with no aspen regeneration. The increase in water supply to this wetland is presumably from loss of trees in the surrounding watershed.

stream terraces may be weak after erosion and stream incision have reduced the available soil moisture. In such cases, we could attempt to raise the water table through stream restoration (e.g., sediment capture), or plan for aspen growth only on lower sites. We have also observed situations where locations that were formerly suitable for aspen became too wet as a result of a change in water-table depth and duration (fig. 22). In this situation, aspen regeneration may need to shift uphill from its original location for the clone to survive, and conifer removal and fencing should accommodate this.

Conifer Removal

Removal of competing conifers is considered essential for strong aspen regeneration (Jones et al. 2005). Even our least shade-tolerant conifer, western juniper (Minore 1979), can out-compete aspen (Wall et al. 2001). Mature competing conifers can suppress aspen overstory trees, and conifers of any size can suppress growth of aspen suckers. In addition, conifers compete strongly for soil moisture with aspen in an environment where moisture is often in short supply. Fortunately, our management experience has shown that even severely suppressed aspen will respond to conifer removal with new suckering, provided that live stems are present. A trenching study by Shepperd et al. (2001) found that a dense aspen root system persisted in mixed stands where half of the basal area consisted of conifers.

Managers in our area agree that all conifers should be removed in treated aspen stands, except for those that must be retained to meet other management objectives (e.g., large-tree conservation or stream shading). Conifer removal from a buffer zone around an aspen stand is also advised to permit more light and heat to reach the stand and thereby stimulate regeneration, and to allow for some clonal expansion. A buffer may extend 50 ft or more outside the existing live or dead aspen perimeter (see the discussion below).

Girdling of conifers is also effective in removing conifer competition and preferred when harvest is not possible or snags are needed (fig. 23).

In situations where managers face opposition to conifer removal, they may be asked how much conifer overstory can be left while still allowing for adequate aspen regeneration. To our knowledge, all studies published to date have involved complete conifer removal. The consensus among aspen managers in the Blue Mountains is that aspen suckering and growth are inhibited to some degree by any amount of competing conifers. To test this position, we reviewed data from an unpublished survey of 155 aspen stands on the Malheur and Wallowa-Whitman National Forests and nearby Bureau of Land Management (BLM) lands in 1999 and 2000, by Lynda Cobb and Martin Vavra of Oregon State University. They recorded the number of aspen suckers in a 30-m (98-ft)-diameter circular plot (or two randomly selected quarters of a 15-m (49-ft)-circular plot where sprouts were very dense). The canopy cover of

Figure 23–Girdling of conifers to reduce competition in an aspen stand.

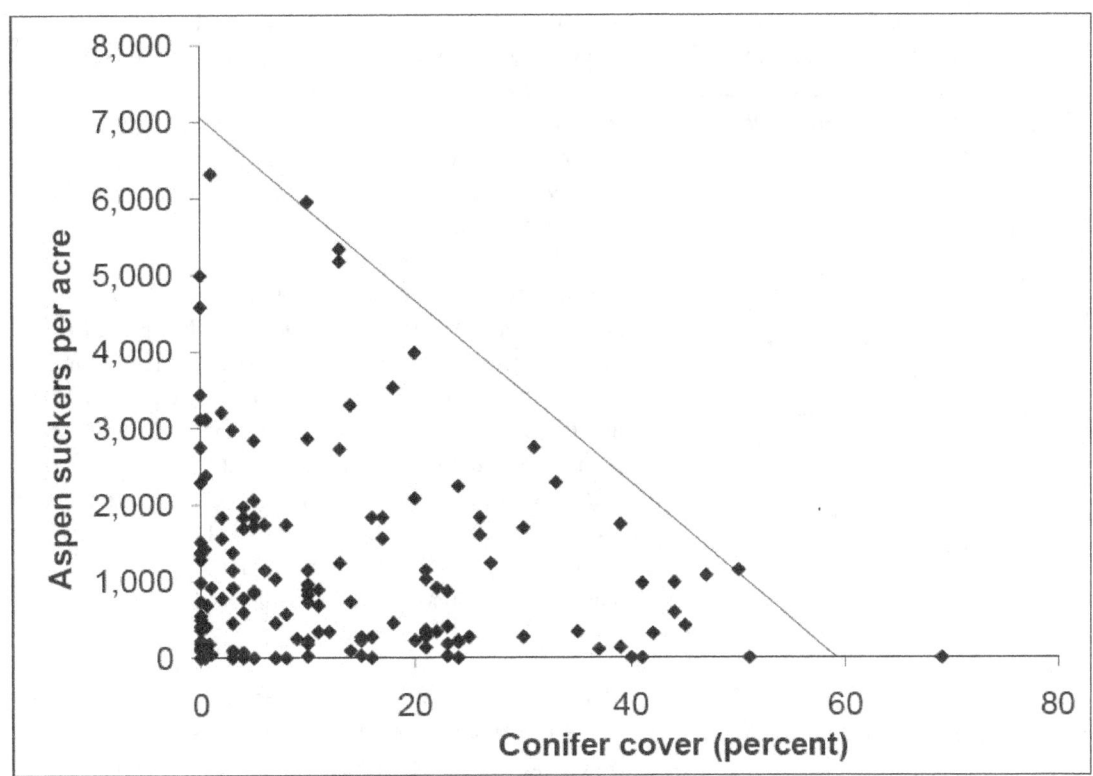

Figure 24—A plot of aspen suckers (count per acre) vs. conifer canopy cover for 155 aspen stands on the Malheur and Wallowa-Whitman National Forests and nearby Bureau of Land Management lands in 1999 and 2000, sampled by Lynda Cobb and Martin Vavra of Oregon State University. The trend line traces the maximum sucker count observed for a given conifer canopy cover.

conifers was also recorded at the center and margins of the 30-m plots at the four cardinal directions, using a spherical densiometer. The data were collected on plots with livestock fencing (n = 6), deer-elk fencing (n = 35), and no fencing (n = 114). Plots with small cages were omitted from this analysis because their extent and effect was unknown. We pooled the fenced and unfenced stands here because the sample size for fenced stands is small and, although sucker density averages were higher in fenced stands, in fact, a wide range occurs in both fenced and unfenced stands.

A comparison of aspen suckers (count per acre) vs. associated conifer canopy cover shows that the maximum possible aspen sucker density decreases steadily with increasing conifer cover from about 7,000 per acre with no conifer overstory to zero at 60-percent conifer overstory canopy cover (fig. 24). The trend line in figure 24 represents the potential for aspen regeneration when conditions are optimal. (Numerous factors can inhibit aspen regeneration, even at low conifer cover, notably herbivory, competition from other plants, presence of a dense aspen overstory, low density or vigor of aspen parent trees, and poor soil conditions.) Just 5 percent of the stands had a relatively high

sucker density of 3,500 per acre or more, and all of these had 20 percent or less conifer cover. The data in figure 24 support the opinion of field managers that any amount of conifer cover inhibits aspen regeneration. Presumably conifer competition suppresses not only the number of suckers but also their growth rate, prolonging the time during which they are vulnerable to browsing.

Although removal of all conifers is most beneficial to aspen, retention of some widely spaced, large conifers for other resource needs is compatible with aspen regeneration. It is likely that aspen in the Blue Mountains historically coexisted with widely spaced large conifers in the park-like stands of old trees that are believed to have dominated here in the past. Where only some conifers can be removed, removal of those on the southeast to southwest portion of the aspen stand will promote soil warming and extra light reaching the soil surface. Retained conifers may also be pruned well up the stem to improve the amount of light reaching the ground.

Aspen regeneration is limited in areas with heavily compacted soils such as concentrated skid trails and landings (Frey et al. 2003, Schier et al. 1985b). The worst compaction occurs from traffic on wet, fine-grained soils. Unfortunately, soils are fine grained and moist to wet for much of the summer on most of our riparian and wetland aspen types (see the section on aspen community classification). Harvest should be timed to occur when soils are either frozen or dry.

Conifer slash disposal–

Two main approaches have been used successfully in the Blue Mountains for disposal of slash from conifer removal in aspen: burning in piles and scattering without burning. When slash is light, the latter is a good option. However, heavy aspen slash has been shown to inhibit suckering in some cases (Frey et al. 2003, Schier et al. 1985b), and it is reasonable to presume that heavy conifer slash would also have a similar effect. Slash can provide some amount of protection from browsing for aspen suckers, although man-

agers in the Blue Mountains believe that browsing pressure is typically too intense here for this method to be effective. Whole-tree yarding of removed conifers may also be used to avoid slash in aspen stands.

Burning small hand piles of slash (approximately 4 ft high by 6 ft diameter) disposes of the slash and can stimulate suckering (fig. 25). Long, hot fires in large slash piles can kill aspen roots entirely under the piles and create invasion sites for weeds, and thus should be avoided (Jones et al. 2005). In most cases, slash piles should be placed a safe distance from residual mature aspen so the fire does not kill them, because our objective is usually to promote suckering in the openings created by conifer removal while preserving as many residual large aspen as possible.

Broadcast burning of slash is likely to kill residual mature aspen but can be very effective in stimulating suckering. Good regeneration has been obtained in our area by this method in conjunction with fencing (fig. 26).

Fencing

Managers agree that physical protection of suckers is critical for aspen regeneration and long-term survival in the Blue Mountains. Combined herbivory by deer, elk, and cattle makes young aspen with uninterrupted growth form (Keigley and Frisina 1998) a rare sight outside of fenced exclosures or talus slopes, where access by hoofed herbivores is restricted (see for example the POTR [RUBBLE, HIGH] aspen community type description in the section on aspen community classification). In many situations, fencing is the only treatment needed to promote successful sucker recruitment (fig. 27). In some places, herbivory is so intense that there appears to be no aspen suckering, but soon after placement of a fence, suckers become apparent. Fencing is needed to allow successful regeneration after conifer removal in most localities. Fencing should be in

Figure 25–Hand pilling of slash for burning after conifer removal from an aspen stand. Slash was considered too much to leave in place and was piled outside of the aspen stand for burning.

Figure 26–Broadcast burning of conifer slash and aspen regeneration. Conifers were removed in 1997. On the left is a 1998 photo of decadent aspen over dense slash from conifer removal. The slash was broadcast burned in 1999 after fence construction, killing overstory aspen. On the right is a 2007 photo with a few remaining aspen snags and healthy aspen regeneration.

A

David Swanson

Figure 28–Response of aspen to fencing on the Walla Walla Ranger District, Umatilla National Forest. The contrast between the aspen exclosure (left) and open area (right) is due to ungulate herbivores; there is no significant soil/site difference. Inside the exclosure, which had been in place for 10 years by the photo date, aspens were up to 15 ft tall. Outside, only a few heavily browsed suckers were located.

B

Cindy Kranich

Diane Shirley

Figure 29–Buck-and-pole fencing to protect aspens.

Figure 27–Response of aspen to fencing. (A) An aspen stand in 2001 on the Prairie City Ranger District, Malheur National Forest. Both trees had crowns that were marginally alive. By 2004, one of the standing trees had fallen and a careful search located about twenty 4- to 6-in-tall suckers in the vicinity. Fencing was placed in the summer of 2004. (B) The same aspen stand in July 2007. Suckers have increased steadily in number and height to over 6 ft.

place before considering any treatments that involve killing overstory aspen to promote regeneration (such as felling or burning). Fencing alone may allow adequate regeneration and thus show further treatments to be unnecessary, and treatments that kill mature aspen without protecting the regeneration could result in loss of the clone.

Stands with abundant browsed suckers and a vigorous overstory (as indicated by a crown:bole ratio of at least 25 percent) are most likely to respond strongly to fencing treat-

ment, but even clones in very poor condition can often be regenerated with fencing alone (fig. 27).

Season of use and intensity of use by cattle, deer, and elk are unique to each time and place, although in many areas the heaviest pressure from all species is in late summer and early fall. Fences that exclude cattle alone are cheaper and have less effect on wildlife, but over much of our area they do not provide adequate protection. Experience in the Blue Mountains shows that cattle fencing is adequate locally where elk are not common or in elk summer range where human traffic prevents animals from lingering long in the aspen stands. Managers who suspect that cattle exclosures will be adequate in an area may want to test the effect of small cattle exclosures before investing in extensive fencing that may ultimately prove inadequate.

Most aspen exclosure fencing in the Blue Mountains consists of either 7- to 8-ft woven wire (fig. 28) or 6-ft

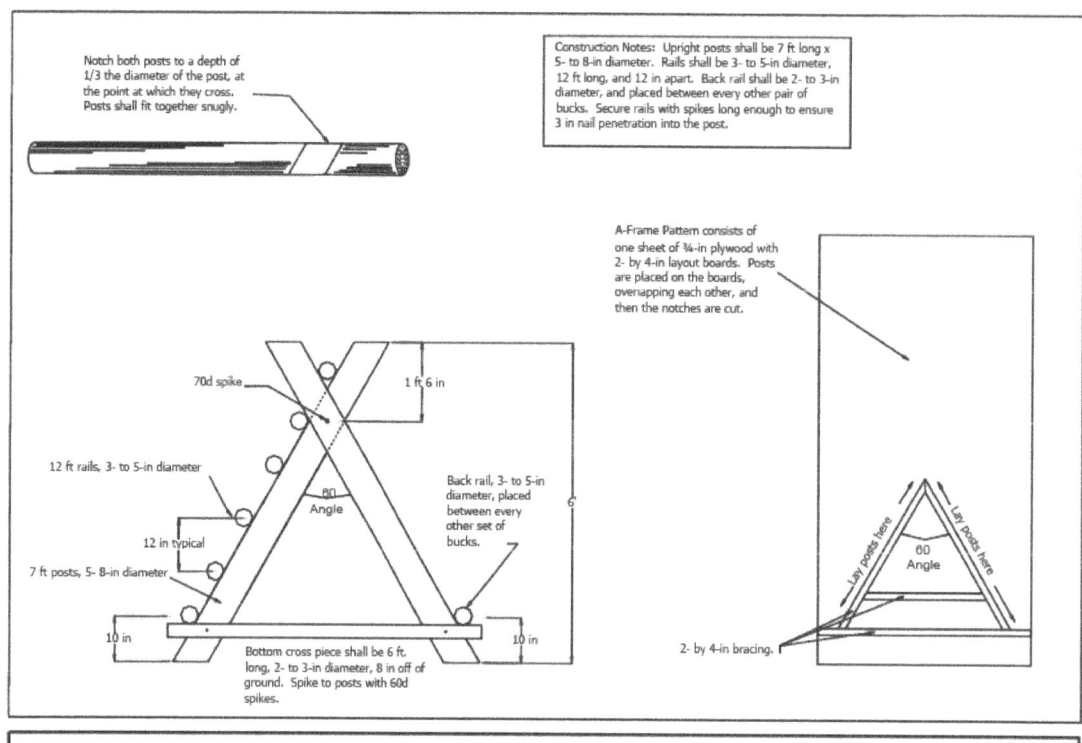

Notch both posts to a depth of 1/3 the diameter of the post, at the point at which they cross. Posts shall fit together snugly.

Construction Notes: Upright posts shall be 7 ft long x 5- to 8-in diameter. Rails shall be 3- to 5-in diameter, 12 ft long, and 12 in apart. Back rail shall be 2- to 3-in diameter, and placed between every other pair of bucks. Secure rails with spikes long enough to ensure 3 in nail penetration into the post.

A-Frame Pattern consists of one sheet of ¾-in plywood with 2- by 4-in layout boards. Posts are placed on the boards, overlapping each other, and then the notches are cut.

70d spike

1 ft 6 in

12 ft rails, 3- to 5-in diameter

60 Angle

Back rail, 3- to 5-in diameter, placed between every other set of bucks.

12 in typical

7 ft posts, 5- 8-in diameter

10 in

10 in

Bottom cross piece shall be 6 ft. long, 2- to 3-in diameter, 8 in off of ground. Spike to posts with 60d spikes.

Lay posts here

Lay posts here

60 Angle

2- by 4-in bracing.

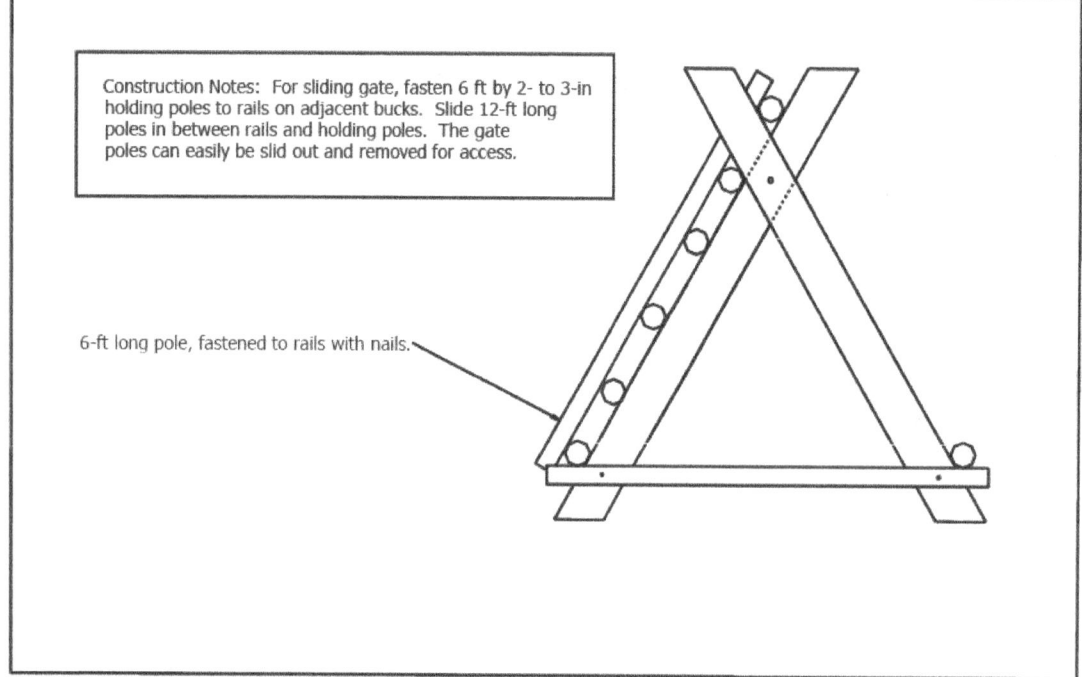

Construction Notes: For sliding gate, fasten 6 ft by 2- to 3-in holding poles to rails on adjacent bucks. Slide 12-ft long poles in between rails and holding poles. The gate poles can easily be slid out and removed for access.

6-ft long pole, fastened to rails with nails.

Figure 30—
Construction diagram of buck-and-pole fencing.

buck-and-pole fencing (fig. 29). The former is very effective but subject to snow damage, and thus should be restricted to lower elevation sites. Woven wire fences are usually 14 gauge and can be constructed from single panels or two 40-in panels joined with hog rings (Rolf 2001). Rolf (2001) also suggested placing two strands of high-tensile wire above the woven wire. Trees (typically conifers) make good corners if available. Some managers consider 5-ft woven wire fencing to be adequate except in the areas of highest elk browsing pressure. Managers agree that, in many situations, several smaller exclosures are easier to maintain than a single large exclosure, and the consequences of a breach less damaging.

Buck-and-pole fences are effective, withstand snow loading, can be constructed mostly with local materials, and are considered by many to have less visual impact than wire fences (fig. 30). Also, the spaces between the rails allow small mammals and grouse access to the stand. Local

Betsy Kaiser

Figure 31–Use of welded-wire rod fence panels to control browsing of hardwood tree plantings.

Vicky Erickson

Figure 32–Circular aspen exclosure constructed from two 16-ft welded-wire rod fence panels.

Michael Tatum

Figure 33–Gabion wire cages 5 years after installation (Prairie City Ranger District, Malheur National Forest). These cages were placed around the few surviving suckers near two decadent parent trees; at that time the suckers were hedged to less than 1 ft tall. Cost was about $25 each in materials, and all were constructed in about an hour.

lodgepole pine stands provide inexpensive materials, and may be used without peeling or treatment. Rails should be at least 3 inches in diameter. These buck-and-pole fences will remain effective with little maintenance for the 15-year period needed for aspen regeneration and then can be allowed to deteriorate and fall in place. Wire fences require a labor-intensive cleanup because fallen wire presents a hazard to wildlife and livestock.

Welded-wire rod livestock panels (5 by 16 ft) have been used to protect hardwoods in the Blue Mountains (fig. 31). These panels are more expensive than rolled wire mesh fencing and are suited to protecting individual trees or small groups of trees. They are easy to install, resistant to snow loads and flooding, and can be disassembled and moved to a new location. Elk are able to reach over the panels and browse about 2 ft into the exclosure. Both square (fig. 31) and circular (fig. 32) layouts have been used. Two 16-ft panels shaped to a circular layout make an exclosure with a diameter of about 10 ft.

Gabion wire cages, 3 ft in diameter and 5 ft tall secured with two or three steel posts have been successful and proven to be cost-effective when 10 or fewer cages will protect a stand; typically this is a few suckers under a nearly dead aspen overstory (fig. 33). Gabion wire is heavy-duty

mesh designed for construction of rock-filled erosion-control structures and the like. Fencing becomes a more cost-effective option when more than about 10 cages are needed. Small exclosures 10 to 20 ft in diameter can also be made quickly with gabion wire and used to protect isolated clumps of aspen or suckers around a few decadent parent trees. Use of light-gauge woven wire for building these cages has proven unsatisfactory, as large ungulates can crush the wire and access the contents of the cage.

Plastic mesh fences (7.5 ft tall) have been used successfully to exclude elk and moose in Montana (Kees 2004). Experience with such fencing in the Blue Mountains has shown that the plastic mesh holds up reasonably well, but steel posts are inadequate for corners, the plastic zip ties break in the cold weather, and the fencing tears loose from the posts. Existing trees provide more secure corners and can be used to create an exclosure of irregular shape; also, where winter browsing is minimal, snow damage can be minimized by letting the fencing down each winter (D. Bartos, 2008, personal communication, aspen ecologist, USDA Forestry Sciences Laboratory, Utah State University).

In regions with intense aspen use by wild and domestic ungulates such as the Blue Mountains, exclosures must be maintained well beyond the point where trees are tall enough for foliage to be out of reach. Antler rubbing, barking, and aggressive browsing that causes stem breakage can kill trees that are otherwise tall enough to be beyond the reach of browsers. Rolf (2001) found that elk in northern Arizona broke down and killed most aspen saplings less than 2 in d.b h. and 12 to 15 ft tall. Barking of larger trees can lead to girdling or disease infection. Fencing is needed until trees reach about 4 in d.b h., which typically requires 10 to 15 years in the Blue Mountains area. Annual maintenance checks are needed to ensure the integrity of exclosures. Removing unsound or standing dead trees that might fall on the fence can reduce maintenance needs.

Felling trees to form a barrier around the perimeter of an aspen clone has been suggested as an alternative to fencing in South Dakota (Kota 2005). Based on observations of herbivores' ability to jump over low fences and also find minor breaches in fences, managers in the Blue Mountains believe that this method may be effective in situations where browsing pressure is light and cattle are the main herbivore, but it would not be effective here in most situations.

Chemical repellents are a potential alternative to fencing for reducing browsing of aspen (Baker et al. 1999). Repellents allow some level of browsing, but this might be acceptable in a healthy regenerating aspen stand with many stems. Some repellents discourage cattle as well as deer and elk (Osko et al. 1993). Repellents are generally effective for at least a month after application, and are most effective if there is little rain. Broadcast application over large areas is cost prohibitive (Baker et al. 1999), but spot-spraying of isolated clones could prove to be more cost-effective than fencing in some situations. Managers in the Blue Mountains report that repellents have been used successfully on conifers, but aspen may prove to be more difficult to protect because of their high palatability and rapid growth rates: new growth after treatment may be browsed because it is unprotected. Several summer and fall treatments would be needed if elk are present for a long period. Repellents may be most promising where cattle are the main herbivore and they are present for a fairly short, well-defined interval.

Fire

Fire is generally beneficial to aspen because it removes competing conifers and stimulates suckering (Jones and DeByle 1985b). Thus prescribed fire is sometimes considered as a management tool to regenerate aspen stands. Prescribed fire has been used successfully to dispose of heavy conifer slash and stimulate suckering (fig. 26). Photo series for quantifying fuels are available for Rocky Mountain aspen (Ottmar et al. 2000). However, there are several important issues to consider before introducing prescribed fire into aspen in the Blue Mountains. First, aspen stands tend to be less flammable than other vegetation types in our area; hence when conditions are favorable for burning in aspen, they may be hazardous in surrounding areas. Slash from conifer removal in an aspen stand (fig. 26) can mitigate this problem by providing highly flammable fuel. Second, fire in aspen should be avoided if aspen suckering is already occurring, because fire in a stand of suckers can be followed by weaker suckering than in the original stand (Perala 1974). Third, postfire herbivory on aspen suckers is often intense and can prevent aspen regeneration (Shirley and Erickson 2001). Studies elsewhere in the West have shown that small patches of regenerating aspen–less than 12 acres according to Mueggler and Bartos (1977), i.e., nearly all of our aspen stands–are likely to fail owing to herbivory. Coarse woody debris from the fire can be a deterrent, but it is generally not effective against elk (Forester et al. 2007), and we suspect it to be ineffective against deer also. Thus, fencing should be in place to protect new suckers in the first growing season after a fire. Fourth, the typical low-intensity prescribed fires used in fuel treatments in our area are designed to remove surface fuels and young conifers without killing large fire-resistant pines and Douglas-firs. These fires can kill mature aspen without removing conifers; as a result, suckers will grow weakly under the conifer overstory. Thus, competing conifers should be felled or girdled before the fire. Finally, severely weakened clones, consisting of just a few suppressed or decadent trees, may not have the carbohydrate reserves to regenerate vigorously after fire. Given the naturally high mortality rate of aspen suckers, the survival of a clone with just a few suckers is uncertain. A safer alternative in the case of a small weakened clone would be to first try to regenerate the clone by conifer removal and fencing or caging.

Wildfires present both opportunities and risks for aspen management. On the one hand, a wildfire can stimulate suckering and renewal of decadent aspen stands, plus it offers a rare opportunity for seed reproduction by aspen (all known examples of seed reproduction by aspen in our area have been after fires). On the other hand, after death of mature aspen in a fire, the survival of a clone is dependent on survival of suckers, which are vulnerable to browsing. Forage produced by other early-seral plants after a large fire may partly distract herbivores from aspen, but loss of aspen clones after fire from herbivory is still a concern.

Figure 34–Suckering response of degenerated aspen clone to felling. This clone responded weakly to conifer removal but regenerated well after felling the decadent overstory aspens, with fence protection.

Reproduction by seed after fires in our area is extremely rare, and seedlings, like suckers, are highly vulnerable to browsing. Steps that managers can take to favor aspen after wildfire include maintaining existing exclosures and constructing new exclosures if possible. Speed is crucial: after the overstory aspen are killed, the number of suckers will be highest in the first growing season and then decline annually in vigor and number under heavy browsing pressure as root reserves are depleted. A second step is reducing herbivory through grazing management. The latter approach is, of course, effective only where livestock are the main herbivores impacting aspen. Exclusion of livestock, at least during the period when they are especially attracted to aspen (late July, August, and September) can be very helpful. This management step should be continued until aspen are large enough to be safe from cattle browsing, which typically requires about 5 years. We know of a few cases where relatively large (10 ac), very vigorous aspen stands in the Blue Mountains burned in wildfires and produced regeneration dense enough to withstand herbivores. However, the increased frequency and severity of wildfires that has been observed in recent decades has not improved the overall situation for aspen in the Blue Mountains.

Aspen Felling and Girdling

Aspen are rarely felled in the Blue Mountains. Because aspen are not managed for wood products in the three national forests of the Blue Mountains, they are not normally harvested here. Harvest to produce stands of various ages for wildlife management (e.g., Gullion 1984) is also not practiced in the Blue Mountains: although the proportion of old aspen age classes is quite high here, the overall rarity of old aspen on the landscape relative to conifer types

and their great wildlife value preclude harvest to improve wildlife habitat.

Girdling aspen is not recommended as a regeneration treatment because it stimulates little suckering (Schier and Smith 1979). Roots of girdled aspen are deprived of the photosynthate that they formerly received from the leaves; meanwhile, cytokinin can escape upward in the xylem of girdled stems, and thus suckering is not stimulated. In fact, girdling is only recommended as a treatment to **eliminate** aspen from a site (Schier and Smith 1979).

Resource managers are faced with a difficult decision at the end of the flow chart in figure 19 when a deteriorating clone has not responded to conifer removal and fencing. If these measures have been in place for 2 or 3 years and no suckering response has occurred, then some managers recommend felling the remaining overstory trees to stimulate suckering (fig. 34). The drawback here is that we lose valuable mature trees, and there is some risk that the clone will fail to sucker and thus be eliminated by the treatment. However, felling may be needed to regenerate a decadent clone as described by Schier (1975): the root system of a clone may gradually die under diseased, declining overmature trees while these trees continue to suppress suckering. Unfortunately, less aggressive measures, such as felling only half of the remaining large trees in a deteriorating clone, result in weak suckering responses. If such a "last resort" felling of aspen is implemented, avoid felling soon after leaf flush, when carbohydrates have been translocated to the tops and root reserves are lowest (Schier 1976). Dormant-season felling is preferred (Schier et al. 1985b). And, of course, ensure that fencing is in place so that the suckers, which may be sparse under a severely weakened clone, are adequately protected.

Mechanical Site Preparation

Mechanical site preparation can stimulate suckering, but it can also lead to root damage that hinders sucker survival and future productivity (see reviews by Frey et al. 2003 and Schier et al. 1985b). For example, disking severs roots, which disconnects them from overstory trees and releases them from apical dominance-related suppression of suckering; it can also increase soil temperatures and reduce competing vegetation. However, the small root segments created by disking have very limited water uptake and receive no energy inputs from neighboring trees. For these reasons, disking is generally not recommended (Schier et al. 1985b).

Separation of lateral roots from existing mature trees by deep soil ripping just outside the canopy limit has been recommended as a way to extend stand boundaries (Shepperd 2001, Shepperd et al. 2006). Suckering from remote roots is stimulated by separation from overstory trees.

Unfortunately this treatment is expensive and also cuts off any carbohydrates that the suckers would receive from the mature trees. In our experience, suckering from distal roots is usually adequate without ripping (e.g., fig. 35).

Thinning

Managers in the Blue Mountains are interested in thinning as a means to speed up the growth of aspen to a size class that is safe from herbivores. Thinning aspen often increases diameter growth rate, whereas height growth rate depends mainly on site quality (Jones and Shepperd 1985). Thus, thinning could shorten the time needed to create robust stands (e.g., trees 4 in d.b.h. or greater) resistant to antler rubbing, barking, and breaking by pushing and trampling.

Some arguments against thinning are as follows. Aspen effectively self-thin in dense postdisturbance stands, and thus artificial thinning is not necessary to the development of productive stands (Frey et al. 2003, Shepperd 1993). A high density of suckers provides some insurance against mortality losses to herbivores or other factors. Also, a dense stand of aspen suckers helps to maintain the root system that will be used by the clone in the future (DesRochers and Lieffers 2001b).

Fencing is crucial for any stands thinned in our area, because herbivore damage is greater in sparse stands (Shepperd 1993). Thinning of dense first-year stands can produce numerous new suckers that must be thinned again (Strothman and Heinselman 1957). Jones and Shepperd (1985) recommended thinning stands at 5 to 10 years of age, when the tallest trees are about 15 ft tall, to a spacing of about 5 by 5 ft (1,500 trees per acre). Thinnings in older stands are generally recommended for saw-log production and are not applicable to the Blue Mountains.

Establishment of Aspen Outside of Existing Stands

Establishment of new aspen stands is desirable to restore lost clones, increase connectivity between existing stands, increase genetic diversity, and improve the opportunity for

Figure 35–Response of aspen to conifer removal and fencing, Geary Aspen Project, Blue Mountain Ranger District, Malheur National Forest. (A) March 1994, prior to treatment. Note the conifer encroachment in the stand behind and stubs from browsed suckers in the foreground. (B) March 1994, after conifer removal. A fence was constructed soon after. (C) August 1995. The densest portions of the stand had approximately 10,000 stems/acre. (D) July 2007. Regeneration was 6 to 10 ft high behind the fence; sparse browsed suckers were outside of the fence.

sexual reproduction by providing a mix of male and female plants (Shirley and Erickson 2001).

Expanding the boundaries of an existing aspen clone is often desirable, both to restore lost historical area and to increase the chances for long-term survival of the clone. For example, an aspen clone squeezed into a narrow zone between dense upland conifers and a wet sedge meadow is in a precarious position, vulnerable to elimination by a minor rise in the water table (figs. 22, 36). Many wetland margin aspen clones would be made safer by conifer removal that would allow them to expand into somewhat drier adjacent areas.

Aspen roots are often found well beyond the perimeter of existing trees. The range of the rooting for a clone can often be estimated by careful search for aborted suckers. Felling conifers and fencing to allow successful production of suckers from these existing roots often yields dramatic results and a rapid increase in the area occupied by aspen stems (fig. 35). As discussed in the "Aspen Biology and Ecology" section, aspen roots can grow laterally at a rate of perhaps 1 yd per year under favorable conditions. Thus it makes sense to extend fencing and conifer treatment beyond any existing stems or aborted suckers if site conditions appear adequate. We have observed clonal expansion to be most successful on the south and southwest sides of existing aspen clones. This is presumably due to the greater light availability and higher soil temperatures to the south and southwest. Thus, a larger zone of conifer removal and fencing to the south or southwest side of a clone is advised. One of our ranger districts, as a rule of thumb, extends conifer removal and fencing 50 ft beyond the last live aspen on the north and east side of a stand and 100 ft to the south and west.

Planting artificially propagated aspen plants is more costly but necessary if the goal is to establish a new stand, rapidly expand a stand far beyond existing boundaries, or

cross barriers to roots such as a stream channel (fig. 37). Planting stock should be derived from local sources, but not necessarily from the clone nearest the planting site; it is often desirable to intersperse material from various local clones to increase genetic diversity and to ensure a mix of male and female plants for sexual reproduction. For more information on propagation and planting see the "Vegetative Propagation" section below.

Choosing appropriate sites–
Clearly any area proposed for planting or expansion of an existing aspen clone must have suitable soil and site conditions, minimal competition from other vegetation, and the usual protection from herbivores. The latter two conditions do not differ from what is required for regenerating aspen clones within their present limit and was discussed previously. The answer to the former question–Where are soil/site conditions correct for expansion of an aspen clone?–is not always obvious, yet must be answered before investment is made in fencing, conifer removal, or planting. Areas adjacent to a vigorous existing clone with similar landform and understory vegetation are good bets for successful expansion. The following guidelines are suggested if the objective is to plant or expand a clone into new areas unlike those currently occupied. They are based on our aspen community classification work.

1. In areas where the upland vegetation is dominated by the dry upland forest potential vegetation group (ponderosa pine or Douglas-fir series vegetation, or dry grand fir plant associations such as grand fir/pinegrass; see Powell et al. 2007 for more information), aspen is usually restricted to riparian or wetland areas where supplemental moisture is available and soils are rich and loamy with a high available water capacity. Look for areas with a diversity of mesic forbs such as those listed for the aspen/mesic forb or aspen/

Figure 36–Aspens on meadow fringe. Aspens in the Blue Mountains often occur in a narrow zone between soils that are too wet and coniferous forest with too little light. If the water table in this meadow were to rise, the few remaining aspens could be killed.

Figure 37–Aspen planted to enlarge a stand. Site conditions in the planted area are similar to the stand with vigorous regeneration in the background, but well beyond the extent of existing roots.

common snowberry plant community types. Areas supporting a dense sod of introduced pasture grasses such as meadow foxtail (*Alopecurus pratensis*), Kentucky bluegrass (*Poa pratensis*), and timothy (*Phleum pratense*) will also usually support aspen (see the aspen/Kentucky bluegrass and aspen/meadow foxtail plant community types in the section on aspen community classification). Note that the presence of the introduced pasture grass, intermediate wheatgrass (*Agropyron intermedium*), alone is not a good indicator of suitability for aspen, because this grass can grow on sites too dry for aspen. Vegetation on proposed aspen sites should be distinctly more lush and diverse than in the adjacent dry upland forest. Areas dominated by wetland grasses and sedges such as aquatic sedge (*Carex aquatilis*) or bluejoint reedgrass (*Calamagrostis canadensis*) can sometimes support aspen, but are often too wet. For optimal aspen growth, the water table should recede at least 2 ft below the surface for most of the growing season (Jones and Debyle 1985c).

2. In areas with upland vegetation dominated by moist upland forest or cold upland forest potential vegetation groups (moist grand fir or subalpine fir potential vegetation; Powell et al. 2007), aspen is still most common in wet areas, but moisture is also adequate for aspen to grow on a variety of upland sites. Thus established aspen clones can be enlarged from wetland margins onto adjacent drier soils, as long as the upland soils are not obviously shallow, droughty, or nutrient-poor. New plantings are most likely to succeed in moist mesic meadow areas such as those described above for the dry upland forest areas. If a new planting of aspen on an upland site is attempted, look for a relatively lush growth of the understory species listed for grand fir series aspen types (see the aspen community classification section), the most widespread of which is the aspen (grand fir)/snowberry plant community type. Mesic forbs such as mountain sweet-cicely (*Osmorhiza chilensis*), western meadowrue (*Thalictrum occidentale*), and nettleleaf horsemint (*Agastache urticifolia*) are good indicators of relatively rich, moist soil where aspen should flourish. As in the previous case, avoid areas with chronically saturated soils dominated by wetland grasses and sedges.

Vegetative Propagation

Stem cuttings of aspen root poorly, so a more elaborate procedure is required. A protocol developed in Denmark by Larsen (1943) has been modified and used with aspen in the Western United States, and is described in detail by Schier (1978) and Schier et al. (1985b). This method involves making root cuttings from an existing stand, developing suckers from the cuttings, then cutting and rooting these suckers. The following section is an account of local experience with this propagation method in the Blue Mountains. (See also propagation protocols assembled by the Native Plant Network at http://www.nativeplantnetwork.org/)

Root collection–

It is best to collect roots in the autumn, following leaf fall in mature trees, when the maximum amount of carbohydrates reside in the root system as opposed to in the apical shoots of stems (fig. 2). Autumn cuttings must be refrigerated for several months after collection, but then the entire subsequent growing season is available for rooted sucker production. Cuttings may also be made in early spring (Schier 1978), although snow and frozen soil may interfere. Root cuttings should not be made during the spring leaf flush, because the high concentrations of auxins in the roots at this time suppress suckering (Scheir 1978).

A good rule of thumb is to collect roots that are, at a minimum, the size of your index finger in diameter. Roots larger than 3 inches in diameter are more cumbersome for the nursery to work with. Pulaskis, hoedads, and shovels have all been used successfully, as has washing roots from the ground using high-pressure water. A small hand trowel comes in handy for more delicate excavation of roots. Root suckers growing in a straight line are excellent indicators of where the mature root is located underground. Mature roots may be as close as 2 in beneath the ground surface but most often are found at a depth of 4 to 6 in. These surface roots take advantage of light rains that do not penetrate to the groundwater level and eventually will turn downward in search of more abundant moisture. It is important to use care when digging to prevent scraping the surface tissue of the roots. This tissue contains the primordia that become root suckers. Heavy-duty branch pruners are used to cut the roots into 8- to 12-in segments. Smaller pruners are useful to remove any suckers. You may leave the suckers intact and simply transplant it to another site; however, our success

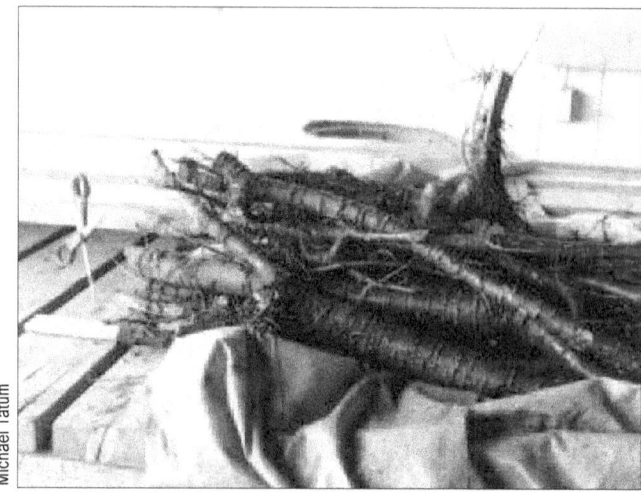

Michael Tatum

Figure 38–Aspen root cuttings after cleaning and before final wrapping. Roots should be kept moist and cold throughout this process.

rate for such transplants has been poor, probably owing to their weak root systems. Excavated roots are placed in large trash bags along with some sort of tag to identify the source of the collection site.

Upon returning to the office, one should futher trim roots and rinse off excess dirt (fig. 38). Rinsing also keeps the roots moist during shipping. We roll the roots up in burlap bags or polypropylene shop towels and then place these in clean plastic trash bags. A tag indicating stand location and elevation is placed in a sealable plastic bag inside the trash bag. This way more than one bag may be shipped in a box. Roots may first be mixed with sphagnum moss before wrapping, which will prevent the formation of mold when the roots are placed in cold storage over winter. Roots should be kept refrigerated until just before shipping. Overnight shipping of roots to the destination nursery reduces the potential for drying or overheating of roots.

Propagation of containerized aspen from collected roots–

Propagation, to date, has been carried out by the U.S. Forest Service J. Herbert Stone Nursery in Medford, Oregon, and the U.S. Forest Service Coeur d'Alene Nursery (Idaho Panhandle National Forest). Cost per plant was about $2.00 from the latter source in 2008 for small quantities (several hundred), not including the cost of root collection, shipping, or outplanting. Root segments received in the fall were washed in a large tub containing a 10-percent alcohol solution, wrapped in polypropylene shop towels or burlap, and stored under refrigeration (Johann Visser, personal communication, culturist, J. Herbert Stone Nursery). In February or early March, root segments were placed in wooden containers measuring 2 by 3 by 6 in. Drainage holes were drilled into the base of the containers. The containers were then filled with a 1-in layer of pure perlite, followed by a 3- to 4-in layer that was 40 percent peat, 40 percent vermiculite,

and 20 percent perlite. Root segments were placed on top of the latter layer and covered with approximately a quarter inch of the same. The medium was moist but not wet to reduce disease. The containers were placed in a greenhouse maintained at 70 to 75 °F. Sprouting took place within 10 days to 2 weeks. When root suckers reached 3 to 4 in tall, they were cut as close as possible to the old root section and the lower leaves removed, and then they were dipped in a commercial rooting hormone containing IBA (indole-3-butyric acid) and placed in individual D-40 (40 in^3) containers or in 1-gal pots filled with a mixture that was 40 percent peat, 40 percent vermiculite, and 20 percent perlite. These were grown in a mist chamber under a 24-hour photoperiod at 90 percent relative humidity and 78 °F (during the day a layer of shade cloth was placed over the chamber to reduce sunlight by 50 percent). Roots emerged within a few weeks on about 70 percent of the cuttings. The plants were fertilized with a solution containing a 21-5-20 ratio of nitrogen, phosphorous, and potash and trace amounts of micronutrients. When the plants appeared to be growing vigorously, they were placed in a greenhouse and grown for 2 to 3 weeks, or until approximately 10 in tall. After the danger of hard frosts had passed, containers were moved outside to a shade house for the remainder of the growing season (fig. 39). The average height at the end of the growing

Figure 40–A shade card improves the survival of planted aspen.

Figure 39–Rooted aspens in 2.5-in diameter by 10-in deep (40 in^3) plastic containers growing in a shade house.

season was 16 in. Once plants had completely hardened off and entered dormancy in late fall, containers were moved into freezer storage until they were needed for outplanting the following spring.

Planting propagated aspen–

Propagating aspen is an expensive venture. It is imperative that planting procedures that will optimize survival are employed. Ensure that site conditions are appropriate, with adequate available soil moisture and removal of competing vegetation; see the previous section for more information. In addition, trees must be planted properly, in adequate densities, and protected from herbivores. Dormant containerized trees should be planted as early in the year as conditions allow.

Warm temperatures and severe drought are common in summer in the Blue Mountains, and preventing tree death from desiccation is a challenge, particularly on more coarse-grained soils along intermittent streams that run dry early in the summer. As temperatures rise to 90 °F and above, the heat load on the young aspen rises dramatically. This often results in dieback of the terminal shoot or death from desiccation. Placing a shade card approximately 2 to 4 in from the planted tree, on the south-southwest side of the tree, blocks much of the afternoon sun, thereby reducing the heat load (fig. 40). It is important that the shade card is placed low enough to protect the root collar of the tree. Even if the aspen terminal dies back to the height of the shade card, the tree usually survives. Most often, a lateral shoot will assume dominance in the subsequent growing season. It is critical to keep the root system alive until the tap roots can grow down to the water table. If successful, the shoot can die back to ground level and the root system will send up a new shoot the following season.

Removing competing vegetation, such as sedges and grasses, will also reduce the competition for moisture. A scalp that is 24 in square is usually sufficient and provides a competition-free environment for the first growing season. Planting on sites that provide adequate soil moisture throughout the growing season, will of course, eliminate the need for the above measures.

Selecting an adequate planting density to ensure successful reforestation is dependant on the predicted survival rate for the site. One high-elevation site with plentiful soil moisture and relatively low heat load from the afternoon sun on the Umatilla National Forest had a survival rate of 99 percent. Favorable predicted survival allows planting at much lower densities with the expectation that surviving trees will send up hundreds of root suckers in the future. This permits the manager to spread a limited number of aspen containers across several planting units.

Rigid, plastic tubing can provide short-term protection from herbivores for planted aspen on a new site. This rela-

tively inexpensive measure will protect the young aspen; if survival is adequate, more expensive measures (e.g., fencing) can be justified. Tubes should be at least 24 in tall and are stapled to 1.5 in square, 30-in tall, wooden hubs. The hubs are pounded into the ground to a depth of 12 in. These hubs hold up much better in the snow than do bamboo stakes. Longer tubes (30 in) provide protection longer for the rapidly growing aspen, but we found that these larger tubes were more easily knocked over by cattle, probably because a proportionally longer segment of the wooden hub was exposed and acted as a lever to push the tube over. Once the aspen has outgrown the tube, the device has served its purpose and it is time to move on to a longer term solution: fencing.

Other vegetative propagation options–

Juvenile shoots of aspen hybrids (*Populus tremuloides* x *P. tremula*) grown from tissue culture have been successfully cut into short (two-node) cuttings and rooted with about 70 percent success rate (Haapala et al. 2004). Multiple batches of greenwood cuttings were made from the same stock by cutting regrowth every 4 weeks. This technique could prove successful with suckers from root cuttings grown in the greenhouse as described above, allowing more plants to be obtained from each root cutting. Aspen have also been successfully propagated by tissue culture derived from seeds (Noh and Minocha 1986).

Propagation of Aspen from Seed

Propagation of aspen from seed is also possible, although abundant seed production events (fig. 41) appear to be rare in our area. Both bare root and containerized methods have been used (Day et al. 2003, Schier et al. 1985b; see also the Native Plant Network at http://www.nativeplantnetwork. org/). Campbell (1984) believed that propagation from seed is faster and cheaper than vegetative propagation. Several issues should be kept in mind when propagating aspen from seeds. Aspen is dioecious, so female clones must be located for seed collection. Sex determination in aspen is not difficult, as the shape, color, and position of male and female floral structures are very distinctive (see photographs in Moench 2000). Although it is possible to determine sex from assessment of dormant buds in the fall, the task is easiest in late spring when trees are in full flower. Female flowers (catkins) emerge later in the season than males, and are most noticeable in May when they are green and fully extended (Moench 2000). The silhouette of a female aspen tree with a heavy seed crop is very striking.

Seed collection must be timed very carefully, because capsules can open quickly and release all seeds in windy weather. Conversely, seed that is collected prematurely will not ripen, and viability will be poor. Seed maturity is best determined by examination of seed color and appearance.

Michael Tatum

Figure 41—Seeds released by aspen on the Malheur National Forest, 19 June, 2008.

Immature seed is glossy and translucent, whereas mature seeds are pink or brown. The collection window typically ranges from late May to mid-June depending on elevation and local weather conditions (Moench 2000). At a given site, however, the range of appropriate collection time can be as narrow as 48 hours (Fung and Hamel 1993). The U.S. Forest Service Coeur d'Alene Nursery (Idaho Panhandle National Forest) recommends that female catkins be collected just before they disperse, and shipped immediately to the nursery for drydown and then sowing within 2 to 3 days (Kent Eggleston, horticulturist, personal communication). Other methods include pruning branches with mature but closed catkins, followed by soaking branches in tubs of water for approximately 5 days until the catkins begin to release cotton. Capsules can be dislodged from the catkins with a vacuum, or gently stripped by hand into a container (Fung and Hamel 1993, Moench 2000).

Aspen seeds lack dormancy and can be sown immediately after collection. Seeds lose viability extremely rapidly (e.g., within 2 to 4 weeks; McDonough 1985) and must be dried and stored cold if not planted. Seeds and seedlings must be kept moist until well established. Under good growing conditions, 1-year-old plants are large enough to plant.

Planting techniques are the same as those described above for vegetatively propagated aspen.

Restoring Understory Plant Diversity in Aspen Stands

Aspen stands in good condition support a diverse herbaceous understory. Heavy grazing not only prevents aspen regeneration, but also can suppress or eliminate native herbs from the understory. Prolonged heavy grazing in mesic aspen meadows will favor Kentucky bluegrass and other introduced sod-forming grasses; see for example the quaking aspen/Kentucky bluegrass plant community type in Crowe and Clausnitzer (1997) and in the aspen community classification section of this study. Plants that are commonly suppressed or eliminated from aspen stands include forbs such as heartleaf arnica (*Arnica cordifolia*), common camas (*Camassia quamash*), mountain sweet-cicely (*Osmorhiza chilensis*), straightbeak buttercup (*Ranunculus orthorhynchus*), starry false solomon's seal (*Smilacina stellata*), sticky geranium (*Geranium viscosissimum*), and western meadowrue (*Thalictrum occidentale*). Natural recolonziation of degraded communities by these plants will be very slow owing to competition from the dense grass sod. However, the fencing that is in place to allow aspen regeneration will also protect herbaceous plantings, and conifer removal allows light to reach the forest floor, both of which present an ideal opportunity for restoration of native herbaceous plants.

A variety of shrubs occur in aspen stands, some of which are preferred browse species and have probably been reduced below their historical abundance by herbivores. These shrubs are potentially even more vulnerable to ungulate herbivory than aspen, because they may be shorter lived and are unable to grow tall enough to entirely escape the herbivores' reach. It is probably no accident that in our area the most common understory shrubs in aspen stands are the less palatable browse species (e.g., snowberry *Symphoricarpos* spp., alder *Alnus* spp., and wax currant *Ribes cereum*) or are defended by thorns (roses *Rosa* spp. and hawthorn *Crataegus* spp.). We suspect that the highly palatable shrubs that occur sporadically in aspen communities in our area are less common than they were historically as a result of browsing, and thus they are good candidates for restoration efforts. On riparian and wetland aspen sites these include red-osier dogwood (*Cornus stolonifera*), chokecherry, and western serviceberry. On upland aspen sites they are chokecherry, bitter cherry (*Prunus emarginata*), Scouler willow (*Salix scouleriana*), Rocky Mountain maple (*Acer glabrum*), and western serviceberry. Riparian and wetland sites dominated by herbaceous species and lacking shrubs of any kind today are typically too wet and are not good candidates for shrub restoration.

However, riparian sites supporting some shrubs today (e.g., snowberry) are potential candidates for plantings to increase shrub diversity. The shrubs listed above for upland sites are quite drought tolerant (with the exception of maple), and could potentially occur over most of the environmental range of upland aspen. Thus, plantings of these species in typical aspen stands to increase understory diversity would be reasonable. The suitability of the driest aspen types (the aspen/pinegrass and aspen/elk sedge plant community types) for shrub restoration is questionable because they lack shrubs today. However, soil and environmental conditions of these types do not differ greatly from upland types with shrub understories, suggesting that shrub restoration may be possible here also.

Before beginning an understory restoration project, be sure that the hydrology of the site has not been altered such that typical aspen-grove species are no longer adapted. This commonly occurs when stream erosion and incision lowers the water table on a streamside terrace. The moist soil of many aspen groves with intact hydrology is ideal for plant propagation.

To select the species to plant, we recommend both searching the site for rare relict occurrences of native plants and classifying your site by this publication and examining the list of typical plants in the type description. Ideally seed will be gathered from the relict plants or from nearby less impacted areas. Planting containerized plants is more reliable than seeding. For many plants, this will require seed pretreatment plus growing in a greenhouse for the equivalent of a growing season. An excellent source for native plant propagation protocols is the Native Plant Network, at http://nativeplants.for.uidaho.edu/.

Competition from existing plants must be controlled to allow establishment of the new plants, especially herbaceous species. Tillage and herbicides are not recommended, because we do not want to endanger the aspen and other native plants. An effective but labor-intensive solution is to place each plant in the center of an area about 3 ft in diameter that has been scalped down to mineral soil. Also effective is to scalp and lay down woven weed-barrier fabric, then place the plants about 2 ft apart by slitting the fabric with an X (personal communication, Chris Hoag, USDA NRCS Plant Materials Center, Aberdeen, Idaho). Most aspen understory plants are moderately shade tolerant, but one should generally avoid patches of dense aspen regeneration or other competing woody vegetation.

Assessment of Aspen Regeneration

Management decisions in aspen stands are driven by stand structure and condition, including the density, size, and condition of aspen regeneration, overstory aspen, and competing conifers (fig. 19). Typically decisions can be based on

a subjective assessment of an aspen stand. For example, the stand in figure 27 clearly had deficient regeneration and was in need of protection from herbivores, whereas the stand in figure 8 clearly would have benefitted from conifer removal. A quick classification of the predominant growth form of aspen regeneration by the system of Keigley and Frisina (1998) and Keigley et al. (2002) will usually determine whether browsing is intense and, hence, fencing or other herbivore-control measures are needed.

Once management actions have been taken, some sort of monitoring program is usually desired to track the success or failure of management actions and assess future needs. Repeat photography is a quick and usually adequate method to track the progress of aspen regeneration treatments. For best results, take photos from permanently marked locations (e.g., a fencepost) that are referenced by a written description and exact coordinates. When obtaining coordinates from the global positioning system (GPS), be sure to record the coordinate system (latitude-longitude, Universal Transverse Mercator, etc.), datum (North American Datum 1983 is recommended), and estimated GPS error (if available) in addition to the coordinates themselves. Record the azimuth of each photograph and bring a copy of previous shots on revisits so the exact view can be matched. A scale reference such as a graduated pole placed a specified distance from the photographer is also helpful. For more information on setting up photographic monitoring points, see Hall (2001).

If quantitative information on stand response to management is needed, permanent monitoring plots may be installed and sampled according to the U.S. Forest Service Common Stand Exam protocols (USDA FS 2008). The following discussion is intended to guide the choice of protocol options to best fit the unique conditions of Blue Mountains aspen stands. Our aspen stands are typically too small for the standard layout of multiple plots in a systematic grid. In some cases, a single fixed-area plot may be established that encompasses most or all of an aspen stand. In other cases, the transect cross-section method is most appropriate, with the transect oriented along the long axis of the stand and plots placed at regular intervals. The transect may be conveniently located with ends at landmarks such as an exclosure fencepost or corner tree.

Aspen regeneration is usually sampled by counting suckers (i.e., by sampling stem density) in fixed-area plots (e.g., Schier 1975). Schier (1975) also counted sucker clumps (stems clustered together in an area no more than 8 inches in diameter), as only one stem per clump would usually survive to maturity. Given our typical sucker densities of a few thousand stems per acre or less, 1/100-ac (11.8-ft radius) plots would usually be appropriate. The number of plots will differ according to the size and density of the stand. For example, in an oblong 1-ac aspen stand approximately 300 ft long, one might place five 1/100-ac plots at 50-ft intervals. The total tree tally, given the typical aspen sucker densities in the Blue Mountains, would range from less than 30 to about 100 stems. Because survival to a height that is safe from herbivores is our main concern, we would normally record the height of all suckers less than 4.5 ft high; both d.b h. and height class for all larger stems up to some threshold value such as 4 in d.b h.; and d.b.h. alone for larger trees.

Aspen Stand Quick Assessment and Desired Future Condition

The following quick assessment system was designed by M.L. Tatum for use in inventory of aspen stands on the Prairie City Ranger District of Malheur National Forest. The canopy layers of individual aspen stands are identified by letters (table 4) and the vigor of each layer is described with a number between 0 and 6 (table 5). The letters and numbers are then combined to produce a stand description code. For example, a stand with a nearly dead aspen understory, an aspen middle story with some good- and some poor-condition individuals, and an overstory in fair condition would be classified as "A4B3C2."

The conifer competition in an aspen stand is described similarly, with letter codes for the conifer canopy layers (table 6) and a number for the conifer competition class of each layer; the latter describes the degree to which the conifer layer is suppressing aspen (table 7). The conifer competition description is particularly useful to identify stands in need of conifer removal.

The aspen layer and conifer competition systems can be combined into a composite aspen assessment code.

Consider the following example aspen stand:

- Understory: aspen are nearly all dead and overtopped by a very thick and heavy carpet of grand fir regeneration; suckers/seedlings of aspen are not achieving any net annual height growth.
- Middlestory: aspen have some good- and some poor-condition individuals and a moderate conifer component that is only affecting some clumps of aspen.
- Overstory: aspen in fair condition with a light conifer overstory.

This stand would be classified as A4B3C2D6E3F1.

The structural classification of an aspen stand (tables 8 and 9) can be derived from the assessment codes. The stand described above would thus be placed into HRV class 3, old forest multistrata.

Once the structural class and area of each aspen stand in a planning area is known, the total acreage of each class can be computed for all aspen stands. Then the proportion of area in each class can be compared to reference conditions to determine how the aspen stands meet the desired structural composition at a landscape scale. A proposed landscape composition of aspen stands is provided in table 10. It suggests management for a dominance of young age classes in aspen stands; this is what we expect was historically present, based on our knowledge of the high historical fire frequency in the Blue Mountains (Heyerdahl et al. 2001). In addition, owing to aspen's short lifespan and tendency for mature trees to become diseased, a high proportion of young age classes is needed to maintain aspen acreage on the landscape. Note that because aspen area as a whole is considered to be in deficit in our area, an increase in younger age classes of aspen should be obtained primarily through expansion of aspen area, not killing of existing old trees.

Table 4–Aspen layer classification

Code	Structural layer	Typical age	Age class	Size group
		Years		
A	Understory	0-25	Suckers to juvenile	Sucker to sapling
B	Midstory	25-75	Immature to early mature	Sapling/poles to large
C	Overstory	75-125+	Late mature to over-mature	Large+

Table 5—Aspen layer vigor classification

Code	Name	Definition
0	Layer absent	No individuals of this structure are present, common sense applies: if you have a clump of three large aspen and there are three suckers, then you shouldn't use this code; if the same three suckers are contained within a 3-ac aspen stand, code them with this code as nonexistent.
1	Vigorous	No evidence of permanent disease (conks); foliage disease may be present but not causing long-term damage; bark is healthy (not seriously damaged); evidence shows very good annual leader/height growth; minor browsing/hedging.
2	Stable	The layer appears to be free and clear to grow; only minor stem or leaf disease; browsing or hedging may be checking most of annual growth; other minor physical damage may have occurred; only occasional cavity excavation. Growth is good to fair.
3	Mixed condition	A significant portion of the individuals in this structural layer meet condition 1 or 2, and a significant portion meet conditions 4 through 6.
4	Declining	Shortening crown ratios, lack of or short annual growth, cavity excavators beginning frequent excavations, disease conks present, heavy browsing/hedging with reduced suckering, suppression or overtopping by other trees, or other physical damage causing serious injury. Occasional dead trees of this layer are present. Growth is poor.
5	Decadent	Nearly dead; frost cracks; broken or split-out tops; major portion of tree dead; many cavities from bird use; typically at least 80 to 90 years old at minimum. Dead trees common of same age. Growth essentially stopped.
6	Dead	

Table 6—Conifer layer classification

Code	Structural layer	Typical age	Age class	Size group
		Years		
D	Understory	0-25	Seedlings to juvenile	Seedlings to sapling
E	Midstory	25-150	Immature to early mature	Poles to large
F	Overstory	150+	Late mature to overmature	Large+

Table 7—Conifer competition classification

Code	Name	Description
0	None	No conifer present in this layer or nearly absent and not competing.
1	Light	Scattered conifer competing lightly with aspen; no significant overtopping, crowding, or suppression.
2	Moderate	Conifer beginning to have an apparent effect on aspen health and vigor across most of the site.
3	Mixed	Some portions of the aspen stand or clumps within stands on aspen are being affected as in (2) moderate, some as in (4) suppressing.
4	Suppressing	Conifer in position to reduce aspen crowns, vigor, growing space and form. Aspen are showing the effects. Some aspen mortality or form deformation.
5	Near lethal	Conifer exerting near lethal effects on aspen. Aspen suffering severe and significant suppression mortality. Significant mortality of middlestory and mature aspen; many are dead or near dead. Most dead aspen are still standing; some of the dead aspen are on the ground. If used to describe understory, aspen in the understory is overtopped with no growing space and showing poor architecture/breakage/abrasion damage.
6	Lethal	Conifer totally dominating the site: overtopping, deforming, shading, crowding, and suppressing aspen, resulting in wholesale mortality. Very few mature aspen surviving. Most of the dead aspen are on the ground, some dead remain standing. If used to describe conifer effect on understory, the understory is stunted, has poor vigor, or consists of dead sprouts.

Table 8—Aspen stand structural classification

HRV class	Number of layers	Aspen canopy layers present or absent			Oldest age group	Structural class[a]	Notes
		A Under-story	B Mid-story	C Over-story			
					Years		
1	3	Present	Present	Present	80+	OFMS	Rare except in stands treated 10 or more years ago.
2	2	Present	Present	Absent/ dead	40-80	SE, UR, YFMS	Overstory dead; a rare condition. May become more common as older burned or treated stands slowly recruit a middle story and regeneration continues.
3	2	Absent/ dead	Present	Present	80+	OFMS	Understory aspen absent or dead; a rare condition.
4	2	Present	Absent/ dead	Present	80+	OFMS	Understory and overstory present; common in treated stands with regeneration under old, decadent overstory. When the magnitude of the regeneration overwhelms the amount of remaining overstory, this will become class 5, and after several more years possibly class 2.
5	1	Present	Absent/ dead	Absent/ dead	0-40	SI	Understory only; a rare condition, usually happens after fire or treatment that kills overstory, or where the stand has expanded to several acres from original few parent trees and labeling the stand as class 7 doesn't make sense because of widespread vigorous regeneration.
6	1	Absent/ dead	Present	Absent/ dead	40-80	SE, UR, YFMS	Middle-story only; a rare condition. May be an older treated stand or older fire-created stand where recruitment of aspen occurred in the past but is not currently present.
7	1	Absent/ dead	Absent/ dead	Present	80+	OFSS	Overstory only; the most common situation in our area. The overstory is usually decadent.
8	0	Absent/ dead	Absent/ dead	Absent/ dead	-	-	All aspen dead. Take care to ensure that no aspens are alive.

[a] For definitions of structural classes, see table 9.

Note: HRV = historical range of variation.

Table 9—Forest Structural Class Definitions

Code	Name	Description
SI	Stand initiation	Following a stand-replacing disturbance such as wildfire or timber harvest, growing space is occupied rapidly by vegetation that either survives the disturbance or colonizes the area. Survivors literally survive the disturbance above ground, or initiate growth from their underground roots or from seeds stored on site. A single-canopy stratum of tree seedlings and saplings is present in this class.
SE	Stem exclusion open canopy or stem exclusion closed canopy	In this stage of development, vigorous, fast-growing trees that compete strongly for available light and moisture occupy the growing space. Because trees are tall and reduce sunlight, understory plants (including smaller trees) are shaded and grow more slowly. Species that need sunlight usually die; shrubs and herbs may become dormant. In this class, establishment of new trees is precluded by a lack of sunlight (stem exclusion closed canopy) or of moisture (stem exclusion open canopy).
UR	Understory reinitiation	As a forest develops, new age classes of trees (cohorts) establish as the overstory trees die or are thinned and no longer fully occupy growing space. Regrowth of understory vegetation then occurs, and trees begin to develop in vertical layers (canopy stratification). This class consists of a sparse to moderately dense overstory with small trees underneath.
YFMS	Young forest multistrata	In this stage of forest development, two or more tree layers are present as a result of canopy differentiation or because new cohorts of trees got established. This class consists of a broken or discontinuous overstory layer with a mix of tree sizes present (large trees are absent or scarce); it provides high vertical and horizontal diversity. This class is also referred to as "multistratum, without large trees" (USDA FS 1995).
OFMS	Old forest multistrata	Many age classes and vegetation layers mark this structural class and it usually contains large, old trees. Decaying fallen trees may also be present that leave a discontinuous overstory canopy. On cool moist sites without recurring underburns, multilayer stands with large trees in the uppermost stratum may be present.
OFSS	Old forest single strata	Many age classes but only a single fairly distinct overstory layer marks this structural class, and it usually contains large, old trees. Decaying fallen trees may also be present that leave a discontinuous overstory canopy.

Table 10—Desired age and structural composition of aspen stands[a]

Age	Structural class[b]	Proportion of aspen stand area
Years		*Percent*
0-40	SI	45-50
40-80	SE, UR, YFMS	45-50
80+	OFMS, OFSS	5-10

[a] Based on historical range of variation (HRV) estimates by M.L. Tatum and K. Schuetz. Applies to aspen stand in areas dominated by the dry upland forest plant association group (Powell et al. 2007). Proportions of aspen stands are based only on acreages of live trees. Note: aspen area as a whole is considered to be in deficit in our area; thus the 0-40- and 40-80-yr age classes should be restored through expansion of aspen area, not killing of existing aspen stands 80 yr and older.

[b] For definitions of structural classes, see table 9.

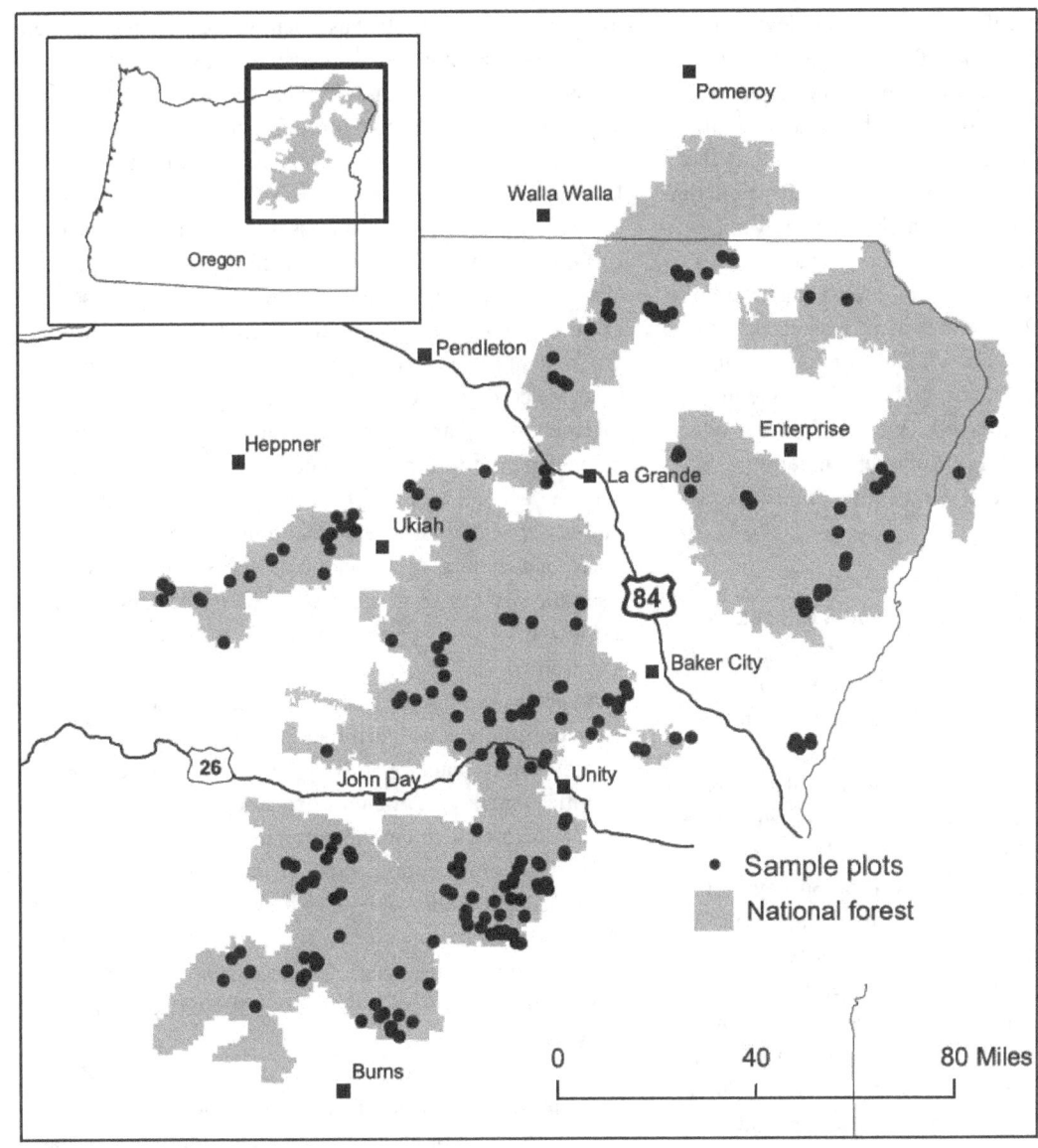

Figure 42–Locations of plots used in the aspen community classification study.

Aspen Community Classification in the Blue Mountains

Study Area

Physiography and geology–
The study area (fig. 42) is dominantly an extensive lava plateau at elevations of 3,500 to 6,500 ft, dissected by some deep canyons with elevations as low as 2,000 ft. Several mountain ranges rise above the plateau to about 9,000 ft elevation. Bedrock is dominantly volcanic rocks that erupted during the Cenozoic Era: primarily basalt, but also andesite and rhyolite. Interbedded with these volcanic rocks are some relatively thin layers of tuffaceous sedimentary rocks. Locally in the southern half of the study area, the older sedimentary and metasedimentary rocks that occur beneath the volcanics are exposed. These consist mostly of graywacke, shale, and argillite deposited in a

marine environment. One large area of granitic rock also occurs in the study area–the Bald Mountain batholith–which is centered in the vicinity of Anthony Lakes, northwest of Baker City, Oregon (Orr and Orr 1999, Walker and McLeod 1991.)

A surface layer of wind-deposited loess or volcanic ash is locally present, particularly on flat or concave slopes where it has escaped erosion and often accumulated after erosion from surrounding slopes. This material is the parent material for the fine-grained soils occupied by many of our aspen stands.

Climate–
The climate of aspen communities in the Blue Mountain region is quite variable owing to their wide elevation range. At lower elevations (below 4,000 ft), the climate is temperate and semiarid, with annual precipitation of 10 to 20 in and ephemeral snow cover in most winters (Western

Regional Climate Center 2007). At the higher elevations, annual precipitation ranges from 20 to 40 in, generally increasing with elevation and from south to north. Annual precipitation is locally 40 to 60 in at high elevations in the Wallowa Mountains and in the northeastern portion of the Umatilla National Forest (USDA NRCS 2007). Precipitation is highly seasonal, with most arriving between November and June; drought conditions are common in late summer. Temperatures generally decrease with increasing elevation, although low temperature extremes in all seasons tend to occur at moderate elevations on valley bottoms surrounded by higher terrain. Summer highs are typically in the high 70s and 80s °F, and lows in the 40s. Winter highs average in the 30s °F and lows in the teens. Summer temperatures in the 90s °F are not unusual, and winter temperatures occasionally fall below 0 °F.

Soils–

Soils of aspen communities are highly variable thanks to aspen's broad range of adaptation. Riparian and wetland aspen occur on fine-grained soils formed in loess and volcanic ash that has been reworked and deposited in low areas. These soils have a high organic matter content, high available water capacity, moderately acid to neutral reaction (pH 5.6 to 7.0), and are seasonally saturated with water within the upper 40 in. Most of these soils classify as Andic Argiudolls or Aquic Pachic Argiudolls (Soil Survey Staff 1999). Aspen communities on upland sites occasionally occur in stoney colluvium or even rock rubble with loamy interstitial material, but in most cases a layer of mixed loess and volcanic ash more than 10 in thick overlies the stoney material. Where the surface loamy layer is more than 20 in thick, it usually becomes more clay-rich with depth. These soils have a rather thin organic-rich surface layer and moderately acid to neutral reaction (pH 5.6 to 7.2). Common soil classifications are Andic Haploxerepts and Andic Haploxeralfs.

Plant Association Concept

This publication uses the conventions for classifying vegetation that have been in use in the Pacific Northwest Region (Region 6) of the Forest Service for several decades. The **plant association** is the fundamental unit of classification. It is based on the **potential** natural vegetation of the site, the plant community that would become established if all successional sequences were completed under the present environmental and floristic conditions (Winthers et al. 2005). Plant associations are named by using both the dominant late-seral overstory species and other species that indicate environmental conditions such as moisture supply and temperature. Because aspen rarely occurs as a late-seral species, few plant associations have aspen as the named

overstory species. A plant association includes the late-seral vegetation for which it is named and all the disturbed and early-seral vegetation that would succeed to that late-seral vegetation. This naming convention does not imply that the late-seral vegetation is or was ever dominant on the landscape.

The **plant community type** is an aggregation of plant communities with similar current composition and structure (Jacoby 1989). Thus plant community types are classes of **existing** as opposed to potential vegetation. In this study, aspen plant community types were created to join and describe communities at early seral stages that are difficult to place into a plant association and for which important management information can be assembled based on the current vegetation. Most of the vegetation classes described in this publication are plant community types; they have a Region 6 ecoclass code and in most cases are based on a sample size of two or more plots. The term **type** is used alone to refer to either plant associations or plant community types.

A **series** is an aggregation of plant associations (and therefore a unit of **potential** vegetation) based on the dominant overstory plants. For example, all of the aspen communities that have a grand fir overstory as their potential vegetation are placed in the grand fir series.

The term **plant community** is used here to refer to an assemblage of plants without reference to classification. In this publication we describe a few aspen plant communities as unique occurrences of aspen that are unlikely to be encountered elsewhere and are not given a Region 6 ecoclass code.

The keys and types are based on the concept of **indicator plants**. The indicator plants selected to define a plant community type or plant association are those plants that are thought to be the most diagnostic of a particular environment. They are plants common enough to be found on a useful number of plots, yet narrow enough in their range of adaptation that their presence tells us something unique about the environment. In the case of plant associations, the indicator plants are native plants diagnostic of the temperature and moisture conditions of the site. For plant community types, they may be either this or indicators of management disturbance such as Kentucky bluegrass in communities with a history of heavy grazing.

Field Methods

This study incorporates plots sampled by Elizabeth Crowe, Rod Clausnitzer, and Terry Hicks (from 1988 to 1997) for riparian plant community classification (Crowe and Clausnitzer 1997); plots sampled by Charlie Johnson (in 2000) and the author (D. Swanson, in 2002-2005) for this study; and a few plots from other upland plant classifications by Blue Mountains area ecologists (Claus-nitzer 1993, Johnson 2004, Johnson and Simon 1987). A total of 219 plots were used, of which 153 were sampled by Swanson.

A 0.93-ac circular reconnaissance plot (72 ft in diameter) was established at each site, and canopy coverage was estimated for all vascular plant species. A plant canopy was defined as the outer perimeter of the plant, including small gaps. Cover was estimated to the nearest 5 percent, with additional cover classes of 3 percent, 1 percent, and trace (present at less than 1 percent cover). Trees were separated into overstory (more than 11 in d.b h.) and understory (less than or equal to 11 in d.b.h.). Ground surface cover was estimated for bare soil, bedrock, rock, gravel, erosion pavement, mosses, lichens, litter, and submerged areas.

Environmental data gathered for each plot included elevation, slope aspect, slope steepness, slope shape, position on slope, landform, and a brief soil description (Soil Survey Division Staff 1993). Soil pH was determined in the field with indicator solutions. Photographs were taken from the plot center at two or more azimuths. To facilitate relocation of plots for future monitoring, each plot center was marked with a metal stake, a reference sign was placed on a tree nearby, GPS coordinates were recorded (after 2002), and narrative directions for locating the plot were recorded.

Classification and Data Analysis Methods

Many aspen communities described here fit into existing aspen-dominated riparian or wetland plant associations or community types (Crowe and Clausnitzer 1997), or they are seral communities of plant associations that have been defined in previous studies (Johnson and Clausnitzer 1992, Johnson and Simon 1987). Thus the keys and community definitions here follow closely the classes and indicator plants used in these earlier studies. As in the previous studies, the keys presented here generally progress from cold-moist to warm-dry environments.

Most of the 83 riparian and wetland aspen plots in this study fit readily into existing plant associations or plant community types defined by Crowe and Clausnitzer (1997). These types are described again here, in most cases with a larger sample size than in the original publication. Fifteen of the riparian and wetland aspen plots fit poorly into existing classes. Most of these (nine plots) are similar to the existing quaking aspen/Kentucky bluegrass plant community type of Crowe and Clausnitzer (1997) but are dominated by a mix of grasses rather than Kentucky bluegrass. These are placed in a new type, aspen/meadow foxtail. The remaining plots are unique and are either placed into their own new plant community types or are described as miscellaneous communities under "Aspen/Tall Shrub Wetland Communities on Slopes."

Existing classifications are less complete for upland aspen communities, and hence more new upland types were created as a part of this study. Plots were first classified into series based on the potential conifer dominant, although in some cases this is not possible owing to lack of conifers or other reliable indicator plants.

Of 136 upland aspen plots, 10 fit readily into three existing grand-fir-series plant associations from Johnson and Clausnitzer (1992) or Johnson and Simon (1987) and are described here under those types, the grand fir/twinflower, grand fir/big huckleberry, and grand fir/Rocky Mountain maple plant associations. Aspen is a very minor seral component of these types and was not included in previous descriptions.

A large number of plots key into existing ponderosa pine/snowberry and Douglas-fir/snowberry types in Johnson and Clausnitzer (1992) or Johnson and Simon (1987) (both common and mountain snowberry) or closely resemble these types despite lack of conifers. Ordination by nonmetric multidimensional scaling (NMS) (McCune and Grace 2002) showed poor separation of these plots into series by community composition, so they are joined here into a new aspen (ponderosa pine–Douglas-fir)/snowberry plant community type.

Many aspen plots also key into existing ponderosa pine/pinegrass, Douglas-fir/pinegrass, or grand fir/pinegrass communities, or resemble these types but lack conifers. Ordination by NMS again showed poor separation of these plots into series by community composition (and diagnostic conifers are often absent), so they were joined into a new aspen/pinegrass type. For the same reasons, aspen plots with elk sedge (with or without conifers) were joined into a new aspen/elk sedge type.

Remaining plots fit poorly into any existing plant associations or community types. Natural groupings in these plots were explored subjectively and by ordination using NMS to define new types.

For some types—the riparian aspen/common snowberry communities, the aspen/mesic forb plant community type, and the aspen (ponderosa pine–Douglas-fir)/snowberry plant community type—tabular data are presented to differentiate phases resulting from grazing-related degradation. The phases were developed as follows: (1) In the aspen/common snowberry communities, two plots with exceptionally high grass cover and one with exceptionally high cover of unpalatable forbs are presented separately. These phases are known from previous studies to result from heavy grazing (Crowe and Clausnitzer 1997). (2) The aspen/mesic forb plant community type covers a range of plots with light to moderate grazing impacts (Crowe and Clausnitzer 1997). This type was divided into "less impacted" and "more impacted" phases based on the proportion of the plant cover in species known to be resistant to grazing based on previous publications (Crowe and Clausnitzer 1997, Johnson and Clausnitzer 1992, Johnson and Simon 1987). Species known to be grazing resistant include introduced sod-forming pasture grasses, most introduced forbs, and certain grazing-resistant native forbs such as false hellebore (*Veratrum* spp.). (3) For the aspen (ponderosa pine–Douglas-fir)/snowberry plant community type, the three phases presented in the table are simply the subjective rating of good, fair, or poor that was recorded in the field.

Soil available water capacity is computed for the upper 40 in of soil by assuming a certain available water capacity for each soil texture, adjusted by the volumetric content of coarse fragments. The assumed water capacities are based on unpublished USDA Natural Resources Conservation Service (NRCS) guidelines and are as follows (in dimensionless units of water volume per soil volume): volcanic ash silt loam–0.34; silty clay loam–0.27; clay loam–0.24; silt loam, loam, or sandy clay loam–0.22; sandy loam–0.15; loamy sand–0.08; and sand–0.05.

Data Presentation

All scientific names follow Hitchcock and Cronquist (1973). All database codes follow the PLANTS National Database (USDA NRCS 2008). All plant species used in this report are listed in appendix B with scientific name, common name, and PLANTS database code. A cross reference to the currently recommended synonym (USDA NRCS 2008) is given in appendix C for cases where the recommended synonym differs from the name used here.

The tables of principal species with each type description present constancy (the percentage of plots on which the species was found) and mean cover computed using only the plots where the plant was present. To be included in the table, a plant must have a constancy of at least 50 percent when the average cover, where present, is 1 percent or less, or a constancy of at least 20 percent when the average cover is more than 1 percent. Average covers of less than 0.5 percent are written as "tr" (trace).

Keys to Aspen Communities of the Blue Mountains

The following keys are based on 219 plots located in the Blue Mountains. They may be used for any site where aspen are currently growing or grew in the past. Because the sample plots used to develop the classification are circular with a diameter of 36 ft, the keys will work best if an area with uniform vegetation approximately this size is chosen. To use the keys, compare the choices listed under "a" and "b" for each number, select the alternative that fits best, note the number given on the right margin and proceed to the lead with that number. Continue until a type name is reached. Turn to the page number indicated and check the type description to make sure that it fits.

Use the "Key to Riparian and Wetland Aspen Vegetation" (p. 51) for sites where a water table is found within 40 in of the surface during at least part of the growing season (wetlands), or for sites located on flood plains or alluvial terraces that have vegetation that is distinctly different from adjacent uplands thanks to flooding or enhanced soil moisture (riparian areas). Use the "Key to Upland Aspen Vegetation" (p. 52) for all other sites.

Key to Riparian and Wetland Aspen Vegetation

1a. Slopes ≤10 percent; riparian and lowland meadow communities..**2**

1b. Slope >10 percent; isolated tall-shrub dominated wetlands on slopes..
....Aspen/Tall Shrub Wetlands Plant Communities on Slopes p. 57

2a. Engelmann spruce (*Picea engelmannii*) cover ≥10 percent, or site capable of such cover................................
....POTR5-PIEN/GLST-CACA4 p. 55

2b. Engelmann spruce cover <10 percent and site not capable of supporting 10 percent Engelmann spruce cover.................**3**

3a. Mountain alder (*Alnus incana*) cover ≥25 percent...**4**

3b. Mountain alder cover <25 percent...**5**

4a. Red-osier dogwood (*Cornus stolonifera*) cover ≥25 percent..POTR5/ALIN2-COST4 p. 56

4b. Red-osier dogwood cover <25 percent...POTR5/ALIN2-SYAL p. 56

5a. Black hawthorn (*Crataegus douglasii*) cover ≥25 percent...POTR5/CRDO2 p. 56

5b. Black hawthorn cover <25 percent..**6**

6a. Common snowberry (*Symphoricarpos albus*) cover ≥25 percent...**7**

6b. Common snowberry cover <25 percent...**8**

7a. Grand fir (*Abies grandis*) cover ≥10 percent or site capable of supporting such cover.....................................
....ABGR/SYAL (FLOODPLAIN) p. 58

7b. Douglas-fir (*Pseudotsuga menzesii*) cover ≥10 percent or site capable of supporting such cover......................
....PSME/SYAL (FLOODPLAIN) p. 58

7c. Ponderosa pine (*Pinus ponderosa*) cover ≥10 percent or site capable of supporting such cover........................
....PIPO/SYAL (FLOODPLAIN) p. 58

7d. Conifer cover <10 percent and conifer potential unknown...POTR5/SYAL p. 58

8a. Aquatic sedge (*Carex aquatilis*) cover ≥25 percent...POTR5/CAAQ p. 62

8b. Aquatic sedge cover <25 percent...**9**

9a. Woolly sedge (*Carex lanuginosa*) cover ≥10 percent...POTR5/CALA30 p. 62

9b. Woolly sedge cover <10 percent...**10**

10a. Yellow sedge (*Carex flava*) cover ≥25...POTR5/CAFL4 p. 65

10b. Yellow sedge cover <25 percent...**11**

11a. Bluejoint reedgrass (*Calamagrostis canadensis*) cover ≥25 percent.............................POTR5/CACA4 p. 66

11b. Bluejoint reedgrass cover <25 percent...**12**

12a. Kentucky bluegrass (*Poa pratensis*) cover ≥25 percent..POTR5/POPR p. 68

12b. Kentucky bluegrass cover <25 percent..**13**

13a. Sum of cover by all grasses (Poaceae) ≥50 percent; introduced pasture grasses, especially meadow foxtail (*Alopecurus pratensis*) usually dominate..POTR5/ALPR3 p. 68

13b. Sum of cover by all grasses <50 percent...POTR5/MESIC FORB p. 68

Key to Upland Aspen Vegetation

1a. Over half of the ground surface is bedrock or rock rubble (rock fragments > 3 in diameter; rock may be partly covered with a thin layer of litter)..**2**

1b. Ground surface dominated by soil, gravel, and/or litter...**3**

2a. Elevation above 6,000 ft.; subalpine fir (*Abies lasiocarpa*) often present...........................POTR5 (RUBBLE, HIGH) p. 72

2b. Elevation below 6,000 ft; wax currant (*Ribes cereum*), creeping Oregon grape (*Berberis repens*), common snowberry (*Symphoricarpos albus*), or hotrock penstemon (*Penstemon deustus*) usually present......POTR5 (RUBBLE, LOW) p. 72

3a. Subalpine fir with total cover ≥10 percent, or site capable of supporting such cover..
....Aspen types of the subalpine fir series p. 75

3b. Subalpine fir cover <10 percent and site not capable of supporting 10 percent subalpine fir cover.........................**4**

4a. Grand fir with total cover ≥10 percent, or site capable of supporting such cover..
....Upland grand fir series aspen type key p. 53

4b. Grand fir with total cover <10 percent and site not capable of supporting 10 percent grand fir cover....................**5**

5a. Ponderosa pine or Douglas-fir with cover ≥10 percent, or site capable of supporting such cover............................
....Upland ponderosa pine and Douglas-fir series aspen type key p. 54

5b. Ponderosa pine or Douglas-fir with cover <10 percent and site not capable of supporting 10 percent ponderosa pine or Douglas-fir..Undefined aspen type

Upland Grand Fir Series Aspen Type Key

1a. Twinflower (*Linnaea borealis*) distributed throughout the stand with cover ≥1 percent ....ABGR/LIBO3 p. 77

1b. Twinflower with cover <1 percent..**2**

2a. Big huckleberry cover (*Vaccinium membranaceum*) ≥5 percent...ABGR/VAME p. 78

2b. Big huckleberry cover <5 percent...**3**

3a. Rocky Mountain maple (*Acer glabrum*) cover ≥5 percent...ABGR/ACGL p. 81

3b. Rocky Mountain maple cover <5 percent..**4**

4a. Oceanspray (*Holodiscus discolor*) cover ≥5 percent..POTR5(ABGR)/HODI p. 83

4b. Oceanspray cover <5 percent..**5**

5a. Snowberry (common snowberry *Symphoricarpos albus* or mountain snowberry *S. oreophilus*) cover ≥5 percent............
....POTR5(ABGR)/SYMPH p. 83

5b. Snowberry (common snowberry and mountain snowberry) cover <5 percent..**6**

6a. Pinegrass (*Calamagrostis rubescens*) cover ≥5 percent..POTR5/CARU p. 95

6b. Pinegrass cover <5 percent...**7**

7a. Elk sedge (*Carex geyeri*) cover ≥5 percent...POTR5/CAGE2 p. 95

7b. Elk sedge cover <5 percent...**8**

8a. Cover by introduced grasses (intermediate wheatgrass *Agropyron intermedium,* orchardgrass *Dactylis glomerata,* etc.) ≥5 percent...POTR5/EXOTIC GRASS p. 95

8b. Cover by introduced grasses <5 percent..Other grand fir series aspen communities p. 86

Upland Ponderosa Pine and Douglas-Fir Series Aspen Type Key

1a. Cover by cherry species (chokecherry *Prunus virginiana* or bitter cherry *P. emarginata*) ≥5 percent..................................2

1b. Cover by cherry species <5 percent..3

2a. Chokecherry cover greater than bitter cherry cover..POTR5/PRVI p. 88

2b. Chokecherry cover less than less than bitter cherry...POTR5(PSME)/PREM p. 90

3a. Snowberry (common snowberry or mountain snowberry) cover ≥5 percent............POTR5(PIPO-PSME)/SYMPH p. 92

3b. Cover by snowberry <5 percent..4

4a. Pinegrass cover ≥5 percent..POTR5/CARU p. 95

4b. Pinegrass cover <5 percent..5

5a. Elk sedge cover ≥5 percent...POTR5/CAGE2 p. 95

5b. Elk sedge cover < 5 percent..6

6a. Cover by introduced grasses (intermediate wheatgrass, orchardgrass, etc.) ≥5 percent....................................
....POTR5/EXOTIC GRASS p. 95

6b. Cover by introduced grasses <5 percent..................Other Douglas-fir and ponderosa pine series aspen communities p. 99

Aspen-Engelmann Spruce Types

Aspen-Engelmann Spruce/Fowl Mannagrass-
Bluejoint Reedgrass Plant Community Type
Populus tremuloides-Picea engelmannii/
Glyceria striata-Calamagrostis canadensis
POTR5-PIEN/GLST-CACA4   HQC113

D. Swanson

WA016

Engelmann spruce is a common riparian and wetland-
margin species in the Blue Mountains. We sampled just
one plot where aspen occurred with significant Engelmann
spruce cover; it is in the Charlie Johnson Research Natural
Area of the Wallowa-Whitman National Forest, at 5,480 ft
elevation. The highly diverse understory is dominated by
various wetland-adapted grasses, including mannagrass
(*Glyceria striata*), bluejoint reedgrass (*Calamagrostis
canadensis*), bentgrass (*Agrostis stolonifera*), and tufted
hairgrass (*Deschampsia cespitosa*). The soil consists of layers of both loess or alluvial silt and volcanic ash, with colors
indicating intermittent saturation below 3 ft depth. This site
is highly productive and aspen is seral to spruce.

Aspen-Tall Shrub Types

Aspen/Mountain Alder–Red-Osier Dogwood Plant Community Type
Populus tremuloides/Alnus incana-Cornus stolonifera

POTR5/ALIN2-COST4   HQS222
(Crowe and Clausnitzer 1997)

Aspen/Mountain Alder-Common Snowberry Plant Community Type
Populus tremuloides/Alnus incana-Symphoricarpos albus

POTR5/ALIN2-SYAL   HQS223
(Crowe and Clausnitzer 1997)

These two plant community types are represented by one plot each sampled by Crowe and Clausnitzer (1997). They occur on nearly level flood plains at 4,300 and 5,000 ft, respectively. Soils consist of silt loam over sand, gravel, and cobbles with a low to moderate available water capacity. Aspen form an open canopy over shrubs, primarily mountain alder (*Alnus incana*), common snowberry (*Symphoricarpos albus*), and, in POTR5/ALIN2-COST4, red-osier dogwood (*Cornus stolonifera*) and chokecherry (*Prunus virginiana*). Herbaceous plants include blue wildrye (*Elymus glaucus*), creeping bentgrass (*Agrostis stolonifera*), asters (*Aster* spp.) and a variety of other forbs at low cover.

These plant communities are a variant of the much more widespread flood-plain alder communities lacking aspen. Aspen occur in these alder communities thanks to their ability to colonize mesic disturbed sites. These ecosystems constantly change owing to flooding and sedimentation, stream channel migration, and succession. Thus long-term management of aspen in these communities would be difficult and unpredictable. Like other aspen communities, they provide valuable wildlife habitat and are vulnerable to browsing.

Aspen/Black Hawthorn Plant Community Type
Populus tremuloides/Crataegus douglasii

POTR5/CRDO2   HQS4

One plot of this community type was sampled on a gentle slope at 4,160 ft elevation in Patterson Basin on the North Fork John Day Ranger District of the Umatilla National Forest. It is on a dark-colored, clay loamy soil with pH of 6.6 to 6.8. A stand of pole-sized aspen with few saplings and minor grand fir occurs over a dense stand of hawthorn (65 percent cover) and common snowberry (*Symphoricarpos albus*) (35 percent cover) with minor rose (*Rosa* sp.) and serviceberry (*Amelanchier alnifolia*). The most abundant herb is the introduced grass meadow foxtail (*Alopecurus pratensis*). Minor amounts of many forbs typical of aspen meadows are present, such as columbine (*Aquilegia formosa*), monkshood (*Aconitum columbianum*), and false Solomon's seal (*Smilacina racemosa*). Sites of this type can probably support Douglas-fir or grand fir, and conifer encroachment could eliminate aspen over time. Both aspen and hawthorn can resprout after disturbance, and competition by hawthorn is likely to reduce the density of aspen regeneration after disturbance. Mechanical treatment of hawthorn may be needed in some cases to allow for aspen regeneration.

Aspen/Tall-Shrub Wetland Plant Communities on Slopes
Populus tremuloides/Tall Shrub
POTR5/Tall Shrub (wetland slope)

D. Swanson

UA042

Aspen have been recorded growing in unusual shrub-rich wetland communities located over seeps or springs on slopes. Three plots of this type were sampled between 4,600 and 5,240 ft elevation on slopes of south or west aspect ranging from 15 to 55 percent. The three plots share no plants in common besides aspen; all have a rich shrub layer dominated by one or more of the following species: mountain alder (*Alnus incana*), black hawthorn (*Crataegus douglasii*), common chokecherry (*Prunus virginiana*), rose (*Rosa*), red elderberry (*Sambucus racemosa*), or common snowberry (*Symphoricarpos albus*). Sedges and forbs are also diverse and abundant, notably Dewey sedge (*Carex deweyana*), cleavers (*Galium aparine*), cowparsnip (*Heracleum lanatum*), and western coneflower (*Rudbeckia occidentalis*).

Riparian Aspen/Common Snowberry Types

Grand Fir/Common Snowberry (Floodplain)
Plant Community Type
Abies grandis/Symphoricarpos albus
ABGR/SYAL (FLOODPLAIN)   CWS314
(Crowe and Clausnitzer 1997)

Douglas-Fir/Common Snowberry (Floodplain)
Plant Association
*Pseudotsuga menziesii/Symphoricarpos
albus*
PSME/SYAL (FLOODPLAIN)   CDS628
(Crowe and Clausnitzer 1997)

Ponderosa Pine/Common Snowberry
(Floodplain) Plant Association
Pinus ponderosa/Symphoricarpos albus
PIPO/SYAL (FLOODPLAIN)   CPS511
(Crowe and Clausnitzer 1997)

Aspen/Common Snowberry Plant
Community Type
Populus tremuloides/Symphoricarpos albus
POTR5/SYAL   HQS221
(Crowe and Clausnitzer 1997)

D. Swanson

UA002

Aspen with an understory dominated by common snowberry occurs fairly frequently in riparian areas. The typical presence of more shade-tolerant conifers shows that aspen forest is a seral stage with a potential vegetation of coniferous trees. Ordination with nonmetric multidimensional scaling shows that our aspen plots in these communities separate poorly based on community composition. Furthermore, conifer species are sometimes absent in aspen communities, making differentiation based on trees unreliable. For this reason, the aspen communities in these four types are joined and described together here.

Environmental features—
Riparian aspen/common snowberry communities occur at moderate elevations, usually in swales or along intermittent stream courses.

Soils—
Soils are fine-grained and high in organic matter, with a neutral to slightly acid pH. The parent material is usually a mixture of weathered volcanic ash and loess, with layers of nearly pure ash in some profiles. A few profiles have some coarse fragments below 20 in depth, hinting at an underlying layer of gravelly alluvium. The surface texture is usually silt loam or silty clay loam, usually becoming more clay-rich with depth (except for fine sandy loam textures in some fresh ash layers). Colors are typically dark throughout the upper 2 or 3 ft of soil, indicating a high organic matter content, except in the ash layers, which tend to be light colored. Some profiles sampled in early June had a water table near the surface, whereas profiles sampled later in the summer were moist but free water was not present. The soil surface is well covered by litter.

Vegetation composition—
Composition data here are divided into three groups: typical communities that presumably have been less impacted by grazing, communities with the herb layer dominated by Kentucky bluegrass (*Poa pratensis*), and a community dominated by unpalatable perennial forbs.

Coniferous trees (ponderosa pine, Douglas-fir, and grand fir) are usually present in the understory and sometimes in the overstory as codominants with aspen. A fairly dense shrub layer is present and dominated by common snowberry. A variety of grasses is present at low cover values. Kentucky bluegrass becomes the dominant herbaceous species on some plots that have been impacted greatly by grazing. A variety of native perennial forbs is present. Plots heavily impacted by grazing become dominated by certain unpalatable forbs, especially false hellebore (*Veratrum* sp.). It appears that some palatable shrub species, such as western serviceberry (*Amelanchier alnifolia*) and red-osier dogwood (*Cornus stolonifera*), may also be eliminated in the more heavily grazing-impacted communities.

Successional relationships—
Succession is toward coniferous forest with snowberry understory. Moisture is probably adequate in most cases to support grand fir, although, as a result of the local seed-source environment, only ponderosa pine or Douglas-fir may be present.

The rate and degree to which grazing-sensitive perennial forbs can recover naturally after reduction of grazing pressure are unknown. The Kentucky bluegrass or unpalatable perennial forbs that dominate heavily impacted areas are likely to persist for some time even if grazing is discontinued.

Fire—
Fire frequency in these communities is strongly dependent on the fire frequency of surrounding uplands. Stands lacking conifers and downed woody debris are unlikely to carry ground fires, although heat from a crown fire in adjacent uplands may kill aspen in the small stands typical of our area. As mature aspen die and conifers become more abundant, the likelihood of fire in an aspen stand increases. Aspen typically resprout vigorously after stand-replacing fires. If, however, burn conditions are less severe (as would be typical of prescribed fires) and some large conifers are present that survive the fire, mature aspen will likely be killed and aspen regeneration will be compromised in the shade of the conifers.

Management considerations—
Conifer competition is intense in these communities, and removal of conifers may be required to allow aspen regeneration. If overstory conifers are present, light prescribed fires are likely to kill aspen without providing enough light for them to regenerate properly. Livestock grazing and wildlife browsing at levels typical of the Blue Mountains today will usually result in hedging of aspen saplings and no recruitment of new pole-sized aspen. Many aspen clones are at risk of dying out as older trees die of old age or shading by conifers. Heavy ungulate pressure also suppresses snowberry, but to a lesser degree than aspen. Heavy grazing can lead to replacement of grazing-sensitive native forbs by Kentucky bluegrass or unpalatable forbs such as false hellebore.

Environmental features

Site

Plots	14
Elevation, mean (range) (ft)	4,130 (3,140-4,900)
Slope, mean (range) (percent)	3 (0-10)
Aspect	Any
Position	Toeslope
Slope shape	Concave or planar

Soil

Available water capacity (in) (n = 14)	6.5 to 10 (moderate to high)
pH (n = 11)	6.0 to 7.0

RIPARIAN AND WETLAND ASPEN PLANT COMMUNITIES

Principal species

Latin name	Common name	Code	Typical (N = 11)	Grass-dominated (N = 2)	Unpalatable forb-dominated (N = 1)
			Cover (%)/constancy (%)		Cover (%)
Overstory trees:					
Picea engelmannii	Engelmann spruce	PIEN			5
Pinus ponderosa	Ponderosa pine	PIPO	15/64		
Populus tremuloides	Quaking aspen	POTR5	16/91	41/100	30
Pseudotsuga menziesii	Douglas-fir	PSME	12/36		
Understory trees:					
Abies grandis	Grand fir	ABGR	4/45		
Pinus ponderosa	Ponderosa pine	PIPO	6/55		
Populus tremuloides	Quaking aspen	POTR5	25/100	45/50	15
Pseudotsuga menziesii	Douglas-fir	PSME	3/45		
Shrubs:					
Amelanchier alnifolia	Western serviceberry	AMAL2	3/55		
Cornus stolonifera	Red-osier dogwood	COST4	8/27		
Crataegus douglasii	Black hawthorn	CRDO2	2/36		
Potentilla fruticosa	Shrubby cinquefoil	POFR4		5/50	
Ribes lacustre	Prickly currant	RILA	2/18		1
Rosa	Rose	ROSA5	2/55		
Rosa nutkana	Nootka rose	RONU	5/9	8/50	
Spiraea betulifolia	Birchleaf spiraea	SPBE2	3/27		
Symphoricarpos albus	Common snowberry	SYAL	47/100	52/100	35
Grasses and grasslike:					
Agrostis stolonifera	Creeping bentgrass	AGST2		20/50	
Alopecurus pratensis	Meadow foxtail	ALPR3	2/18		1
Bromus carinatus	Mountain brome	BRCA5	2/27		
Calamagrostis canadensis	Bluejoint reedgrass	CACA4			5
Calamagrostis rubescens	Pinegrass	CARU	2/27		
Carex deweyana	Dewey sedge	CADE9	3/9	2/50	
Carex geyeri	Elk sedge	CAGE2	9/18	3/50	
Carex microptera	Smallwinged sedge	CAMI7			1
Dactylis glomerata	Orchardgrass	DAGL	3/36		
Elymus glaucus	Blue wildrye	ELGL	2/45	5/50	
Poa pratensis	Kentucky bluegrass	POPR	2/73	42/100	1
Forbs:					
Achillea millefolium	Common yarrow	ACMI2	1/27	6/100	
Aquilegia formosa	Red columbine	AQFO	2/27		
Arnica cordifolia	Heartleaf arnica	ARCO9	2/36		
Aster foliaceus	Leafy aster	ASFO		18/50	
Aster modestus	Few-flowered aster	ASMO3		10/50	
Camassia quamash	Common camas	CAQU2	2/27		
Cerastium nutans	Nodding chickweed	CENU2		6/50	
Cirsium	Thistle	CIRSI		5/50	
Cirsium vulgare	Bull thistle	CIVU	tr/27	2/50	

(continued)

Principal species *(continued)*

Latin name	Common name	Code	Typical (N = 11)	Grass-dominated (N = 2)	Unpalatable forb-dominated (N = 1)
			Cover (%)/constancy(%)		Cover (%)
Forbs *(continued)*:					
Cynoglossum officinale	Common houndstongue	CYOF		20/50	
Fragaria	Strawberry	FRAGA	2/73	8/100	
Galium boreale	Northern bedstraw	GABO2	2/64	18/50	tr
Galium triflorum	Fragrant bedstraw	GATR3	1/9	2/50	
Geranium viscosissimum	Sticky geranium	GEVI2	3/9	3/100	
Geum macrophyllum	Largeleaf avens	GEMA4	2/18	4/100	tr
Iris missouriensis	Rocky Mountain iris	IRMI	1/45	2/50	
Medicago lupulina	Black medick	MELU		3/50	
Osmorhiza chilensis	Mountain sweet-cicely	OSCH	2/36		tr
Potentilla gracilis	Slender cinquefoil	POGR9	2/73		
Ranunculus orthorhynchus	Straightbeak buttercup	RAOR3	4/27		20
Rudbeckia occidentalis	Western coneflower	RUOC2			10
Senecio crassulus	Thickleaf groundsel	SECR	13/18		35
Sidalcea oregana	Oregon checker-mallow	SIOR	4/64		
Smilacina stellata	Starry false Solomon's seal	SMST	2/64	1/50	1
Taraxacum officinale	Common dandelion	TAOF	1/64	8/50	
Thalictrum occidentale	Western meadowrue	THOC	5/45	1/50	tr
Thermopsis montana	Golden-pea	THMO6	5/27		30
Urtica dioica	Stinging nettle	URDI		3/50	
Veratrum	False hellebore	VERAT	11/36		
Veratrum californicum	California false hellebore	VECA2			40
Viola	Violet	VIOLA	2/18	6/100	

Ground surface features

	Cover (%)
Bare ground	1
Bedrock	0
Rock	0
Gravel	0
Moss, lichen	2
Litter	97

Herbaceous Aspen Meadow Types

Aspen/Aquatic Sedge Plant Community Type
Populus tremuloides/Carex aquatilis
POTR5/CAAQ   HQM212
(Crowe and Clausnitzer 1997)

Aspen/Woolly Sedge Plant Association
Populus tremuloides/Carex lanuginosa
POTR5/CALA30   HQM211
(Crowe and Clausnitzer 1997)

This is the wettest aspen plant community in the Blue Mountain region, and these sites are probably marginal for aspen survival because of wetness. Two plots were sampled, both near 4,100 ft elevation on nearly level concave topography. Soils are fine-grained (silt loam or sitly clay loam), dark-colored owing to high organic-matter content, and waterlogged within a foot of the surface for at least part of the summer. Our one soil pH sample is slightly acid. The soil surface is covered nearly completely by litter.

A few subalpine fir and Engelmann spruce trees occur in the understory, but the tree layer is dominated by aspen. Shrubs are nearly absent, and the herbaceous layer is dominated by aquatic sedge (*Carex aquatilis*) and bluejoint reedgrass (*Calamagrostis canadensis*). One of the plots also has abundant false hellebore (*Veratrum californicum*) and groundsel (*Senecio crassulus*).

Survival of aspen on these sites is tenuous owing to the high water table, because aspen roots require an aerated soil layer above the water table. However, wetness and water table fluctuations may give aspen a competitive advantage over conifers and allow it to persist for long periods. If a few aspen can survive a multiyear wet period, in subsequent drought years, they can expand by cloning into the dense sedge-grass vegetation where seedling establishment by conifers on this substrate is unlikely. Management actions (fencing, conifer removal) that allow aspen clones to expand to adjacent drier sites could improve their chances for survival over the long term.

The description below is based on five plots of this type that were sampled by Crowe and Clausnitzer (1997) and one additional plot sampled for the present study.

Environmental features—
This type occurs in wet basins or on flood plains.

Soils—
Soils consist of a thick layer (at least 2 ft) of silt loam, silty clay loam, or clay loam, probably derived from reworked volcanic ash and loess. Soils are dark-colored owing to high organic matter content. In early summer the soil profile is saturated with water, and a water table was present within 30 in of the surface in all studied profiles.

Vegetation composition—
Aspen dominate the tree layer, and conifers are uncommon. Shrub cover is also low. The understory is dominated by herbaceous plants, especially woolly sedge, blue wildrye (*Elymus glaucus*), Kentucky bluegrass (*Poa pratensis*), and a variety of forbs dominated by starry false Solomon's seal (*Smilacina stellata*).

Successional relationships—
Wetness limits succession to conifers on these sites. Conditions dry enough for conifers occur during dry episodes and on dry microsites, but dense sod limits site colonization by conifers.

Fire—
Fire is probably very rare in these communities because of the high moisture content of soils and vegetation through the summer. However, fire is possible during multiyear

droughts. In addition, these communities usually occur in small patches surrounded by forest where severe crown fires are possible, and heat from these fires may kill aspen. Resprouting of aspen after such fires is likely, although removal of trees from the watershed could result in greater yield of water to the depressions where the aspen/woolly sedge communities occur. In such cases, aspen may be unable to resprout in their former positions on the land-scape, although they may survive by expanding upslope onto slightly drier habitats.

Management considerations—
Conifer competition is generally not an issue in aspen/woolly sedge communities, although conifer removal may be necessary to allow aspen survival in cases where multi-year drought allows conifers to colonize these wetlands. Aspen are likely to expand uphill onto adjacent slightly drier sites if conifers are removed there; this would provide a more secure place for aspen in a future multiyear wet episode. Aspen regeneration is strongly inhibited by cattle grazing and browsing by deer and elk.

Environmental features

Site

Plots	6
Elevation, mean (range) (ft)	5,110 (4,780-5,510)
Slope, mean (range) (percent)	2 (0-5)
Aspect	None
Position	Toeslope or flat
Slope shape	Concave, planar, or undulating

Soil

Plots	5
Available water capacity (in)	7 to 11 (moderate to high)

Principal species

Latin name	Common name	Code	Cover/constancy
			Percent
Overstory trees:			
Populus tremuloides	Quaking aspen	POTR5	56/100
Abies grandis	Grand fir	ABGR	2/33
Understory trees:			
Populus tremuloides	Quaking aspen	POTR5	11/100
Shrubs:			
Symphoricarpos albus	Common snowberry	SYAL	2/33
Grasses and grasslike:			
Carex lanuginosa	Woolly sedge	CALA30	36/100
Carex nebrascensis	Nebraska sedge	CANE2	2/33
Elymus glaucus	Blue wildrye	ELGL	25/50
Juncus balticus	Baltic rush	JUBA	2/33
Phleum pratense	Common timothy	PHPR3	2/33
Poa pratensis	Kentucky bluegrass	POPR	7/83
Trisetum canescens	Tall trisetum	TRCA21	3/33
Forbs:			
Arnica chamissonis	Chamisso arnica	ARCH3	14/33
Aster	Aster	ASTER	5/50
Camassia quamash	Common camas	CAQU2	2/33
Fragaria	Strawberry	FRAGA	6/67
Galium boreale	Northern bedstraw	GABO2	2/50
Galium triflorum	Fragrant bedstraw	GATR3	4/33
Iris missouriensis	Rocky Mountain iris	IRMI	13/33
Mentha arvensis	Field mint	MEAR4	18/33
Smilacina stellata	Starry false Solomon's seal	SMST	17/83
Taraxacum officinale	Common dandelion	TAOF	1/67
Thalictrum occidentale	Western meadowrue	THOC	8/50
Trifolium longipes	Longstalk clover	TRLO	10/50

Ground surface features

	Cover (%)
Bare ground	
Bedrock	1
Rock	0
Gravel	0
Moss, lichen	0
Litter	6
Submerged	85
	8

Aspen/Yellow Sedge Plant Community Type
Populus tremuloides/Carex flava
POTR5/CAFL4   HQG113

D. Swanson

WA031

An aspen grove in a wetland was sampled near Tipton
Summit in the Wallowa-Whitman National Forest (5,110 ft
elevation). This community is dominated by various grass-
like wetland plants, including sedges (*Carex flava* and *C.
athrostachya*), spikerush (*Eleocharis acicularis*), and rush
(*Juncus nevadensis*). A few forb species are also present,
notably greater creeping spearwort (*Ranunculus flammula*).
The soil consists of light-colored silt loam volcanic ash over
silty clay loam at 22-in depth. Soil colors indicate seasonal
saturation, but no water table was within 2 ft of the surface
in mid-July 2004. The pH is quite acid for an aspen site, 5.4
to 5.8. Dried algae on the ground surface indicate standing
water in the spring. This plot is an example of the diversity of wetland settings where aspen can occur in the Blue
Mountains, and strongly fluctuating soil moisture conditions probably aid aspen by reducing conifer competition.

Aspen/Bluejoint Reedgrass Plant Community Type
Populus tremuloides/Calamagrostis canadensis

POTR5/CACA4   HQM123

(Crowe and Clausnitzer 1997)

R. Clausnitzer

UW1991

Environmental features—

This type occurs on flat or slightly concave areas with rather wet soils at moderate elevations.

Soils—

Soils consist of a thick layer (at least 2 ft) of clay loam or silty clay loam, probably derived from reworked volcanic ash and loess; extremely gravelly material occurs below the clayey material in two profiles. Soils are dark-colored owing to high organic matter content. In early summer the soil profile is saturated with water, but by late summer it typically dries to a moist state. Soil pH is slightly to moderately acid.

Vegetation composition—

Aspen is the only common overstory tree; conifers are sometimes present in the understory, but fluctuating high water tables probably hinder the survival of larger conifers. Shrubs are rare or absent, and the herb layer is dominated by bluejoint reedgrass. A variety of forbs is also present, notably leafy aster (*Aster foliaceus*), buttercup (*Ranunculus* spp.), thickleaf groundsel (*Senecio crassulus*), starry false Solomon's seal (*Smilacina stellata*), and false hellebore (*Veratrum* spp.).

Successional relationship—

In general, succession is toward grand fir, subalpine fir, or Engelmann spruce forest. However, several factors act to maintain aspen on these sites. Fluctuations in the water table, specifically multiyear episodes where the water table remains near the surface for the entire summer, can cause widespread mortality of trees, particularly larger trees (including aspen). In a well-stocked aspen stand, a few aspen are likely to survive on drier microsites, and then expand vegetatively during a subsequent multiyear dry episode. Meanwhile, conifer seedling establishment is inhibited by the dense herbaceous vegetation and litter. The result is persistent presence of aspen with few conifers.

Fire—

Fire is probably very rare in these communities because of the high moisture content of soils and vegetation through the summer. However, fire is possible during multiyear droughts. In addition, these communities usually occur in small patches surrounded by dense fir forest where severe crown fires are possible, and heat from these fires may kill aspen. Resprouting of aspen after such fires is likely, although removal of trees from a watershed could result in greater yield of water to the depressions where the aspen/ bluejoint reedgrass communities occur. In such cases, aspen may be unable to resprout in their former positions on the landscape, although they may survive by sprouting on slightly drier habitats upslope.

Management considerations—

Conifer competition is generally not an issue in aspen/bluejoint reedgrass communities, although conifer removal may be necessary to allow aspen survival in special cases where multiyear drought allows conifers to colonize these wetlands. Aspen are likely to expand uphill onto adjacent slightly drier sites if conifers are removed there; this would provide a more secure place for aspen in a future multiyear wet episode. Aspen regeneration is strongly inhibited by cattle grazing and browsing by deer and elk.

Environmental features

Site

Plots	7
Elevation, mean (range) (ft)	4,490 (4,035-5,040)
Slope, mean (range) (percent)	1 (0-2)
Aspect	None
Position	Toeslope or flat
Slope shape	Concave or planar

Soil

Available water capacity (in) (n = 4)	6.5 to 11 (moderate to high)
pH (n = 3)	5.6 to 6.4

Principal species

Latin name	Common name	Code	Cover/constancy
Overstory trees:			*Percent*
Populus tremuloides	Quaking aspen	POTR5	41/100
Understory trees:			
Abies grandis	Grand fir	ABGR	3/29
Abies lasiocarpa	Subalpine fir	ABLA	2/29
Pinus contorta	Lodgepole pine	PICO	3/29
Populus tremuloides	Quaking aspen	POTR5	36/100
Grasses and grasslike:			
Alopecurus pratensis	Meadow foxtail	ALPR3	3/29
Calamagrostis canadensis	Bluejoint reedgrass	CACA4	57/100
Carex microptera	Smallwinged sedge	CAMI7	2/71
Deschampsia cespitosa	Tufted hairgrass	DECE	19/29
Forbs:			
Aconitum columbianum	Columbian monkshood	ACCO4	2/29
Aster foliaceus	Leafy aster	ASFO	10/43
Ranunculus orthorhynchus	Straightbeak buttercup	RAOR3	4/43
Ranunculus uncinatus	Little buttercup	RAUN	3/43
Senecio crassulus	Thickleaf groundsel	SECR	31/57
Smilacina stellata	Starry false Solomon's seal	SMST	15/71
Thermopsis montana	Golden-pea	THMO6	4/43
Veratrum californicum	California false hellebore	VECA2	14/57
Veratrum viride	Green false hellebore	VEVI	6/29
Viola	Violet	VIOLA	3/29

Ground surface features

	Cover (%)
Bare ground	10
Bedrock	0
Rock	0
Gravel	0
Moss, lichen	14
Litter	63

Aspen/Kentucky Bluegrass Plant
Community Type
Populus tremuloides/Poa pratensis
POTR5/POPR   HQM122
(Crowe and Clausnitzer 1997)

Aspen/Mesic Forb Plant Community Type
*Populus tremuloides/*Mesic Forb
POTR5/MESIC FORB   HQM511
(Crowe and Clausnitzer 1997)

Aspen/Meadow Foxtail Plant Community Type
Populus tremuloides/Alopecurus pratensis
POTR5/ALPR3   HQM611

These three types are mesic (moderately moist) aspen
meadows and together are the most widespread aspen communities in the Blue Mountains. They are drier than the
preceding aspen-sedge community types. They have moist,
nutrient-rich soils with nearly neutral pH, all properties that
create an ideal environment for the growth of aspen. Three
communities are treated together here because they appear
to result mainly from differences in past history of grazing,
browsing, and colonization by various exotic grasses. The
aspen/mesic forb plant community type is the most pristine and the other two (POTR5/POPR and POTR5/ALPR3)
are highly impacted. In the tables "Principal species" and
"Ground surface features" below, the POTR5/MESIC

FORB communities are split into two groups according to
level of grazing impacts. The "POTR5/MESIC FORB (less
impacted)" plots have Kentucky bluegrass (*Poa pratensis*)
cover of 10 percent or less, and cover by all exotic grasses
and forbs plus grazing-tolerant native forbs is less than 25
percent. (Grazing-tolerant mesic forbs include common
dandelion *Taraxacum officinale*, false hellebore *Veratrum*
spp., longstalk clover *Trifolium longipes*, lupines *Lupinus*
spp., and yarrow *Achillea millefolium*). The "POTR5/
MESIC FORB (more impacted)" communities have
Kentucky bluegrass cover of more than 10 percent or exotic
grasses and forbs plus grazing-tolerant native forbs cover
of 25 percent or more. They are transitional in composition
to the POTR5/POPR and POTR5/ALPR3 types, which are
dominated by exotic grasses.

Environmental features—
Mesic aspen meadows occur on gentle to nearly level slopes
at midelevations. They are often situated in a swale or small
valley that supports an intermittent stream. These aspen
stands are often quite small (an acre or less), although in a
exceptional cases they may occupy 5 to 10 ac.

Soils—
Soils are fine-grained and high in organic matter, with a
neutral to slightly acid pH. The parent material is usually
a mixture of weathered volcanic ash and loess, with layers
of nearly pure ash in some profiles; coarse fragments are
usually absent. The surface texture is usually silt loam or
silty clay loam, often becoming more clay-rich with depth
(except for fine sandy loam textures in some fresh ash layers). Colors are typically dark throughout the upper 2 or 3 ft

of soil, indicating a high organic-matter content, except in the ash layers, which tend to be light colored. A water table is observed in some profiles below a depth of 24 in, usually in early summer (June). Later in the summer the soil is usually moist, but free water is not present. The soil surface is well covered by litter, even in the more grazing-disturbed stands, thanks to the vigorous rhizomatous grasses (Kentucky bluegrass, meadow foxtail, and others).

Vegetation composition—
Aspen generally dominate over an understory of forbs and grass. Coniferous trees are most common in the understory, but are occasionally codominant with aspen. Most of the coniferous tree species that inhabit the Blue Mountains can occur in mesic meadows together with aspen; ponderosa pine is most common. Shrub cover is low, with common snowberry (*Symphoricarpos albus*) the only common shrub. The understory in relatively pristine POTR5/MESIC FORB communities is dominated by a diverse assemblage of native forbs. Several of these forbs decline with grazing pressure, notably common camas (*Camassia quamash*), mountain sweet-cicely (*Osmorhiza chilensis*), straightbeak buttercup (*Ranunculus orthorhynchus*), starry false Solomon's seal (*Smilacina stellata*), and western meadowrue (*Thalictrum occidentale*). Understories in POTR5/ALPR3 communities are dominated by large grasses, especially introduced pasture species such as meadow foxtail and timothy (*Phleum pratense*), but also some native species such as blue wildrye (*Elymus glaucus*). Kentucky bluegrass is also common. The community type is named after the most common large introduced pasture grass (meadow foxtail), but this species is not always present. Kentucky bluegrass dominates in the highly impacted POTR5/POPR communities. Weedy forbs such as houndstongue (*Cynoglossum officinale*) and Canada thistle (*Cirsium arvense*) are present on the more grazing-impacted sites, but the highly competitive sod-forming grasses prevent them from dominating.

Successional relationships—
Succession is toward conifer forest in almost all cases. High water tables may at times restrict the growth of conifers, but not to the degree that they do in the wetter aspen meadows described previously. Moisture is probably adequate to support grand fir, but in many environments the seed source is mainly ponderosa pine or occasionally lodgepole pine, so these are the most important competing conifers. These communities may succeed to the lodgepole pine/Kentucky bluegrass plant community type (CLM112), the ponderosa pine/Kentucky bluegrass (CPM112) plant community type, or some as yet undefined grand fir series plant community. Shading by these conifers will suppress and could eliminate aspen from a meadow, although aspen often are able to persist on the margins of openings with a fluctuating high

water table where mature conifers may be killed by wetness and conifer seedlings have difficulty establishing.

The rate and ultimate outcome of understory plant recovery by succession if grazing disturbance is reduced is not well known. Kentucky bluegrass is highly competitive with the native forbs and once established may dominate for many years even after exclusion of grazing. If heavy grazing has produced a community dominated by bluegrass with some larger pasture grasses such as meadow foxtail or timothy, exclusion of grazing may allow the taller grasses to gradually replace Kentucky bluegrass by succession.

Fire—
Fire is probably rare in early seral mesic aspen meadows owing to the low flammability of fuels. As aspen die to produce surface woody fuels and conifers fill in, the likelihood of fire increases, as does fire severity. In addition, these communities usually occur in small patches surrounded by conifer forest where severe crown fires are possible, and heat from these fires may kill aspen. Fire frequency is highly dependent on the fire frequency of the neighboring upland forests. In the absence of fire, aspen is gradually eliminated by competing conifers.

Management considerations—
Mesic aspen meadows are highly productive and attractive to livestock and wild ungulates. Browsing pressure is intense in most parts of the study area; aspen are strongly hedged and regeneration is minimal outside of exclosures. Gradual death of old aspen trees and continuing hedging of regeneration could lead to complete loss of some aspen clones. Prolonged grazing pressure also tends to eliminate many native perennial forbs, which are replaced by the more grazing-tolerant grasses, especially Kentucky bluegrass. As mentioned above, we are uncertain about rate of recovery (or even the possibility of recovery) of a diverse native forb community where many species have been eliminated by grazing. Management should emphasize measures that prevent loss of vulnerable native forbs. Conifers are more shade tolerant and longer lived than aspen and compete strongly with aspen; thus conifer removal may be needed to ensure survival of aspen clones.

Environmental features

Site

Plots	46
Elevation, mean (range) (ft)	5,035 (3,930-6,240)
Slope, mean (range) (percent)	4 (0-20)
Aspect	All
Position	Footslope, toeslope
Slope shape	Concave or planar

Soil

Available water capacity (in) (n = 43)	6.5 to 10.5 (moderate to high)
pH (n = 31)	6.2 to 7.0

Principal species

Latin name	Common name	Code	POTR5/ MESIC FORB (less impacted) 16 plots	POTR5/ MESIC FORB (more impacted) 11 plots	POTR5/ALPR3 9 plots	POTR5/POPR 10 plots
			Cover (%)/constancy(%)			
Overstory trees:						
Pinus ponderosa	Ponderosa pine	PIPO	15/25	8/18	7/33	12/20
Populus tremuloides	Quaking aspen	POTR5	32/81	18/82	35/89	51/80
Understory trees:						
Juniperus occidentalis	Western juniper	JUOC	1/31	6/45	1/22	6/30
Pinus contorta	Lodgepole pine	PICO	8/12	10/18	4/33	5/20
Pinus ponderosa	Ponderosa pine	PIPO	4/44	17/55	3/33	3/50
Populus tremuloides	Quaking aspen	POTR5	31/88	26/100	24/67	11/90
Pseudotsuga menziesii	Douglas-fir	PSME	2/25	2/27	tr/11	1/20
Shrubs:						
Berberis repens	Creeping Oregon grape	BERE	2/25	tr/0		
Ribes cereum	Wax currant	RICE	3/12	2/27		1/10
Rosa	Rose	ROSA5	2/31	4/27	15/11	2/10
Symphoricarpos albus	Common snowberry	SYAL	3/50	5/73	4/56	5/70
Grasses and grasslike:						
Agrostis scabra	Rough bentgrass	AGSC5	tr/6		15/22	
Agrostis stolonifera	Creeping bentgrass	AGST2			48/22	
Alopecurus pratensis	Meadow foxtail	ALPR3			37/44	
Bromus carinatus	Mountain brome	BRCA5	3/6	6/64	1/22	5/50
Calamagrostis rubescens	Pinegrass	CARU	4/25			
Carex lanuginosa	Woolly sedge	CALA30				5/20
Carex microptera	Smallwinged sedge	CAMI7	1/31		9/44	7/30
Dactylis glomerata	Orchardgrass	DAGL	2/19	1/9	15/22	tr/30
Elymus glaucus	Blue wildrye	ELGL	3/31	4/73	32/33	4/20
Festuca occidentalis	Western fescue	FEOC		5/9	10/11	20/20
Juncus balticus	Baltic rush	JUBA	tr/6		4/33	3/10
Phleum pratense	Common timothy	PHPR3	3/38	2/27	8/67	3/30
Poa pratensis	Kentucky bluegrass	POPR	5/62	13/82	8/89	52/100
Trisetum canescens	Tall trisetum	TRCA21	8/25	2/36	9/56	4/10
Forbs:						
Achillea millefolium	Common yarrow	ACMI2	1/62	2/82	3/67	2/100
Actaea rubra	Red baneberry	ACRU2				2/20
Allium geyeri	Geyer's onion	ALGE	12/38	12/27		tr/10
Aquilegia formosa	Red columbine	AQFO	7/19	7/55	tr/11	3/50
Arenaria macrophylla	Bigleaf sandwort	ARMA18	25/6	tr/18		2/20
Arnica cordifolia	Heartleaf arnica	ARCO9	3/38	2/18	1/11	2/30
Aster foliaceus	Leafy aster	ASFO	14/25	15/9	2/22	2/20
Camassia quamash	Common camas	CAQU2	6/50	2/36	8/22	
Cirsium arvense	Canada thistle	CIAR4		tr/18		2/20
Cirsium vulgare	Bull thistle	CIVU	1/25	2/45	tr/33	1/40
Collinsia parviflora	Small flowered blue-eyed Mary	COPA3	tr/6	tr/18		2/30

(continued)

Principal species *(continued)*

Latin name	Common name	Code	POTR5/ MESIC FORB (less impacted) 16 plots	POTR5/ MESIC FORB (more impacted) 11 plots	POTR5/ALPR3 9 plots	POTR5/POPR 10 plots
			Cover (%)/constancy(%)			
Collomia linearis	Narrowleaf collomia	COLI2		tr/9		2/20
Cynoglossum officinale	Common houndstongue	CYOF		6/36		1/30
Delphinium depauperatum	Slim larkspur	DEDE2	1/19			2/20
Epilobium	Willowherb	EPILO	tr/6		2/22	
Fragaria	Strawberry	FRAGA	2/81	6/73	4/67	6/90
Galium aparine	Cleavers	GAAP2	4/31	1/36	1/33	1/50
Galium boreale	Northern bedstraw	GABO2	4/56	8/82	1/44	5/60
Geranium viscosissimum	Sticky geranium	GEVI2	1/12	2/27		1/20
Geum macrophyllum	Largeleaf avens	GEMA4	1/19		2/44	2/40
Iris missouriensis	Rocky Mountain iris	IRMI	16/25	25/9	55/11	4/20
Lupinus	Lupine	LUPIN	1/6			3/20
Nemophila parviflora	Smallflower nemophila	NEPA		1/9		13/20
Osmorhiza chilensis	Mountain sweet-cicely	OSCH	8/44	4/27	1/44	1/50
Penstemon globosus	Globe penstemon	PEGL5	4/19	3/18	4/22	
Penstemon procerus	Small flowered penstemon	PEPR2	3/6	3/9	1/11	3/20
Perideridia gairdneri	Gairdner's yampah	PEGA3	5/19	tr/9	2/22	tr/10
Potentilla gracilis	Slender cinquefoil	POGR9	1/50	3/55	5/56	1/50
Prunella vulgaris	Self-heal	PRVU			4/22	2/20
Ranunculus orthorhynchus	Straightbeak buttercup	RAOR3	6/50	1/9	1/22	1/10
Ranunculus uncinatus	Little buttercup	RAUN	2/75	8/55	8/22	8/50
Senecio crassulus	Thickleaf groundsel	SECR	20/44	25/27	16/33	20/20
Sidalcea oregana	Oregon checker-mallow	SIOR	4/62	1/45	3/56	4/60
Smilacina stellata	Starry false Solomon's seal	SMST	6/50	1/27	tr/22	1/50
Taraxacum officinale	Common dandelion	TAOF	3/69	6/82	2/67	3/70
Thalictrum occidentale	Western meadowrue	THOC	16/50	4/55	8/22	2/60
Trifolium longipes	Longstalk clover	TRLO	2/31	24/27	6/22	3/30
Veratrum	False hellebore	VERAT	1/6		1/22	14/20
Verbascum thapsus	Common mullein	VETH		tr/18		2/20
Viola adunca	Early blue violet	VIAD	2/12	4/45	1/11	1/30
Viola nuttallii	Nuttall's violet	VINU2			tr/11	2/20

Ground surface features

	POTR5/MESIC FORB (less impacted) 16 plots	POTR5/MESIC FORB (more impacted) 11 plots	POTR5/ALPR3 9 plots	POTR5/POPR 10 plots
	Cover (%)			
Bare ground	3	7	1	8
Bedrock	0	0	0	0
Rock	0	0	0	0
Gravel	0	0	0	0
Moss, lichen	3	2	2	1
Litter	96	91	97	91

Talus and Rock Outcrop Aspen Types

Aspen (Rubble, High) Plant Community Type
Populus tremuloides (Rubble, High)
POTR5 (RUBBLE, HIGH)   HQR101

D. Swanson

UA046

Aspen (Rubble, Low) Plant Community Type
Populus tremuloides (Rubble, Low)
POTR5 (RUBBLE, LOW)   HQR102

C. Johnson

QA076

Aspen are occasionally found growing out of crevices between large rocks in rubble fields, talus slopes, and fractured rock outcrops. Survival of aspen on these sites is favored by several factors. The poor footing for hoofed animals discourages browsing by deer, elk, and cattle. Rain and snowmelt are shed from the rock surfaces and concentrated in the crevices where the aspen root, providing a better moisture supply than would be available on a less rocky site. Once established, aspen can propagate by cloning as their roots follow the network of cracks and crevices between rocks.

Environmental features—
The high and low variants of rubble aspen communities are well separated by elevation, with the former occurring above 6,000 ft and the latter below 6,000 ft elevation. Otherwise settings are similar: steep slopes of various aspects and soils dominated by coarse fragments.

Vegetation composition—
The plant cover on these communities is quite sparse owing to the lack of soil, and composition is highly variable. At high elevations, subalpine fir are often present but with low cover. Oregon boxwood (*Pachistima myrsinites*), western hawkweed (*Hieracium albertinum*), and a variety of other plants are sometimes present but have low cover. At lower elevations, common associated plants are ponderosa pine, wax currant (*Ribes cereum*), common snowberry (*Symphoricarpos albus*), elk sedge (*Carex geyeri*), fireweed (*Epilobium angustifolium*), and hotrock penstemon (*Penstemon deustus*). The ground surface is mostly bedrock or loose rock and gravel, with litter present in the gaps between rocks.

Successional relationships—
These communities are probably not transient seral stages: cover by other trees is kept low by the lack of soil, allowing aspen to persist indefinitely.

Fire effects—
Ground fires cannot move across the ground owing to lack of fuel. However, the rubble fields and rock outcrops in our area are often rather small, and trees on them are vulnerable to damage by heat from crown fires in surrounding forests. If trees are killed by such a fire, aspen should resprout readily, whereas conifers will reestablish with difficulty by seed.

Management considerations—
Rubble sites are valuable natural refugia for aspen. As a result of their natural protection from conifer encroachment and herbivory, these aspen stands are typically in better condition than aspen stands on sites without rock rubble. Aspen can propagate naturally from these refugia out onto adjacent areas by seed or root cloning where conditions are suitable.

Environmental features

	POTR5 (RUBBLE, HIGH)	POTR5 (RUBBLE, LOW)
Plots	4	14
Elevation, mean (range) (ft)	6,758 (6,440-7,050)	5,040 (4,540-5,650)
Slope, mean (range) (percent)	32 (10-58)	57 (25-95)
Aspect	All	All
Position	Shoulder, backslope	Backslope, footslope
Slope shape	Convex, planar	Convex, planar, concave

Principal species

Latin name	Common name	Code	POTR5 (RUBBLE, HIGH) 4 plots	POTR5 (RUBBLE, LOW) 14 plots
			Cover (%)/constancy(%)	
Overstory trees:				
Abies lasiocarpa	Subalpine fir	ABLA	5/25	
Pinus ponderosa	Ponderosa pine	PIPO		11/29
Populus tremuloides	Quaking aspen	POTR5		13/50
Understory trees:				
Abies grandis	Grand fir	ABGR	4/25	11/21
Abies lasiocarpa	Subalpine fir	ABLA	3/75	
Pinus contorta	Lodgepole pine	PICO	8/25	6/43
Pinus ponderosa	Ponderosa pine	PIPO		2/43
Populus tremuloides	Quaking aspen	POTR5	44/100	29/79
Pseudotsuga menziesii	Douglas-fir	PSME		2/21
Shrubs:				
Amelanchier alnifolia	Western serviceberry	AMAL2	tr/25	2/50
Arctostaphylos uva-ursi	Kinnikinnick	ARUV		7/29
Berberis repens	Creeping Oregon grape	BERE		3/64
Ceanothus velutinus	Snowbrush ceanothus	CEVE	40/25	tr /14
Cornus stolonifera	Red-osier dogwood	COST4	10/25	
Pachistima myrsinites	Oregon boxwood	PAMY	9/50	6/29
Prunus virginiana	Common chokecherry	PRVI		8/36
Ribes cereum	Wax currant	RICE		12/57
Salix scouleriana	Scouler willow	SASC	3/25	11/29
Spiraea betulifolia	Birchleaf spiraea	SPBE2	1/25	4/29
Symphoricarpos albus	Common snowberry	SYAL	1/25	16/71
Symphoricarpos oreophilus	Mountain snowberry	SYOR2		7/21
Vaccinium scoparium	Grouse huckleberry	VASC	1/75	10/21
Grasses and grasslike:				
Agropyron spicatum	Bluebunch wheatgrass	AGSP		8/21
Bromus carinatus	Mountain brome	BRCA5	2/75	1/14
Calamagrostis rubescens	Pinegrass	CARU		4/43
Carex	Sedge	CAREX	6/50	
Carex geyeri	Elk sedge	CAGE2	1/25	6/86
Sitanion hystrix	Bottlebrush squirreltail	SIHY	tr /25	2/21
Stipa occidentalis	Western needlegrass	STOC2	tr /75	1/7

UPLAND ASPEN COMMUNITIES

Principal species

Latin name	Common name	Code	POTR5 (RUBBLE, HIGH) 4 plots	POTR5 (RUBBLE, LOW) 14 plots
			Cover (%)/constancy(%)	
Forbs:				
Achillea millefolium	Common yarrow	ACMI2	1/75	1/21
Apocynum androsaemifolium	Spreading dogbane	APAN2		3/21
Arnica cordifolia	Heartleaf arnica	ARCO9	3/25	2/14
Artemisia ludoviciana	Western mugwort	ARLU	15/25	
Cymopterus terebinthinus foeniculaceus	Turpentine cymopterus	CYTEF	3/25	
Epilobium angustifolium	Fireweed	EPAN2		2/64
Fragaria	Strawberry	FRAGA		4/43
Hackelia micrantha	Blue stickseed	HAMI	3/25	
Helianthella uniflora	Little sunflower	HEUN	5/25	
Heuchera cylindrica	Roundleaf alumroot	HECY2		16/21
Hieracium albertinum	Western hawkweed	HIAL	2/75	0/7
Lupinus sulphureus subsaccatus	Sulphur lupine	LUSUS3	5/25	
Mertensia ciliata	Ciliate bluebells	MECI3	3/25	
Paeonia brownii	Brown's peony	PABR	3/25	
Penstemon attenuatus	Sulfur penstemon	PEAT3	10/25	
Penstemon deustus	Hotrock penstemon	PEDE4		2/50
Penstemon fruticosus	Shrubby penstemon	PEFR3	3/25	2/14
Phlox austromontana	Mountain phlox	PHAU3	5/25	
Potentilla arguta convallaria	Tall cinquefoil	POARC	4/50	tr /14
Valeriana sitchensis	Sitka valerian	VASI	3/25	

Ground surface features

	POTR5 (RUBBLE,HIGH) 4 plots	POTR5 (RUBBLE,LOW) 14 plots
	Cover (%)	
Bare ground	6	2
Bedrock	12	14
Rock	44	51
Gravel	16	1
Moss, lichen	0	4
Litter	21	30

Aspen Types of the Subalpine Fir Series

Aspen(Subalpine Fir)/Western Coneflower Plant Community Type
Populus tremuloides (Abies lasiocarpa)/ Rudbeckia occidentalis

POTR5(ABLA)/RUOC2 HQC114

Aspen are present although rare in plant communities with subalpine fir potential in the Blue Mountains. Here the soil is more fine-grained than the rock rubble sites described previously. Two of the sample plots are in burned areas, one in a clearcut, the fourth on a mountain slope with fir parkland. Elsewhere in the Rocky Mountains, aspen is a common early seral species on sites with subalpine fir potential (Peet 2000), and it is likely that our sample does not portray the full range of subalpine fir sites that aspen could occupy in the Blue Mountains.

Environmental features—
The four plots sampled are on hillslopes.

Soils—
Soils formed in stoney colluvium or weathered bedrock. A loamy surface layer with few stones is present in some profiles, ranging in thickness up to 2 ft. Below is very to extremely gravelly or cobbly loamy soil. Available water holding capacity is low to moderate.

Vegetation composition—
Aspen are absent from one of the plots because they failed to regenerate after a fire, although snags from mature aspen are present. Subalpine fir is sometimes present in the understory. One plot has bitter cherry (*Prunus emarginata*) shrubs. The understory layer is dominated by grasses and the disturbance-adapted forb western coneflower (*Rudbeckia occidentalis*). Skunk-leaved polemonium

(*Polemonium pulcherrimum*), a common associate of subalpine fir, is common. Some forb species typical of mid-elevation aspen stands (such as nettleleaf horsemint *Agastache urticifolia* and western meadowrue *Thalictrum occidentale*) are also present.

Successional relationships—
Succession should be toward subalpine fir forest in most cases, although poor site conditions may lead to open forest stands that allow aspen to persist for a long time.

Fire—
Fires in subalpine fir forests are infrequent but typically of high severity. Fires generally favor aspen, which can resprout afterward without conifer competition. However, the failure of aspen to resprout on one of these subalpine fir plots shows that small clones can on occasion be eliminated by fire, probably when severe fire kills a shallow root system.

Management considerations—
Aspen is probably capable of growing in many subalpine fir plant associations in the Blue Mountains as a seral species, but it is rare. The mixed- to stand-replacement fires typical of these communities should favor aspen, although fire suppression, browsing, competition by lodgepole pines, and lack of propagules (either seeds or preexisting aspen that could resprout) combine to make aspen quite uncommon.

Environmental features

Site

Plots	4
Elevation, mean (range) (ft)	6,245 (4,840-6,870)
Slope, mean (range) (percent)	32 (6-62)
Aspect	All
Position	Backslope
Slope shape	Planar or concave

Soil

Available water capacity (in) (n = 3)	3.5 to 7.5 (low to moderate)
pH (n = 3)	5.8 to 6.4

UPLAND ASPEN COMMUNITIES

Principal species

Latin name	Common name	Code	Cover/constancy
Overstory trees:			*Percent*
Abies grandis	Grand fir	ABGR	3/25
Abies lasiocarpa	Subalpine fir	ABLA	10/25
Pinus contorta	Lodgepole pine	PICO	5/25
Populus tremuloides	Quaking aspen	POTR5	17/75
Understory trees:			
Abies grandis	Grand fir	ABGR	3/25
Populus tremuloides	Quaking aspen	POTR5	16/75
Shrubs:			
Prunus emarginata	Bitter cherry	PREM	25/25
Sambucus	Elderberry	SAMBU	5/25
Symphoricarpos albus	Common snowberry	SYAL	3/50
Grasses and grasslike:			
Bromus carinatus	Mountain brome	BRCA5	15/75
Bromus vulgaris	Columbia brome	BRVU	20/25
Carex microptera	Smallwinged sedge	CAMI7	3/25
Elymus glaucus	Blue wildrye	ELGL	15/50
Trisetum canescens	Tall trisetum	TRCA21	3/25
Forbs:			
Achillea millefolium	Common yarrow	ACMI2	8/50
Agastache urticifolia	Nettleleaf horsemint	AGUR	2/100
Anaphalis margaritacea	Common pearly-everlasting	ANMA	2/75
Arenaria macrophylla	Bigleaf sandwort	ARMA18	3/25
Arnica cordifolia	Heartleaf arnica	ARCO9	3/25
Aster foliaceus	Leafy aster	ASFO	5/25
Aster modestus	Few-flowered aster	ASMO3	3/25
Collomia		COLLO	5/50
Delphinium glaucum	Sierra larkspur	DEGL3	10/25
Epilobium angustifolium	Fireweed	EPAN2	3/25
Fragaria	Strawberry	FRAGA	10/25
Hackelia micrantha	Blue stickseed	HAMI	2/75
Heracleum lanatum	Cowparsnip	HELA4	3/50
Osmorhiza occidentalis	Western sweetroot	OSOC	2/50
Phacelia hastata	Silverleaf phacelia	PHHA	3/25
Phacelia heterophylla	Varileaf phacelia	PHHE2	3/25
Polemonium pulcherrimum	Skunk-leaved polemonium	POPU3	5/100
Rudbeckia occidentalis	Western coneflower	RUOC2	24/100
Sidalcea oregana	Oregon checker-mallow	SIOR	3/25
Thalictrum occidentale	Western meadowrue	THOC	1/100
Viola	Violet	VIOLA	2/50

Ground surface features

	Cover (%)
Bare ground	15
Bedrock	5
Rock	7
Gravel	1
Moss, lichen	0
Litter	72

Aspen Types of the Grand Fir Series

Grand Fir/Twinflower Plant Association
Abies grandis/Linnaea borealis
ABGR/LIBO3
CWF311 (Johnson and Simon 1987)
CWF312 (Johnson and Clausnitzer 1992)

D. Swanson

UA021

One plot containing aspen was sampled from this plant association. It is located at 4,320 ft elevation on a gently sloping bench in the northern Blue Mountains. The soil consists of 20 in of fine-grained volcanic ash over gravelly sandy clay loam, with a pH of 6.2 to 6.6. A sparse overstory of Engelmann spruce, western larch, and Douglas-fir is present, with abundant understory aspen (35 percent cover) and grand fir seedlings and saplings (20 percent cover). The shrub and herb layer is dominated by twinflower (*Linnaea borealis*), false Solomon's seal (*Smilacina racemosa*), prince's pine (*Chimaphila umbellata*), and rose (*Rosa gymnocarpa*). This plant association of rather moist and rich sites is capable of supporting seral aspen, but aspen are rare here, probably owing to conifer competition and herbivory. The high cover of false Solomon's seal (20 percent) is unusual for this plant association and may be an effect of enhanced nutrient cycling provided by aspen.

Grand Fir/Big Huckleberry Plant Association
Abies grandis/Vaccinium membranaceum
ABGR/VAME
CWS211 (Johnson and Simon 1987)
CWS212 (Johnson and Clausnitzer 1992)

C. Johnson

1089

Aspen is a rare early-seral component in this widespread plant association.

Environmental features—
These communities occur in a variety of settings at moderate elevations on moderate slopes.

Soils—
Soils are well-drained and lack a water table or any other sign of wetness. Two of the soils studied formed in stoney colluvium or residuum from bedrock, with low available water capacity and slightly to moderately acid pH. Profiles consist of very gravelly or cobbly loamy material. The third study profile is more typical of the plant association and has over 2 ft of silty volcanic ash over very gravelly loam and a high available water capacity.

Vegetation composition—
Aspen share the tree layer with a variety of conifers, including Douglas-fir, grand fir, ponderosa pine, western larch, and lodgepole pine. The understory is rich in shrubs, especially big huckleberry (*Vaccinium membranaceum*), Scouler's willow (*Salix scouleriana*), birchleaf spiraea (*Spiraea betulifolia*), and many others. Pinegrass (*Calamagrostis rubescens*), strawberry (*Fragaria* sp.), western meadowrue (*Thalictrum occidentale*), and other herbaceous plants form a rather sparse ground cover. These communities differ from typical early seral ABGR/VAME communities in that lodgepole pine is lacking or less abundant than aspen.

Successional relationships—
Aspen is a seral species that will be replaced by more shade-tolerant conifers unless disturbance interrupts succession. Ponderosa pine, Douglas-fir, and grand fir are all possible successors to aspen, and grand fir is likely to dominate over the long term in the absence of disturbance. Competion from the shade-intolerant but fast-growing conifers western larch and lodgepole pine can also limit aspen growth.

Fire—
Moist grand fir plant associations such as this are believed to have historically had a mixed fire regime. Occasional moderate- to high-severity fires removed the overstory and allowed aspen to resprout or regenerate by seed with minimal competition. Fire suppression has probably led to loss of seral aspen communities.

Management consideration—
Conifer competition is intense in these communities, and removal of overstory conifers is usually required to allow aspen regeneration. If overstory conifers are present, light prescribed fires are likely to kill aboveground parts of aspen without providing enough light for aspen suckers to thrive. Soil moisture should be adequate for aspen plantings in ABGR/VAME plant associations where aspen are lacking. These shrub-rich communities provide minimal forage for livestock and are rarely grazed by livestock. However, aspen are preferred wildlife browse and their growth is often suppressed by browsing; protection of aspen from browsing will often be needed to allow aspen regeneration to survive. The early-seral plot listed separately in the tables below probably established by seed into a clearcut. At sampling, the single aspen seedling in the plot had been browsed repeatedly and appeared unlikely to survive.

Environmental features

Site	
Plots	5
Elevation, mean (range) (ft)	4,810 (3,980-5,450)
Slope, mean (range) (percent)	22 (15-30)
Aspect	All
Position	All
Slope shape	All
Soil	
Available water capacity (in) (n = 3)	2 to 9 (low to high)
pH (n = 3)	5.8 to 6.6

Principal species

Latin name	Common name	Code	ABGR/VAME 4 plots	ABGR/VAME very early seral 1 plot
			Cover (%)/constancy(%)	Cover (%)
Overstory trees:				
Larix occidentalis	Western larch	LAOC	35/25	
Pinus contorta	Lodgepole pine	PICO	5/25	
Pinus ponderosa	Ponderosa pine	PIPO	15/50	
Populus tremuloides	Quaking aspen	POTR5	3/25	
Pseudotsuga menziesii	Douglas-fir	PSME	3/25	
Understory trees:				
Abies grandis	Grand fir	ABGR	7/75	
Larix occidentalis	Western larch	LAOC	10/50	3
Picea engelmannii	Engelmann spruce	PIEN	1/50	tr
Pinus contorta	Lodgepole pine	PICO	55/25	8
Pinus ponderosa	Ponderosa pine	PIPO	1/25	2
Populus tremuloides	Quaking aspen	POTR5	16/100	tr
Pseudotsuga menziesii	Douglas-fir	PSME	6/50	
Shrubs:				
Acer glabrum	Rocky Mountain maple	ACGL	3/25	
Amelanchier alnifolia	Western serviceberry	AMAL2	10/50	
Ceanothus velutinus	Snowbrush ceanothus	CEVE	4/50	5
Lonicera utahensis	Utah honeysuckle	LOUT2	6/50	
Pachistima myrsinites	Oregon boxwood	PAMY	2/75	
Prunus emarginata	Bitter cherry	PREM	10/25	1
Ribes lacustre	Prickly currant	RILA	3/25	
Salix scouleriana	Scouler's willow	SASC	9/100	3
Sorbus scopulina	Cascade moutain-ash	SOSC2	3/25	
Spiraea betulifolia	Birchleaf spiraea	SPBE2	10/100	
Symphoricarpos albus	Common snowberry	SYAL	30/25	
Vaccinium membranaceum	Big huckleberry	VAME	30/100	1
Vaccinium scoparium	Grouse huckleberry	VASC	6/50	1
Grass and grasslike:				
Agrostis scabra	Rough bentgrass	AGSC5	tr/25	1
Calamagrostis rubescens	Pinegrass	CARU	11/75	
Carex geyeri	Elk sedge	CAGE2	4/50	
Carex rossii	Ross' sedge	CARO5	10/25	5
Festuca occidentalis	Western fescue	FEOC	1/25	tr
Forbs:				
Achillea millefolium	Common yarrow	ACMI2	1/50	15
Anaphalis margaritacea	Common pearly-everlasting	ANMA		3
Antennaria microphylla	Rosy pussytoes	ANMI3	tr/25	1
Arnica cordifolia	Heartleaf arnica	ARCO9	2/50	
Aster conspicuus	Showy aster	ASCO3	10/25	
Epilobium angustifolium	Fireweed	EPAN2	1/50	tr
Fragaria	Strawberry	FRAGA	2/100	20
Gayophytum decipiens	Deceptive groundsmoke	GADE2	tr/25	3
Lupinus sericeus	Silky lupine	LUSE4	20/25	
Solidago missouriensis	Missouri goldenrod	SOMI2		1
Thalictrum occidentale	Western meadowrue	THOC	5/50	
Valeriana	Valerian	VALER	5/25	
Vicia americana	American vetch	VIAM		1

Ground surface features

	ABGR/VAME 4 plots	ABGR/VAME, very early seral 1 plot
	Cover (%)	
Bare ground	9	40
Bedrock	0	0
Rock	2	0
Gravel	1	1
Moss, lichen	1	10
Litter	86	50

Grand Fir/Rocky Mountain Maple Plant Association

Abies grandis/Acer glabrum

ABGR/ACGL
CWS912 (Johnson and Simon 1987)
CWS541 (Johnson and Clausnitzer 1992)

D. Swanson

UA041

Aspen occasionally occur in this plant association, usually on somewhat atypical sites where slope instability or snow avalanches have limited conifer competition.

Environmental features—
The communities occur on steep slopes at moderate elevations. Two of the plots are in distinct snow avalanche tracks, and a third is on a steep slope (48 percent) that was obviously unstable.

Soils—
Soils are formed in coarse-grained colluvial material with low available water capacity and slightly acid pH. Textures are very to extremely gravelly to bouldery loam or sandy loam.

Vegetation composition—
Overstory conifers are sparse owing to slope instability or avalanches. Overstory aspen may be present as bent, leaning, or gnarled forms. Understory grand fir and aspen are common. Shrubs are abundant, with Rocky Mountain maple dominant. A rich assemblage of grasses and forbs is also present, notably blue wildrye (*Elymus glaucus*), nettle-leaf horsemint (*Agastache urticifolia*), strawberry (*Fragaria* sp.), and blue stickseed (*Hackelia micrantha*). The cover by herbaceous vegetation, especially grasses, is higher on these aspen plots than for other ABGR/ACGL plots that we have sampled, probably thanks to the light conifer overstory.

Successional relationships—
Seedling grand firs are usually present and suggest succession toward a grand fir forest with a few maples persisting

in their shade. However, disturbance by avalanches or by soil instability will maintain some sites indefinitely in an early seral, shrub- and herb-dominated condition.

Fire—
The typical vegetation dominated by deciduous shrubs and moist forbs is likely to carry fire only under extreme conditions, although these plants could be killed by intense heat of a fire in adjacent conifer stands. If extreme weather or conifer encroachment allow fire to burn through these communities, it is likely to be followed by resprouting of aspen and shrubs.

Management considerations—
On sites where natural disturbance does not limit conifer growth, aspen would benefit from conifer removal. Establishment of aspen from seed for plantings is likely to be limited by shrub competition. Dense and tall shrubs may help to reduce browsing of aspen.

Environmental features

Site

Plots	4
Elevation, mean (range) (ft)	5,460 (5,240-5,720)
Slope, mean (range) (percent)	34 (23-48)
Aspect	South and west
Position	Backslope
Slope shape	Planar

Soil

Available water capacity (in) (n = 2)	2 to 4.5 (low)
pH (n = 2)	6.0 to 6.6

UPLAND ASPEN COMMUNITIES

Principal species

Latin name	Common name	Code	Cover/constancy
Overstory trees:			*Percent*
Abies grandis	Grand fir	ABGR	7/25
Populus tremuloides	Quaking aspen	POTR5	20/50
Pseudotsuga menziesii	Douglas-fir	PSME	5/25
Understory trees:			
Abies grandis	Grand fir	ABGR	16/75
Picea engelmannii	Engelmann spruce	PIEN	3/25
Populus tremuloides	Quaking aspen	POTR5	12/75
Shrubs:			
Acer glabrum	Rocky Mountain maple	ACGL	26/100
Berberis repens	Creeping Oregon grape	BERE	15/50
Prunus emarginata	Bitter cherry	PREM	4/50
Rubus parviflorus	Thimbleberry	RUPA	3/25
Salix scouleriana	Scouler's willow	SASC	3/25
Sambucus cerulea	Blue elderberry	SACE3	3/25
Spiraea betulifolia	Birchleaf spiraea	SPBE2	15/25
Symphoricarpos albus	Common snowberry	SYAL	7/75
Symphoricarpos oreophilus	Mountain snowberry	SYOR2	5/25
Grasses and grasslike:			
Bromus carinatus	Mountain brome	BRCA5	20/50
Calamagrostis rubescens	Pinegrass	CARU	18/50
Carex geyeri	Elk sedge	CAGE2	10/50
Carex hoodii	Hood's sedge	CAHO5	10/50
Elymus glaucus	Blue wildrye	ELGL	17/100
Forbs:			
Achillea millefolium	Common yarrow	ACMI2	4/50
Agastache urticifolia	Nettleleaf horsemint	AGUR	10/100
Aster conspicuus	Showy aster	ASCO3	10/25
Aster foliaceus	Leafy aster	ASFO	3/50
Delphinium occidentale	Western larkspur	DEOC	6/50
Fragaria	Strawberry	FRAGA	16/100
Hackelia micrantha	Blue stickseed	HAMI	13/75
Hieracium albiflorum	White hawkweed	HIAL2	2/75
Hydrophyllum fendleri	Fendler's waterleaf	HYFE	5/25
Phacelia hastata	Silverleaf phacelia	PHHA	3/25
Polemonium pulcherrimum	Skunk-leaved polemonium	POPU3	3/25
Pteridium aquilinum	Braken fern	PTAQ	25/50
Rudbeckia occidentalis	Western coneflower	RUOC2	5/25
Senecio serra	Tall butterweed	SESE2	5/25
Thalictrum occidentale	Western meadowrue	THOC	1/75
Thlaspi fendleri	Wild candytuft	THFE3	5/25
Urtica dioica	Stinging nettle	URDI	5/25
Valeriana sitchensis	Sitka valerian	VASI	3/25
Viola	Violet	VIOLA	6/50

Ground surface features

	Cover (%)
Bare ground	12
Bedrock	0
Rock	16
Gravel	2
Moss, lichen	4
Litter	66

Aspen (Grand Fir)/Oceanspray Plant Community Type
Populus tremuloides (Abies grandis)/ Holodiscus discolor

POTR5(ABGR)/HODI   HQC115

Two aspen plots were sampled with grand fir potential vegetation and an understory dominated by oceanspray (*Holodiscus discolor*). One plot is located at 4,680 ft on a shoulder slope on the east side of Bobsled Ridge, in the southwest part of the Walla Walla Ranger District, Umatilla National Forest. The soil is a dark-colored clay loam at least 3 ft thick with pH of 6.6 to 7.0 and a high water-holding capacity. Overstory tree cover is less than 10 percent and consists of a mix of grand fir, western larch, and Douglas-fir. Aspen saplings are abundant in a dense shrub understory of oceanspray, common snowberry (*Symphoricarpos albus*) and lesser amounts of western trumpet honeysuckle (*Lonicera ciliosa*), big huckleberry (*Vaccinium membranaceum*), mallow ninebark (*Physocarpus malvaceus*), Scouler's willow (*Salix scouleriana*), and mountain ash (*Sorbus scopulina*), over diverse forbs. This rich and diverse community resembles communities of both the Douglas-fir/oceanspray and grand fir/Rocky Mountain maple plant associations (Johnson and Clausnitzer 1992, Johnson and Simon 1987). Aspen are thriving and competing well with the tall shrubs. Once aspen are established in such a community, disturbance such as severe wildfire should favor them over conifers, because rapidly growing aspen suckers can compete with shrubs and conifer seed establishment is difficult among resprouting shrubs.

The second plot of this type is on a steep, rocky, southeast-facing slope at 4,440 ft elevation in the far western end of the Heppner Ranger District, Umatilla National Forest. The soil is stoney silt loam to a depth of 8 in, over very stoney silt loam, with pH of 6.6. The overstory is dominated by grand fir and Douglas-fir, with minor suppressed aspen. The understory is rather sparse and consists of aspen, oceanspray (*Holodiscus discolor*) and traces of other mesic shrubs, over sparse blue wildrye (*Elymus glaucus*) and forbs such as trailplant (*Adenocaulon bicolor*) and Sierran peavine (*Lathyrus nevadensis*). The plot is located below a talus aspen community that provides a refugium and propagule source for aspen to colonize nearby forests such as this.

Aspen (Grand Fir)/Snowberry Plant Community Type
Populus tremuloides (Abies grandis)/ Symphoricarpos

POTR5(ABGR)/SYMPH   HQC116

Aspen occurs with snowberry understory in communities capable of supporting grand fir. Most key into existing grand fir/pinegrass, grand fir/hearleaf arnica, or grand fir/elk sedge plant associations (Johnson and Clausnitzer 1992, Johnson and Simon 1987) and have environmental settings similar to these types. However, both aspen and significant shrub cover are unusual for these existing types, and thus this new type was created.

Environmental features—
Usually occurs on gentle to moderately steep hillslopes with southerly aspect and planar to concave shape.

Soils—
Soils are well drained and formed in a colluviated mixture of volcanic ash and loess over stoney colluvium or clay-rich subsoil. Surface textures are usually loam or silt loam at least 10 in thick. Very to extremely gravelly loamy material occurs within 3 ft of the surface in about half of the profiles. In other cases, the subsoil consists of clay loam or gravelly clay loam. Soil pH is moderately acid to neutral. Soil

available water capacity ranges widely but is usually moderate to high.

Vegetation composition—

Ponderosa pine, Douglas-fir, and grand fir are all common associates of aspen, and are especially common as understory species. Shrub cover is substantial, and either species of snowberry (common *Symphoricarpos albus* or mountain *S. oreophilus*) may be present. The understory is dominated by grasses, most often pinegrass (*Calamagrostis rubescens*), and also elk sedge (*Carex geyeri*); forb cover is typically low, with heartleaf arnica (*Arnica cordifolia*) and strawberry (*Fragaria* sp.) the most abundant forbs.

Successional relationships—

Overstory shading by conifers and browsing by elk and deer should, over time, reduce or eliminate aspen and snowberry in most stands, thereby converting them into communities typical of the grand fir/pinegrass or grand fir/elk sedge plant associations.

Fire—

Dry mixed-conifer forests in the Blue Mountains historically had frequent low- or mixed-severity fires (Heyerdahl et al. 2001). This fire regime helped to maintain open stands of large pines or pines plus Douglas-firs, while keeping grand fir numbers low. This type of fire regime has ambiguous effects on aspen. On the one hand, canopy openings created by fires (especially in patches of mixed or high-intensity fire) are good places for aspen to resprout or establish from seed. However, low-intensity fires that kill aboveground parts of aspen without killing overstory conifers force aspen to resprout under conifers where they are unlikely to thrive. Most understory species in these communities resprout strongly after light- to moderate-severity fires.

Management considerations—

Conifer competition is intense in these communities, and removal of conifers is usually required to allow aspen regeneration. If a conifer overstory is present, light prescribed fires are likely to kill aspen without providing enough light for them to grow after resprouting. Livestock grazing and wildlife browsing at levels typical of the Blue Mountains today will usually result in hedging of aspen saplings and no recruitment of new pole-sized aspen. Many aspen clones are at risk of dying out as older trees die of old age or shading by conifers. Heavy ungulate pressure also suppresses snowberry. Effects of heavy livestock grazing on understory herbaceous species are subtle, because this layer is dominated by shrubs and grazing-resistant pine-

grass and elk sedge. The more grazing-sensitive species (especially native forbs) are always rather sparse owing to shading and competition. We would expect heavy grazing to reduce or eliminate some of the native forbs, such as mountain sweet-cicely (*Osmorhiza chilensis*) and western meadowrue (*Thalictrum occidentale*).

Environmental features

Site

Plots	22
Elevation, mean (range) (ft)	5,230 (3,110-6,265)
Slope, mean (range) (percent)	16 (0-38)
Aspect	Usually south
Position	All
Slope shape	Usually planar or concave

Soil

Available water capacity (in) (n = 20)	3.0 to 10.5 (low to high)
pH (n = 18)	6.0 to 6.8

Principal species

Latin name	Common name	Code	Cover/constancy
Overstory trees:			*Percent*
Abies grandis	Grand fir	ABGR	12/27
Pinus ponderosa	Ponderosa pine	PIPO	14/32
Populus tremuloides	Quaking aspen	POTR5	22/77
Pseudotsuga menziesii	Douglas-fir	PSME	5/32
Understory trees:			
Abies grandis	Grand fir	ABGR	9/68
Pinus ponderosa	Ponderosa pine	PIPO	9/45
Populus tremuloides	Quaking aspen	POTR5	27/86
Pseudotsuga menziesii	Douglas-fir	PSME	2/32
Shrubs:			
Berberis repens	Creeping Oregon grape	BERE	4/36
Symphoricarpos albus	Common snowberry	SYAL	15/64
Symphoricarpos oreophilus	Mountain snowberry	SYOR2	22/36
Grasses and grasslike:			
Bromus carinatus	Mountain brome	BRCA5	6/59
Calamagrostis rubescens	Pinegrass	CARU	24/50
Carex geyeri	Elk sedge	CAGE2	23/41
Elymus glaucus	Blue wildrye	ELGL	8/50
Poa pratensis	Kentucky bluegrass	POPR	5/45
Trisetum canescens	Tall trisetum	TRCA21	7/36
Forbs:			
Achillea millefolium	Common yarrow	ACMI2	2/91
Antennaria microphylla	Rosy pussytoes	ANMI3	2/23
Arnica cordifolia	Heartleaf arnica	ARCO9	7/32
Collomia linearis	Narrowleaf collomia	COLI2	2/23
Fragaria	Strawberry	FRAGA	4/73
Geranium viscosissimum	Sticky geranium	GEVI2	2/23
Hackelia micrantha	Blue stickseed	HAMI	2/27
Osmorhiza chilensis	Mountain sweet-cicely	OSCH	2/41
Potentilla gracilis	Slender cinquefoil	POGR9	3/23
Sidalcea oregana	Oregon checker-mallow	SIOR	2/23
Thalictrum occidentale	Western meadowrue	THOC	2/41

Ground surface features

	Cover (%)
Bare ground	10
Bedrock	0
Rock	0
Gravel	0
Moss, lichen	0
Litter	90

Other Grand Fir Series Aspen Communities

We sampled several other plots with aspen and grand fir potential. These are unique occurrences that demonstrate the ecological range of aspen, but appear unlikely to occur elsewhere.

The Dooley Mountain seed tree exclosure aspen. This unique occurrence of aspen is in a fenced seed tree plantation of ponderosa pines east of Beaver Mountain in the Baker Ranger District of Wallowa Whitman National Forest. It is on a gentle slope at 5,495 ft elevation. Large ponderosa pines and smaller lodgepole pines were present here before the Dooley Mountain Fire of 1989. A potential vegetation of grand fir/pinegrass or related plant association is most likely. Today's vegetation is sparse and dominated by a sedge (*Carex concinnoides*) and the grass Idaho fescue (*Festuca idahoensis*), with lesser amounts of yarrow (*Achillea millefolium*), fireweed (*Epilobium angustifolium*), and pinegrass (*Calamagrostis rubescens*). These aspen are a rare example of natural aspen seed establishment. The nearest seed source trees are probably at least 2 mi away. Aspen are scattered throughout the exclosure but are growing very poorly, with gnarled stems and dwarfed leaves suggestive of nutrient deficiency. The soil consists of gravelly loam with little organic matter and a pH of 5.6, near the lower limit for aspen growth. Acidification of the soil by previous conifer forest has made this site marginal for aspen. Of five stems sampled for DNA by V. Erickson (see the genetics sections of this report), four were genetically unique, indicating establishment of at least four different seeds (app. A).

Aspen–Engelmann spruce–grand fir/forb snowdrift community. This plot is on a shoulder slope on the lee side of a windswept ridgetop where a large snowdrift accumulates. It is at 5,000 ft near Black Mountain in the southwest part of the Walla Walla Ranger District, Umatilla National Forest. Aspen are gnarled and leaning, probably owing to downslope creep of the deep snowdrift. The overstory is dominated by Engelmann spruce and grand fir with suppressed aspen. Grand fir dominates the tree understory with aspen also present. Shrubs are absent and the herb layer is dominated by an unusual mix of forbs characteristic of moist (groundsel [*Senecio crassulus*]) and dry (stonecrop [*Sedum stenopetalum*]) sites, reflecting the ecotonal position of the plot along the transition from a dry, rocky ridge to a moist snowbed. Snowdrifts can favor aspen by providing supplemental moisture while suppressing conifers.

Other Grand Fir Series Aspen Communities
(continued)

Aspen/thimbleberry-bracken fern-starry false Solomon's seal community. This plot is located at 5,900 ft in a moist concavity above the Imnaha River near where it leaves the Eagle Cap Wilderness area. The aspen grove has a dense understory of thimbleberry (*Rubus parviflorus*), bracken-fern (*Pteridium aquilinum*), and starry false Solomon's seal (*Smilacina stellata*). Potential vegetation here is likely to be grand fir.

Aspen Types of the Ponderosa Pine and Douglas-Fir Series

Aspen/Chokecherry Plant Community Type
Populus tremuloides/Prunus virginiana
POTR5/PRVI   HQS5

D. Swanson

WA011

Vegetation composition—
The only plant species in common between all of the plots are aspen, chokecherry, and snowberry. Shrub cover is high and dominated by chokecherry, common snowberry, and the dwarf shrub, creeping Oregon grape (*Berberis repens*). Grasses have more cover than forbs, although droughty soils and competition from trees and shrubs limit both. The most abundant herbaceous plant is currently cheatgrass (*Bromus tectorum*), although originally the understory was probably dominated by elk sedge (*Carex geyeri*) and native sod-forming grasses such as blue wildrye (*Elymus glaucus*) or mountain brome (*Bromus carinatus*).

Successional relationships—
Colonization and increase of ponderosa pine, western juniper (*Juniperus occidentalis*), or Douglas-fir over time is likely.

Fire—
These communities typically occur in dry forest environments that historically had frequent low-intensity fires.

Management considerations—
Communities with aspen, chokecherry, and snowberry were probably more common in the past. A combination of conifer encroachment and herbivory have probably caused conversion of many communities to ponderosa pine or Douglas-fir over snowberry. The state of chokecherry in the Blue Mountains is much like aspen, declining because of shading by conifers and ungulate herbivory. Steps should be taken to preserve these communities where they still remain.

Aspen occurs locally in groves with an understory of chokecherry, a tall shrub. The plots described here have little in common beyond the rather warm and dry environment and the presence of aspen, chokecherry, and common snowberry (*Symphoricarpos albus*).

Environmental features—
The plots occur at moderate elevations on mostly steep, south-facing slopes.

Soils—
Soils range from very rocky and droughty on steep slopes to one plot in a swale on a hillslope with a deep loamy soil.

Environmental features

Site	
Plots	4
Elevation, mean (range) (ft)	4,600 (3,480-6,015)
Slope, mean (range) (percent)	40 (20-75)
Aspect	Mostly south
Position	Backslope or footslope
Slope shape	Planar or convex

Soil	
Available water capacity (in) (n = 3)	Variable
pH (n = 3)	6.8 to 7.6

Principal species

Latin name	Common name	Code	Cover/constancy
Overstory trees:			*Percent*
Populus tremuloides	Quaking aspen	POTR5	10/25
Understory trees			
Populus tremuloides	Quaking aspen	POTR5	44/100
Shrubs:			
Amelanchier alnifolia	Western serviceberry	AMAL2	3/25
Artemisia tridentata	Big sagebrush	ARTR2	10/25
Berberis repens	Creeping Oregon grape	BERE	17/75
Chrysothamnus viscidiflorus	Green rabbitbush	CHVI8	5/25
Crataegus douglasii	Black hawthorn	CRDO2	3/25
Philadelphus lewisii	Lewis' mock-orange	PHLE4	5/25
Prunus emarginata	Bitter cherry	PREM	5/25
Prunus virginiana	Common chokecherry	PRVI	34/100
Ribes aureum	Golden currant	RIAU	3/25
Rosa	Rose	ROSA5	10/25
Rosa woodsii	Woods' rose	ROWO	16/50
Symphoricarpos albus	Common snowberry	SYAL	11/100
Grasses and grasslike:			
Agropyron intermedium	Intermediate wheatgrass	AGIN2	5/25
Bromus carinatus	Mountain brome	BRCA5	20/25
Bromus tectorum	Cheatgrass	BRTE	10/50
Carex geyeri	Elk sedge	CAGE2	3/50
Elymus glaucus	Blue wildrye	ELGL	3/50
Poa juncifolia	Alkali bluegrass	POJU	3/25
Trisetum canescens	Tall trisetum	TRCA21	3/25
Forbs:			
Agastache urticifolia	Nettleleaf horsemint	AGUR	5/25
Apocynum androsaemifolium	Spreading dogbane	APAN2	1/75
Clematis ligusticifolia	Western clematis	CLLI2	3/25
Madia glomerata	Cluster tarweed	MAGL2	5/25
Osmorhiza chilensis	Mountain sweet-cicely	OSCH	5/25
Penstemon deustus	Hotrock penstemon	PEDE4	3/25
Smilacina stellata	Starry false Solomon's seal	SMST	3/25
Vicia americana	American vetch	VIAM	2/50

Ground surface features

	Cover (%)
Bare ground	10
Bedrock	0
Rock	6
Gravel	4
Moss, lichen	6
Litter	74

Aspen (Douglas-Fir)/ Bitter Cherry Plant Community Type

Populus tremuloides (Pseudotsuga menziesii)/Prunus emarginata

POTR5(PSME)/PREM   HQC117

D. Swanson

UA040

This plant community type is particularly common on Lookout Mountain in Baker County (BLM administered lands), where three of our four plots are located. This unique area lacks pines (ponderosa or lodgepole), and grand fir and larch are narrowly restricted to moist sites. This leaves room for Douglas-fir and aspen to occupy a wider variety of sites than elsewhere in the Blue Mountains.

Environmental features—
Examples of this community type occur on rather steep, droughty south- and west-facing slopes at moderate elevations.

Soils—
The limited sample suggests rocky soils formed in colluvium from bedrock, with low available water capacity.

Vegetation composition—
Douglas-fir is frequently present along with aspen and it probably represents the potential on most sites. Shrubs are abundant and dominated by bitter cherry, mountain snowberry (*Symphoricarpos oreophilus*), and creeping Oregon grape (*Berberis repens*). Blue wildrye (*Elymus glaucus*) is the only common grass. Forbs are diverse and lush in spite of the rather dry sites, with nettleleaf horsemint (*Agastache urticifolia*) the most common and mountain sweet-cicely (*Osmorhiza chilensis*) also important.

Successional relationships—
Succession should lead to Douglas-fir forest in the absence of disturbance.

Fire—
The aspen, deciduous shrubs, and forbs make this community less flammable than others in the dry forest zone. The natural fire regime is probably frequent light fires or mixed fires. It is dominated by species that resprout vigorously after fire.

Management considerations—
These unique communities are diverse and contain a variety of plants that are vulnerable to heavy grazing or wildlife browsing. They may have been more abundant in the past and have been converted to Douglas-fir/mountain snowberry communities.

Environmental features

Site	
Plots	4
Elevation, mean (range) (ft)	5,310 (4,900-5,910)
Slope, mean (range) (percent)	30 (22-42)
Aspect	South and west
Position	Shoulder, backslope, or footslope
Slope shape	All

Principal species

Latin name	Common name	Code	Cover/constancy
			Percent
Overstory trees:			
Populus tremuloides	Quaking aspen	POTR5	25/75
Pseudotsuga menziesii	Douglas-fir	PSME	22/50
Understory trees:			
Abies lasiocarpa	Subalpine fir	ABLA	3/25
Juniperus occidentalis	Western juniper	JUOC	3/25
Populus tremuloides	Quaking aspen	POTR5	20/100
Shrubs:			
Berberis repens	Creeping Oregon grape	BERE	28/50
Crataegus douglasii	Black hawthorn	CRDO2	40/25
Prunus emarginata	Bitter cherry	PREM	22/100
Prunus virginiana	Common chokecherry	PRVI	6/50
Symphoricarpos oreophilus	Mountain snowberry	SYOR2	18/75
Grasses and grasslike:			
Elymus glaucus	Blue wildrye	ELGL	18/75
Forbs:			
Achillea millefolium	Common yarrow	ACMI2	2/75
Agastache urticifolia	Nettleleaf horsemint	AGUR	16/100
Clarkia rhomboidea	Common clarkia	CLRH	5/25
Collinsia parviflora	Small flowered blue-eyed Mary	COPA3	3/50
Descurainia richardsonii	Mountain tansymustard	DERI2	9/50
Galium aparine	Cleavers	GAAP2	4/50
Hackelia micrantha	Blue stickseed	HAMI	3/25
Hydrophyllum fendleri	Fendler's waterleaf	HYFE	5/25
Osmorhiza chilensis	Mountain sweet-cicely	OSCH	15/50
Osmorhiza occidentalis	Western sweetroot	OSOC	4/50
Phacelia	Phacelia	PHACE	6/50
Phacelia heterophylla	Varileaf phacelia	PHHE2	3/50
Rudbeckia occidentalis	Western coneflower	RUOC2	5/25
Senecio serra	Tall butterweed	SESE2	15/25
Sidalcea oregana	Oregon checker-mallow	SIOR	3/25
Smilacina racemosa	Western false Solomon's seal	SMRA	3/25
Thalictrum occidentale	Western meadowrue	THOC	2/50
Urtica dioica	Stinging nettle	URDI	3/25
Vicia americana	American vetch	VIAM	5/25

Ground surface features

	Cover (%)
Bare ground	6
Bedrock	0
Rock	1
Gravel	1
Moss, lichen	0
Litter	92

Aspen (Ponderosa Pine–Douglas-Fir)/Snowberry Plant Community Type

Populus tremuloides (Pinus ponderosa-Pseudotsuga menziesii)/Symphoricarpos

POTR5(PIPO-PSME)/SYMPH   HQC118

C. Johnson

QA300

Aspen occur occasionally in dry upland forests of ponderosa pine and Douglas-fir with an understory dominated by common (*Symphoricarpos albus*) or mountain (*S. oreophilus*) snowberry. These communities are seral stages in one of the following plant associations (Johnson and Clausnitzer 1992, Johnson and Simon 1987): Douglas-fir/common snowberry (PSME/SYAL, CDS622 or CDS624); Douglas-fir/mountain snowberry (PSME/SYOR, CDS623 or CDS625); ponderosa pine/common snowberry (PIPO/SYAL, CPS522 or CPS524); or ponderosa pine/mountain snowberry (PIPO/SYOR, CPS525).

These are seral communities in which aspen will be replaced by ponderosa pine or Douglas-fir over time if there is no disturbance. According to Johnson and Clausnitzer (1992), the mountain snowberry plant associations are on slightly drier sites than their common snowberry counterparts. However, in the aspen data set there was complete overlap in plant community composition between common and mountain snowberry-dominated plots; thus they are treated together here. Also, owing to the similarity in plant communities between the two series, and frequent difficulty in determining which conifer is the potential in early seral stages, snowberry communities from both the ponderosa pine and Douglas-fir series are joined here.

The data are summarized in condition classes based on subjective field determination of past grazing pressure as follows: "poor" typically has severely hedged aspen with evidence of trampling and weedy understory plant species; "good" has a diverse understory composition and healthy aspen regeneration; "fair" is intermediate.

Environmental features—
These communities occur at moderate elevations and on gentle to moderately steep slopes of mostly south aspect.

Soils—
Soils are well drained and formed in colluvium derived from loess, volcanic ash, and weathered bedrock. Available water capacity in the upper 40 in ranges greatly, and pH ranges from moderately acid to neutral. Surface textures are silt loam or loam, becoming more gravel-rich and in some cases more clay-rich with depth. Very or extremely gravelly material occurs below 16 in depth in most profiles, but reaches the surface in a few.

Vegetation composition—
Ponderosa pine and Douglas-fir are common with aspen in the overstory and understory. A variety of shrubs may be present, with snowberry by far the most common. Snowberry and aspen regeneration cover are lower in plots judged to be in poor condition. The herbaceous layer is rich in grasses and elk sedge (*Carex geyeri*). Elk sedge declines on plots in poor condition, whereas Kentucky bluegrass (*Poa pratensis*) increases. Forb cover is fairly low, and the most abundant species on good sites (heartleaf arnica [*Arnica cordifolia*], strawberry [*Fragaria* sp.], mountain sweet-cicely [*Osmorhiza chilensis*], and western meadowrue [*Thalictrum occidentale*]) showed declines on the plots in poor condition. Other forb species (Sierran peavine [*Lathyrus nevadensis*] and starry false Solomon's seal [*Smilacina stellata*]) were sometimes present on plots in good condition but conspicuously absent from plots in poor condition. Plots in poor condition also had more bare soil exposed.

Successional relationships—
Without disturbance, these communities will succeed to a conifer-dominated state. On sites with a Douglas-fir potential, both it and ponderosa pine will become dominant over aspen, with snowberry usually persisting in the understory. On sites not suitable for firs, aspen will be replaced by ponderosa pine, with snowberry usually persisting in the understory.

Fire—
Dry ponderosa pine and mixed-conifer forests historically had frequent low- or mixed-severity fires (Heyerdahl et

al. 2001). This fire regime helped to maintain open stands of large pines or pines and Douglas-firs. This type of fire regime has ambiguous effects on aspen. On the one hand, canopy openings created by fires (especially in patches of mixed- or high-intensity fire) are good places for aspen to resprout or establish from seed. However, low-intensity fires that kill aboveground parts of aspen without killing over-story conifers force aspen to resprout under conifers where they are unlikely to thrive. Most understory species in these communities resprout strongly after light- to moderate-severity fires.

Management considerations—
Conifer competition is intense in these communities, and removal of conifers may be required to allow aspen regen-eration. If a conifer overstory is present, light prescribed fires are likely to kill aspen without providing enough light for them to thrive after resprouting. These sites are near the dry limit for survival of aspen in the Blue Mountains, so plantings of aspen may fail owing to drought. Livestock grazing and wildlife browsing at levels typical of the Blue

Mountains today will usually result in hedging of aspen saplings and no recruitment of new pole-sized aspen. Many aspen clones are at risk of dying out as trees die of old age or shading by conifers. Heavy ungulate pressure also suppresses snowberry and other shrubs. Heavy livestock grazing also leads to the decline of elk sedge and grazing-sensitive native forbs such as mountain sweet-cicely, sticky geranium (*Geranium viscosissimum*), and western meadowrue.

E░ ░░░░ ░░░░░░░░░░

S░░░
Plots	29
Elevation, mean (range) (ft)	5,040 (3,440-6,920)
Slope, mean (range) (percent)	22 (4-58)
Aspect	Mainly east and south
Position	Backslope, footslope
Slope shape	All

S░ ░░
Available water capacity (in) (n = 22)	2.5 to 10 (low to high)
pH (n = 20)	6.0 to 7.0

P░░░░░░░░░░░

L░░ ░░░ ░	C░░ ░ ░ ░ ░ ░ ░	C░░░	░ ░ ░ ░░░░░ ░░░░░ ░ ░ ░░░	░░ ░░░░░░ ░░░░ ░ ░░░	P░ ░ ░ ░ ░ ░ ░ ░░░ ░ ░ ░░░
			Cover (%)/constancy(%)		
Overstory trees:					
Pinus ponderosa	Ponderosa pine	PIPO	18/80	20/78	12/60
Populus tremuloides	Quaking aspen	POTR5	17/47	17/89	26/80
Pseudotsuga menziesii	Douglas-fir	PSME	23/20	12/22	
Understory trees:					
Juniperus occidentalis	Western juniper	JUOC	2/27	4/67	11/80
Pinus ponderosa	Ponderosa pine	PIPO	7/53	12/89	19/100
Populus tremuloides	Quaking aspen	POTR5	32/93	10/89	2/100
Pseudotsuga menziesii	Douglas-fir	PSME	13/40	8/33	
Shrubs:					
Amelanchier alnifolia	Western serviceberry	AMAL2	2/27	6/22	2/40
Berberis repens	Creeping Oregon grape	BERE	3/80	4/56	1/60
Ribes cereum	Wax currant	RICE	2/33	4/78	3/60
Rosa	Rose	ROSA5	1/40	1/33	3/20
Salix scouleriana	Scouler's willow	SASC	1/7	14/33	
Spiraea betulifolia	Birchleaf spiraea	SPBE2	6/13	2/22	tr/20
Symphoricarpos albus	Common snowberry	SYAL	24/80	31/56	7/80
Symphoricarpos oreophilus	Mountain snowberry	SYOR2	43/20	21/44	15/20
Grasses and grasslike:					
Bromus carinatus	Mountain brome	BRCA5	1/33	3/56	20/20
Calamagrostis rubescens	Pinegrass	CARU	15/27	20/44	5/20

P (continued)

L	C	C			P
			Cover (%)/constancy(%)		
Carex geyeri	Elk sedge	CAGE2	29/73	24/67	3/20
Dactylis glomerata	Orchardgrass	DAGL	tr/7	2/22	tr/40
Elymus glaucus	Blue wildrye	ELGL	2/40	7/56	12/40
Festuca occidentalis	Western fescue	FEOC	5/20	10/11	1/20
Koeleria cristata	Prairie junegrass	KOCR			3/20
Phleum pratense	Common timothy	PHPR3	2/13	tr/11	5/20
Poa juncifolia	Alkali bluegrass	POJU			5/20
Poa pratensis	Kentucky bluegrass	POPR	3/40	2/44	11/60
Sitanion hystrix	Bottlebrush squirreltail	SIHY		4/44	2/40
Stipa occidentalis	Western needlegrass	STOC2	9/40	7/33	1/20
Trisetum canescens	Tall trisetum	TRCA21	3/20	1/11	
Forbs:					
Achillea millefolium	Common yarrow	ACMI2	1/80	1/100	4/80
Arenaria macrophylla	Bigleaf sandwort	ARMA18	1/13	1/44	1/60
Arnica cordifolia	Heartleaf arnica	ARCO9	5/40	2/33	
Collinsia parviflora	Small flowered blue-eyed Mary	COPA3	2/13		3/20
Epilobium angustifolium	Fireweed	EPAN2	2/27	5/11	
Fragaria	Strawberry	FRAGA	7/67	2/67	3/40
Frasera speciosa	Giant frasera	FRSP	3/7	2/22	
Galium bifolium	Thinleaf bedstraw	GABI	5/7		35/20
Galium boreale	Northern bedstraw	GABO2	4/47	3/11	1/20
Geranium viscosissimum	Sticky geranium	GEVI2	3/40	6/22	1/20
Hackelia micrantha	Blue stickseed	HAMI	5/20		1/20
Iris missouriensis	Rocky Mountain iris	IRMI	1/13	1/11	15/20
Lathyrus nevadensis	Sierran peavine	LANE3	6/27		
Lupinus	Lupine	LUPIN		tr/11	6/40
Osmorhiza chilensis	Mountain sweet-cicely	OSCH	6/67	4/78	3/60
Osmorhiza occidentalis	Western sweetroot	OSOC	3/20		
Sidalcea oregana	Oregon checker-mallow	SIOR	2/27	tr/22	1/60
Smilacina stellata	Starry false Solomon's seal	SMST	28/20	3/11	tr/20
Solidago missouriensis	Missouri goldenrod	SOMI2	3/27		
Taraxacum officinale	Common dandelion	TAOF	1/40	4/44	2/40
Thalictrum occidentale	Western meadowrue	THOC	11/53	1/22	

			P		
	Cover (%)				
Bare ground	2	5	12		
Bedrock	0	0	0		
Rock	2	1	0		
Gravel		0	1		
Moss, lichen	0	0	0		
Litter	96	94	87		

Aspen/Pinegrass Plant Community Type
Populus tremuloides/Calamagrostis rubescens
POTR5/CARU   HQG114

C. Johnson

QA273

Aspen/Elk Sedge Plant Community Type
Populus tremuloides/Carex geyeri
POTR5/CAGE2   HQG112 (Johnson 2004)

C. Johnson

7024

Aspen/Exotic Grass Plant Community Type
Populus tremuloides/Poaceae
POTR5/EXOTIC GRASS   HQC115

D. Swanson

WA012

Aspen occur as a seral species in a variety of warm, dry, upland forest plant associations with understory layers dominated by pinegrass (*Calamagrostis rubescens*), elk sedge (*Carex geyeri*), or introduced grasses that have replaced these species. The potential vegetation on these sites may be ponderosa pine (PIPO/CARU, CPG221 or PIPO/CAGE2, CPG222 plant associations), Douglas-fir (PSME/CARU, CDG112 and CDG121 or PSME/CAGE2, CDG111 plant associations), or grand fir (ABGR/CARU, CWG112 and CWG113 or ABGR/CAGE2, CWG111 plant associations). (These types are all defined in Johnson and Clausnitzer 1992, Johnson and Simon 1987). However, the late-seral conifers needed to determine the potential vegetation are often not present. Fortunately the site characteristics and understory vegetation of aspen communities from the three pinegrass plant associations are quite similar to one another, so they are treated together here. The same is true for aspen communities of the three elk sedge plant associations, and they are also joined here under a broadened concept of the aspen/elk sedge plant community type originally defined by Johnson (2004).

Environmental features—
Aspen/pinegrass and aspen/elk sedge community types are found on sites with moderate elevations, slope steepness, and available soil moisture. Earlier studies (Johnson and Clausnitzer 1992, Johnson and Simon 1987) have determined that pinegrass requires slightly more warmth and moisture than elk sedge.

Soils—
Soils are well-drained and lack a water table or any other signs of wetness. They generally have a moderate available water capacity and slightly acid to neutral pH. They formed in a variety of materials, including volcanic ash, loess, colluvium, and alluvium. Soils have a surface layer of loam or silt loam at least 10 in thick and sometimes gravelly (up to 35 percent gravel). In some profiles, this material continues beyond the depth of observation, whereas in others it is underlain by either more clay-rich material or very gravelly loamy material.

Vegetation composition—
Ponderosa pine, Douglas-fir, lodgepole pine, or grand fir may be present depending on the potential of the site, availability of seed, and stand history. Shrubs and forbs are typically sparse, and the understory is dominated by grass or sedge, usually pinegrass or elk sedge. Other common plants are mountain brome (*Bromus carinatus*), heartleaf arnica (*Arnica cordifolia*), and strawberry (*Fragaria* sp.). Where the community was disturbed and artificially seeded (POTR5/exotic grass in the table below), exotic species such as intermediate wheatgrass (*Agropyron intermedium*) may dominate.

Successional relationships—

Aspen is a seral species that will be replaced by conifers unless disturbance interrupts succession. Ponderosa pine, Douglas-fir, and grand fir are all possible successors to aspen. Where moisture is limiting, succession is likely to end with ponderosa pine or mixed pine and Douglas-fir, and moister sites may be colonized by the more shade-tolerant grand fir.

Fire—

Warm dry upland forests with pinegrass or elk sedge understory are well known for their frequent, low-intensity fires (Heyerdahl et al. 2001). The three dominant conifers of these sites–ponderosa pine, Douglas-fir, and grand fir–have fire-resistant bark that allows mature trees to survive light fires. Light underburns are likely to kill some or all of the aspen while allowing overstory conifers to survive. High-severity fires that remove the overstory and allow aspen to resprout (or, rarely, establish from seed) without competition are needed if aspen is to be maintained by fire.

Management considerations—

Conifer competition is intense in these communities, and removal of conifers may be required to allow aspen regeneration. If overstory conifers are present, light prescribed fires are likely to kill aspen without providing enough light for vigorous resprouting of aspen. These sites are near the dry limit for survival of aspen in the Blue Mountains, so plantings of aspen may fail owing to drought. Livestock grazing and wildlife browsing at levels typical of the Blue Mountains today will usually result in hedging of saplings and no recruitment of new pole-sized aspen. Many aspen clones are at risk of dying out as older trees die of old age or shading by conifers. Native understory vegetation is composed largely of grazing-tolerant grasses and sedges (pinegrass and elk sedge) and forbs with fairly low palatability; thus native understory vegetation can persist even as heavy grazing and browsing lead to the loss of aspen.

E

	POT␣␣CA␣U	POT␣␣CA␣E␣	POT␣␣E␣␣␣ ␣␣␣␣
S␣␣␣			
Plots	20	13	3
Elevation, mean (range) (ft)	5,550 (4,740-6,600)	5,460 (4,540-7,060)	5,460 (4,800-6,300)
Slope, mean (range) (percent)	14 (2-40)	19 (3-52)	25 (10-40)
Aspect	All (more often S)	All	N
Position	All	All	Backslope, footslope
Slope shape	Convex, planar, concave	Convex, planar, concave	Concave, planar
S␣␣␣			
Available water capacity (in)	4.5 to 7 (moderate) (n = 10)	3 to 10 (low to high) (n = 9)	2 to 8 (low to high) (n = 3)
pH	5.6 to 6.8 (n = 9)	6.0 to 7.0 (n = 9)	6.0 to 8.2 (n = 3)

P␣␣␣␣␣␣␣␣␣␣

L␣␣␣ ␣␣␣	C␣␣␣␣␣␣␣	C␣␣␣	POT␣␣CA␣U ␣␣ ␣␣␣	POT␣␣CA␣E␣ ␣␣ ␣␣␣	POT␣␣␣␣␣␣ ␣␣␣␣␣ ␣␣␣
			Cover (%)/constancy(%)		
Overstory trees:					
Abies grandis	Grand fir	ABGR	12/10	20/15	5/33
Pinus contorta	Lodgepole pine	PICO	1/5	6/23	10/33
Pinus ponderosa	Ponderosa pine	PIPO	22/55	16/38	
Populus tremuloides	Quaking aspen	POTR5	28/70	19/92	10/33
Pseudotsuga menziesii	Douglas-fir	PSME	28/25	24/31	20/33
Understory trees:					
Abies grandis	Grand fir	ABGR	4/45	3/46	2/67
Pinus contorta	Lodgepole pine	PICO	17/30	7/31	
Pinus ponderosa	Ponderosa pine	PIPO	6/65	11/69	6/67
Populus tremuloides	Quaking aspen	POTR5	13/95	12/92	75/100
Pseudotsuga menziesii	Douglas-fir	PSME	8/35	4/54	tr/33

(continued)

P░░░░░░░░░░ (continued)

L░░░ ░░░ ░	C░░ ░ ░ ░ ░ ░	C░░░	POT░ ░░CA░ U ░░ ░░░░	POT░ ░░CA░ E░ ░░ ░░░░	POT░ ░░░░░░ ░░░░░░ ░ ░░░
			Cover (%)/constancy(%)		
Shrubs:					
Arctostaphylos uva-ursi	Kinnikinnick	ARUV	3/5	21/23	
Artemisia tridentata	Big sagebrush	ARTR2	tr/5		1/67
Berberis repens	Creeping Oregon grape	BERE	1/35	2/38	
Chrysothamnus viscidiflorus	Green rabbitbush	CHVI8			1/67
Ribes cereum	Wax currant	RICE	2/20	4/31	
Spiraea betulifolia	Birchleaf spiraea	SPBE2	5/5		3/33
Symphoricarpos albus	Common snowberry	SYAL	2/30	2/69	3/67
Symphoricarpos oreophilus	Mountain snowberry	SYOR2	4/30	2/8	
Grasses and grasslike:					
Agropyron intermedium	Intermediate wheatgrass	AGIN2	tr/5		62/67
Agrostis scabra	Rough bentgrass	AGSC5			10/33
Bromus carinatus	Mountain brome	BRCA5	5/25	4/62	3/67
Calamagrostis rubescens	Pinegrass	CARU	29/100	2/31	1/33
Carex	Sedge	CAREX	5/5	1/8	3/33
Carex geyeri	Elk sedge	CAGE2	25/70	42/100	
Dactylis glomerata	Orchardgrass	DAGL	1/10	3/8	3/67
Festuca idahoensis	Idaho fescue	FEID		4/23	
Festuca rubra	Red fescue	FERU2			10/33
Melica subulata	Alaska oniongrass	MESU		4/23	
Poa nervosa	Wheeler's bluegrass	PONE2		4/23	
Poa pratensis	Kentucky bluegrass	POPR	6/20	2/31	
Stipa occidentalis	Western needlegrass	STOC2	4/20	2/46	
Trisetum canescens	Tall trisetum	TRCA21	5/10	5/31	tr/33
Forbs:					
Achillea millefolium	Common yarrow	ACMI2	1/85	2/92	1/100
Arenaria macrophylla	Bigleaf sandwort	ARMA18	3/15	2/31	tr/100
Arnica cordifolia	Heartleaf arnica	ARCO9	7/45	28/31	2/67
Cirsium arvense	Canada thistle	CIAR4	1/5		1/67
Collinsia parviflora	Small flowered blue-eyed Mary	COPA3	3/5	3/23	
Epilobium angustifolium	Fireweed	EPAN2	2/25	1/23	
Fragaria	Strawberry	FRAGA	6/95	9/92	1/67
Hieracium albertinum	Western hawkweed	HIAL	2/45	2/23	1/67
Hieracium albiflorum	White hawkweed	HIAL2	1/40	1/62	tr/33
Lupinus	Lupine	LUPIN	6/35		
Lupinus caudatus	Tailcup lupine	LUCA	10/20	8/23	
Medicago lupulina	Black medick	MELU			5/33
Osmorhiza chilensis	Mountain sweet-cicely	OSCH	5/40	2/77	1/33
Polemonium pulcherrimum	Skunk-leaved polemonium	POPU3			3/33
Sedum stenopetalum	Wormleaf stonecrop	SEST2	tr/5	2/23	10/33
Senecio serra	Tall butterweed	SESE2			2/67
Taraxacum officinale	Common dandelion	TAOF	1/20	2/62	tr/100
Thalictrum occidentale	Western meadowrue	THOC	2/25	8/38	
Trifolium longipes	Longstalk clover	TRLO		13/15	15/33
Viola adunca	Early blue violet	VIAD	3/30	2/62	tr/33

⬚ ⬚⬚⬚⬚ ⬚⬚⬚⬚⬚ ⬚⬚⬚⬚⬚

	POT⬚⬚CA⬚ U ⬚⬚ ⬚⬚⬚	POT⬚⬚CA⬚ E⬚ ⬚⬚ ⬚⬚⬚	POT⬚ ⬚⬚⬚⬚⬚ ⬚⬚⬚⬚⬚ ⬚ ⬚⬚⬚
	Cover (%)		
Bare ground	5	6	14
Bedrock	0	0	0
Rock	1	1	2
Gravel	1	2	3
Moss, lichen	3	0	0
Litter	90	91	81

Other Douglas-Fir and Ponderosa Pine Series Aspen Communities

Aspen (Douglas-fir)/showy aster community. This plot is in a dense aspen thicket on the upper canyon slope of Needham Butte in the southeastern Wallowa Valley Ranger District of Wallowa-Whitman National Forest. It is on a steep north-facing slope at 5,220 ft elevation. Elsewhere in the Imnaha-Hells Canyon region, sites like this are usually occupied by Douglas-fir over ninebark (*Physocarpus malvaceus*), common snowberry (*Symphoricarpos albus*), and other shrubs, or thickets of these shrubs without trees. For reasons probably related more to site history than to environmental conditions, a vigorous aspen clone is present instead, with widely scattered Douglas-fir. Shrubs are absent and the understory is a rich assortment of forbs dominated by showy aster (*Aster conspicuous*) and Missouri goldenrod (*Solidago missouriensis*).

Aspen/blue wildrye community. This plot describes a strongly regenerating aspen clone 6 years after the 1994 Little Malheur Fire. It is on a north-facing slope at 5,650 ft elevation in the Prairie City Ranger District of Malheur National Forest. The grasses blue wildrye (*Elymus glaucus*, 60 percent cover) and bottlebrush squirreltail (*Sitanion hystrix,* 20 percent cover) are dominant. These two species are vigorous postfire resprouters like aspen. An aspen-grass community is likely to persist here for some time; the long-term trajectory is unknown.

Other Douglas-Fir and Ponderosa Pine Series
Aspen Communities *(continued)*

Aspen/bluebunch wheatgrass community. Aspen were recorded cloning after fire up a slope vegetated mainly by bluebunch wheatgrass (*Agropyron spicatum*), western needlegrass (*Stipa occidentalis*), bottlebrush squirreltail (*Sitanion hystrix*), wax currant (*Ribes cerum*), and annual forbs. The plot is located on a north-facing footslope adjacent to a riparian zone at 5,090 ft on the Prairie City Ranger District of Malheur National Forest. Sites dominated by bunchgrasses are nearly always too dry to support aspen; this plot represents a rare exception to the rule that sites moist enough to support aspen will also support rhizomatous grasses and sedges rather than bunchgrass.

Slender cinquefoil-yarrow-timothy community. This unusual occurrence of aspen is at 5,370 ft elevation on a nearly treeless plateau near Marr Flat in the southern part of the Wallowa Valley Ranger District, Wallowa-Whitman National Forest. The plot is listed here, although it is not certain if ponderosa pine is truly the potential vegetation. The soil consists of about 2 ft of silty loess over gravelly clay loam that overlies basalt bedrock. Depressions on the flat are occupied by vernal pools. The vegetation consists of grazing-resistant unpalatable forbs (slender cinquefoil [*Potentilla gracilis*], yarrow [*Achillea millefolium*]) and introduced grasses (timothy [*Phleum pratense*] and Kentucky bluegrass [*Poa pratensis*]). This community results from historical overgrazing, and it is difficult to reconstruct the original vegetation, although a moist steppe community such as one of the Idaho fescue–prairie junegrass plant associations is likely. Small aspen sprouts inside cages are all that persist today, but large fallen aspen trunks show that mature trees can survive here too. The strongly contrasting soil water regime on sites like this is inhospitable to trees, and aspen survival is probably marginal.

Acknowledgments

Charles G. Johnson, Jr., former Area Ecologist for the Blue Mountains National Forests, provided the original impetus for this work. The authors gratefully acknowledge technical review comments by Dale Bartos (Aspen Ecologist, U.S. Forestry Sciences Laboratory, Logan, UT) Tom Demeo (Regional Ecologist, U.S. Forest Service Pacific Northwest Region), and Mary Manning (Regional Ecologist, U.S. Forest Service Northern Region), editorial review by Lynn Sullivan (U.S. Forest Service, Pacific Northwest Research Station), and publication layout by Adrianna Sutton. Thanks also to Marty Vavra and Edward DePuit (U.S. Forest Service, Pacific Northwest Research Station) for sponsoring this work as a Pacific Northwest Research Station publication. Primary funding for this publication was provided by the U.S. Forest Service Region 6 Ecology Program. The National Park Service, Alaska Region, contributed time for D.K. Swanson to complete this project after his departure from the U.S. Forest Service.

Metric Equivalents

When you know:	Multiply by:	To find:
Inches (in)	2.54	Centimeters
Feet (ft)	.3048	Meters
Yards (yd)	.914	Meters
Miles (mi)	1.609	Kilometers
Square feet (ft^2)	.093	Square meters
Acres (ac)	.405	Hectares
Square feet per acre (ft^2/ac)	.229	Square meters per hectare
Cubic inches (in^3)	16.4	Milliliters
Gallons (gal)	3.78	Liters
Degrees Fahrenheit (°F)	Subtract 32 and then divide by 1.8	Celsius degrees
Trees per acre	2.47	Trees per hectare

References

Altman, B. 2000. Conservation strategy for landbirds in the northern Rocky Mountains of eastern Oregon and Washington. Version 1.0. Oregon-Washington Partners in Flight. http://www.orwapif.org/consplan html. (7 May 2008).

Baker, F.S. 1925. Aspen in the central Rocky Mountain region. Bulletin 1291. Washington, DC: U.S. Department of Agriculture. 47 p.

Baker, D.L.; Andelt, W.F.; Burnham, K.P.; Shepperd, W.D. 1999. Effectiveness of Hot Sauce® and Deer Away® repellents for deterring elk browsing of aspen sprouts. Journal of Wildlife Management. 63(4): 1327–1336.

Barnes B.V. 1966. The clonal growth habit of American aspens. Ecology. 47(3): 439–447.

Barnes, B.V. 1975. Phenotypic variation of trembling aspen in western North America. Forest Science. 21(3): 319–328.

Bates, P.C.; Sucoff, E.; Blinn, S.R. 1998. Short-term flooding effects on root suckering of quaking aspen. Northern Journal of Applied Forestry. 15(4): 169–173.

Bright, G.A. 1994. An extensive reconnaissance of the Wenaha National Forest in 1913. Powell, D.C., ed. Tech. Pub. F14-SO-08-94. Pendleton, OR: U.S. Department of Agriculture, Forest Service, Umatilla National Forest. 56 p.

Buell, M.F.; Buell, H.F. 1959. Aspen invasion of prairie. Bulletin of the Torrey Botanical Club. 86(4): 264–269.

Callan, B.E. 1998. Diseases of *Populus* in British Columbia: a diagnostic manual. Victoria, BC: Natural Resources Canada, Canadian Forest Service. 157 p.

Campbell, R.B. 1984. Asexual vs. sexual propagation of quaking aspen. In: Murphy, P.M., ed. The challenge of producing native plants for the Intermountain area. Proceedings, Intermountain Nurseryman's Association 1983 conference. Gen. Tech. Rep. INT-GTR-168. Ogden, UT: U.S. Department of Agriculture, Forest Service, Intermountain Forest and Range Experiment Station: 61–65.

Chen, H.Y.H.; Klinka, K.; Kabzems, R.D. 1998. Site index, site quality, and foliar nutrients of trembling aspen: relationships and predictions. Canadian Journal of Forest Research. 28: 1743–1755.

Clausnitzer, R.R. 1993. The grand fir series of northeastern Oregon and southeastern Washington: successional stages and management guide. R6-ECO-TP-050-93. Portland, OR: U.S. Department of Agriculture, Forest Service, Pacific Northwest Region. 193 p.

Cobb, L. 1997. Diurnal breeding birds in aspen (*Populus tremuloides*) communities on the Malheur National Forest, 1997. A summary report to the Malheur National Forest. Prairie City, OR: Grant County Bird Club. 22 p.

Cochran, P.H.; Berntsen, C.M. 1973. Tolerance of lodgepole and ponderosa pine seedlings to low night temperatures. Forest Science. 19(4): 272–280.

Crowe, E.A.; Clausnitzer, R.R. 1997. Mid-montane wetland plant associations of the Malheur, Umatilla, and Wallowa-Whitman National Forests. Tech. Pap. R6-NR-ECOL-TP-22-97. Baker City, OR: U.S. Department of Agriculture, Forest Service, Wallowa-Whitman National Forest. 299 p.

Davidson, R.W.; Hinds T.E.; Hawksworth, F.G. 1959. Decay of aspen in Colorado. Station Paper 45. Fort Collins, CO: U.S. Department of Agriculture, Forest Service, Rocky Mountain Forest and Range Experiment Station. 14 p.

Day, M.W. 1944. The root system of aspen. American Midland Naturalist. 32(2): 502–509.

Day, R.A.; Walter, R.P.; Kozar, J.J.; Bricker, S.J.; Bowers, J.G. 2003. Propagation protocol for bareroot bigtooth and quaking aspen using seeds. Native Plants Journal. 4(2): 125–128.

Debyle, N.V. 1985a. Animal impacts. In: DeByle, N.V.; Winokur, R.P., eds. Aspen: ecology and management in the Western United States. Gen. Tech. Rep. RM-119. Fort Collins, CO: U.S. Department of Agriculture, Forest Service, Rocky Mountain Forest and Range Experiment Station: 115–123.

Debyle, N.V. 1985b. Wildlife. In: DeByle, N.V.; Winokur, R.P., eds. Aspen: ecology and management in the Western United States. Gen. Tech. Rep. RM-119. Fort Collins, CO: U.S. Department of Agriculture, Forest Service, Rocky Mountain Forest and Range Experiment Station: 135–152.

Debyle, N.V. 1985c. Water and watershed. In: DeByle, N.V.; Winokur, R.P., eds. Aspen: ecology and management in the Western United States. Gen. Tech. Rep. RM-119. Fort Collins, CO: U.S. Department of Agriculture, Forest Service, Rocky Mountain Forest and Range Experiment Station: 153–160.

Demmer, R.; Beschta, R.L. 2008. Recent history (1988-2004) of beaver dams along Bridge Creek in central Oregon. Northwest Science. 82(4): 309–318.

DesRochers, A.; Lieffers, V.J. 2001a. The coarse-root system of mature *Populus tremuloides* in declining stands in Alberta, Canada. Journal of Vegetation Science. 12: 355–360.

DesRochers, A.; Lieffers, V.J. 2001b. Root biomass of regenerating aspen (*Populus tremuloides*) stands of different densities in Alberta. Canadian Journal of Forest Research. 31: 1012–1018.

Farmer, R.E. 1963. Effect of light intensity on growth of *Populus tremuloides* cuttings under two temperature regimes. Ecology. 44: 409–411.

Finley, W.L. 1937. The beaver–conserver of soil and water. Transactions North American Wildlife Conference. 2: 295–297.

Forester, J.D.; Anderson, D.P.; Turner, M.G. 2007. Do high-density patches of coarse wood and regenerating saplings create browsing refugia for aspen (*Populus tremuloides* Michx.) in Yellowstone National Park (USA)? Forest Ecology and Management. 253: 211–219.

Fortin, D.; Beyer, H.L.; Boyce, M.S.; Smith, D.W.; Duchesne, T.; Mao, J.S. 2005. Wolves influence elk movements: behavior shapes a trophic cascade in Yellowstone National Park. Ecology. 86(5): 1320–1330.

Frey, B.R.; Lieffers, V.J.; Landhäusser, S.M.; Comeau, P.G.; Greenway, K.J. 2003. An analysis of sucker regeneration of trembling aspen. Canadian Journal of Forest Research. 33: 1169–1179.

Fung, M.Y.P.; Hamel, B.A. 1993. Aspen seed collection and extraction. Tree planters' Notes. 44(3): 98–100.

Galbraith, W.A.; Anderson, E.W. 1971. Grazing history of the Northwest. Journal of Range Management. 24(1): 6–12.

Gary, H.L. 1968. Soil temperatures under forest and grassland cover types in northern New Mexico. Res. Note RM-118. Fort Collins, CO: U.S. Department of Agriculture, Forest Service, Rocky Mountain Forest and Range Experiment Station. 11 p.

Gifford, G.F. 1966. Aspen root studies on three sites in northern Utah. American Midland Naturalist. 75(1): 132–141.

Grant, M.C. 1993. The trembling giant. Discover. 14: 83–89.

Gullion, G.W. 1984. Managing northern forests for wildlife. Coraopolis, PA: Ruffed Grouse Society. 72 p.

Haapala, T.; Pakkanen, A.; Pulkkinen, P. 2004. Variation in survival and growth of cuttings in two clonal propagation methods for hybrid aspen (*Populus tremula* x *P. tremuloides*). Forest Ecology and Management. 193: 345–354.

Halofsky, J.S.; Ripple, W.J. 2008. Fine-scale predation risk on elk after wolf reintroduction in Yellowstone National Park, USA. Oecologia. 155: 869–877.

Halofsky, J.S.; Ripple, W.J.; Beschta R.L. 2008. Recoupling fire and aspen recruitment after wolf reintroduction in Yellowstone National Park, USA. Forest Ecology and Management. 256: 1004–1008.

Hall, F.C. 2001. Ground-based photographic monitoring. Gen. Tech. Rep. PNW-GTR-503. Portland, OR: U.S. Department of Agriculture, Forest Service, Pacific Northwest Research Station. 340 p.

Heyerdahl, E.K.; Brubaker, L.B.; Agee, J.K. 2001. Spatial controls of historical fire regimes: a multiscale example for the interior West, USA. Ecology. 82(3): 660–678.

Hinds, T.E. 1985. Diseases. In: DeByle, N.V.; Winokur, R.P., eds. Aspen: ecology and management in the Western United States. Gen. Tech. Rep. RM-119. Fort Collins, CO: U.S. Department of Agriculture, Forest Service, Rocky Mountain Forest and Range Experiment Station: 87–106.

Hitchcock, C.L.; Cronquist, A.C. 1973. Flora of the Pacific Northwest. Seattle, WA: University of Washington. 730 p.

Holsten, E.; Hennon, P.; Trummer, L.; Schultz, M. 2001. Insects and disease of Alaskan forests. R10-TP-87. Juneau, AK: U.S. Department of Agriculture, Forest Service, Alaska Region. 242 p.

Hungerford, R.D. 1988. Soil temperatures and suckering in burned and unburned aspen stands in Idaho. Res. Note. INT-378. Ogden, UT: U.S. Department of Agriculture, Forest Service, Intermountain Research Station. 6 p.

Irwin, L.L.; Cook, J.G.; Riggs, R.A.; Skovlin, J.M. 1994. Effects of long-term use by big game and livestock in the Blue Mountains forest ecosystems. Gen. Tech. Rep. PNW-GTR-325. Portland, OR: U.S. Department of Agriculture, Forest Service, Pacific Northwest Research Station. 49 p.

Jackson, M.B. 1993. Are plant hormones involved in root shoot communication? In: Callow, J.A., ed. Advances in botanical research. London: Academic Press: 104–187.

Jacoby, P.W., ed. 1989. A glossary of terms used in range management. Denver, CO: Society for Range Management. 20 p.

Johnson, C.G., Jr. 2004. Alpine and subalpine vegetation of the Wallowa, Seven Devils and Blue Mountains. R6-NR-ECOL-TP-03-04. Portland, OR: U.S. Department of Agriculture, Forest Service, Pacific Northwest Region. 611 p. plus appendixes.

Johnson, C.G., Jr.; Clausnitzer, R.R. 1992. Plant associations of the Blue and Ochoco Mountains. R6-ERW-TP-036-92. Portland, OR: U.S. Department of Agriculture, Forest Service, Pacific Northwest Region. 208 p.

Johnson, C.G., Jr.; Simon, S.A. 1987. Plant associations of the Wallowa-Snake Province. R6-ECOL-TP-255A-86. Portland, OR: U.S. Department of Agriculture, Forest Service, Pacific Northwest Region. 400 p. plus appendixes.

Johnson, M.D. 2001. Region 6 inventory and monitoring system: field procedures for the Current Vegetation Survey. Version 2.04. Portland, OR: U.S. Department of Agriculture, Forest Service, Pacific Northwest Region. 151 p. http://www.fs fed.us/r6/survey/document.htm. (7 March 2008).

Jones, B.E.; Rickman, T.H.; Vazquez, A.; Sado, Y.; Tate, K.W. 2005. Removal of encroaching conifers to regenerate degraded aspen stands in the Sierra Nevada. Restoration Ecology. 13(2): 373–379.

Jones, J.R.; Debyle, N.V. 1985a. Climates. In: DeByle, N.V.; Winokur, R.P., eds. Aspen: ecology and management in the Western United States. Gen. Tech. Rep. RM-119. Fort Collins, CO: U.S. Department of Agriculture, Forest Service, Rocky Mountain Forest and Range Experiment Station: 57–64.

Jones, J.R.; Debyle, N.V. 1985b. Fire. In: DeByle, N.V.; Winokur, R.P., eds. Aspen: ecology and management in the Western United States. Gen. Tech. Rep. RM-119. Fort Collins, CO: U.S. Department of Agriculture, Forest Service, Rocky Mountain Forest and Range Experiment Station: 77–81.

Jones, J.R.; Debyle, N.V. 1985c. Soils. In: DeByle, N.V.; Winokur, R.P., eds. Aspen: ecology and management in the Western United States. Gen. Tech. Rep. RM-119. Fort Collins, CO: U.S. Department of Agriculture, Forest Service, Rocky Mountain Forest and Range Experiment Station: 65–70.

Jones, J.R.; Shepperd, W.D. 1985. Intermediate treatments. In: DeByle, N.V.; Winokur, R.P., eds. Aspen: ecology and management in the Western United States. Gen. Tech. Rep. RM-119. Fort Collins, CO: U.S. Department of Agriculture, Forest Service, Rocky Mountain Forest and Range Experiment Station: 209–216.

Kay, C.E. 1994. The impact of native ungulates and beaver on riparian communities in the Intermountain West. Natural Resources and Environmental Issues. 1: 23–24.

Kees, G. 2004. Fencing out wildlife: plastic mesh fences and electric fences monitored by satellite telemetry. Tech. Rep. 0424-2838-MTDC. Missoula, MT: U.S. Department of Agriculture, Forest Service, Missoula Technology and Development Center. 18 p.

Keigley, R.B.; Frisina, M.R. 1998. Browse evaluation by analysis of growth form. Volume I. Methods for evaluating condition and trend. Helena, MT: Montana Fish Wildlife & Parks. 153 p.

Keigley, R.B.; Frisina, M.R.; Fager, C.W. 2002. Assessing browse trend at the landscape level. Part 1: preliminary steps and field survey. Rangelands. 24(3): 28–33.

Kemperman, J.A.; Barnes, B.V. 1976. Clone size in American aspens. Canadian Journal of Botany. 54: 2603–2607.

Keyser, T.L.; Smith, F.W.; Shepperd, W.D. 2005. Trembling aspen response to a mixed-severity wildfire in the Black Hills, South Dakota, USA. Canadian Journal of Forest Research. 35: 2679–2685.

Korstian, C.F. 1921. Effect of late spring frost upon forest vegetation in the Wasatch Mountains of Utah. Ecology. 2(1): 47–52.

Kota, A. 2005. Fences and on-site forest materials as ungulate barriers to promote aspen persistence in the Black Hills. Logan, UT: College of Natural Resources, Utah State University. 74 p. M.S. thesis

Laird, W.E. 1997. Soil survey of Baker Country area, Oregon. U.S. Department of Agriculture, Natural Resources Conservation Service. http://soils.usda.gov/survey/printed_surveys/. (29 Jan 2009).

Lamontagne, M.; Margolis, H.; Bigras, F. 1998. Photosynthesis of black spruce, jack pine, and trembling aspen after artificially induced frost during the growing season. Canadian Journal of Forest Research. 28: 1–12.

Landhäusser, S.M.; Lieffers, V.J. 1998. Growth of *Populus tremuloides* in association with *Calamagrostis canadensis.* Canadian Journal of Forest Research. 28: 396–401.

Larsen, C.M. 1943. Stiklinger af urteagtige skud paa rødder of bævreasp og graapoppil. [Cuttings from herbaceous shoots on the roots of aspen and gray poplar.] Dansk Skovforening Tidsskrift. 28: 96–113.

Lawrence, W.T.; Oechel, W.C. 1983. Effects of soil temperature on the carbon exchange of taiga seedlings. II. Photosynthesis, respiration, and conductance. Canadian Journal of Forest Research. 13: 850–859.

Lieffers, V.J.; Landhäusser, S.M.; Hogg, E.H. 2001. Is the wide distribution of aspen a result of its stress tolerance? In: Shepperd, W.D.; Binkley, D.; Bartos, D.L.; Stohlgren, T.J.; Eskew, L.C., comps. Sustaining aspen in western landscapes. Proceedings RMRS-P-18. Fort Collins, CO: U.S. Department of Agriculture, Forest Service, Rocky Mountain Research Station: 311–323.

Losin, N.; Floyd, C.H.; Schweitzer, T.E.; Keller, S.J. 2006. Relationship between aspen heartwood rot and the location of cavity excavation by a primary cavity-nester, the red-naped sapsucker. The Condor. 108(3): 706–710.

Lu, E.-Y.; Sucoff, E.I. 2003. Responses of quaking aspen seedlings to solution calcium and aluminum. Journal of Plant Nutrition. 26: 97–123.

Maine, J.S.; Horton, K.W. 1966. Vegetative propagation of *Populus* spp. I. Influence of temperature on formation and initial growth of aspen suckers. Canadian Journal of Botany. 44(9): 1183–1189.

Manier, D.J.; Laven, R.D. 2002. Changes in landscape patterns associated with the persistence of aspen (*Populus tremuloides* Michx.) on the western slope of the Rocky Mountains, Colorado. Forest Ecology and Management. 167: 263–284.

McCune, B.; Grace, J.B. 2002. Analysis of ecological communities. Gleneden Beach, OR: MJM Software Design. 300 p.

McDonough, W.T. 1985. Sexual reproduction, seeds, and seedlings. In: DeByle, N.V.; Winokur, R.P., eds. Aspen: ecology and management in the Western United States. Gen. Tech. Rep. RM-119. Fort Collins, CO: U.S. Department of Agriculture, Forest Service, Rocky Mountain Forest and Range Experiment Station: 25–28.

Minore, D. 1979. Comparative autoecological characteristics of northwestern tree species: a literature review. Gen. Tech. Rep. PNW-GTR-87. Portland, OR: U.S. Department of Agriculture, Forest Service, Pacific Northwest Forest and Range Experiment Station. 72 p.

Moench, R.D. 2000. Aspen seed collection. Nursery Information Series. Fort Collins, CO: Colorado State Forest Service. 7 p. http://csfs.colostate.edu/pdfs/aspenseed.pdf. (29 May 2009).

Mueggler, W.F. 1988. Aspen community types of the Intermountain Region. Gen. Tech. Rep. INT-GTR-250. Ogden, UT: U.S. Department of Agriculture, Forest Service, Intermountain Research Station. 135 p.

Mueggler, W.F. 1989. Age distribution and reproduction of intermountain aspen stands. Western Journal of Applied Forestry. 4(2): 41–45.

Mueggler, W.F.; Bartos, D.L. 1977. Grindstone Flat and Big Flat exclosures–a 41-year record of changes in clearcut aspen communities. Res. Pap. INT-195. Ogden, UT: U.S. Department of Agriculture, Forest Service, Intermountain Research Station. 16 p.

Noh, E.-W.; Minocha, S.C. 1986. High efficiency shoot regeneration from callus of quaking aspen (*Populus tremuloides* Michx.). Plant Cell Reports. 5: 464–467.

Ontko, A.G. 1993. Thunder over the Ochoco. Vol I. The gathering storm. Bend, OR: Maverick Publications. 436 p.

Oregon Department of Agriculture. 2008. Oregon state noxious weed list. http://www.oregon.gov/ODA/PLANT/WEEDS/statelist2.shtml. (1 April 2008).

Orr, E.L.; Orr, W.N. 1999. Geology of Oregon. Dubuque, IA: Kendall/Hunt. 254 p.

Osko, T.J.; Hardin, R.T.; Young, B.A. 1993. Research observation: chemical repellants to reduce grazing intensity on reclaimed sites. Journal of Range Management. 46: 383–386.

Ottmar, R.D.; Vihanek, R.E.; Wright, C.S. 2000. Stereo photo series for quantifying natural fuels. Volume III: Lodgepole pine, quaking aspen, and gambel oak types in the Rocky Mountains. PMS 832. Boise, ID: National Wildfire Coordinating Group, National Interagency Fire Center. 85 p.

Parker, J. 1955. Annual trends in cold hardiness of ponderosa pine and grand fir. Ecology. 36(3): 378–380.

Peet, R.K. 2000. Forests and meadows of the Rocky Mountains. In: Barbour, M.G.; Billings, W.D., eds. North American terrestrial vegetation. Cambridge, United Kingdom: Cambridge University: 75–121.

Perala, D.A. 1974. Prescribed burning in an aspen-mixed hardwoods forest. Canadian Journal of Forest Research. 4: 222–228.

Perala, D.A. 1990. Quaking aspen. In: Burns, R.M.; Honkala, B.H., tech. coords. Silvics of North America: 2. Hardwoods. Agric. Handb. 654. Washington, DC: U.S. Department of Agriculture, Forest Service: 555–569.

Powell, D.C. 2008. Early livestock grazing in the Blue Mountains. http://www fs.fed.us/r6/uma/publications/centennial. (26 Feb 2009).

Powell, D.C.; Johnson, C.G., Jr.; Crowe, E.A.; Wells, A.; Swanson, D.K. 2007. Potential vegetation hierarchy for the Blue Mountains Section of northeastern Oregon, southeastern Washington, and west-central Idaho. Gen. Tech. Rep. PNW-GTR-709. Portland, OR: U.S. Department of Agriculture, Forest Service, Pacific Northwest Research Station. 87 p.

Richardson, T.W.; Heath, S.K. 2004. Effects of conifers on aspen-breeding bird communities in the Sierra Nevada. San Luis Obispo, CA: Transactions of the Western Section of the Wildlife Society. 40: 68–81.

Riggs, R.A.; Tiedemann, A.R.; Cook, J.G.; Ballard, T.M.; Edgerton, P.J.; Vavra, M.; Krueger, W.C.; Hall, F.C.; Bryant, L.D.; Irwin, L.L.; DelCurto, T. 2000. Modification of mixed-conifer forests by ruminant herbivores in the Blue Mountains Ecological Province. Res. Pap. PNW-RP-527. Portland, OR: U.S. Department of Agriculture, Forest Service, Pacific Northwest Research Station. 77 p.

Ripple, W.J.; Beschta, R.L. 2007. Restoring Yellowstone's aspen with wolves. Biological Conservation. 138: 514–518.

Ripple, W.J.; Larsen, E.J.; Renkin, R.A.; Smith, D.W. 2001. Trophic cascades among wolves, elk and aspen on Yellowstone National Park's northern range. Biological Conservation. 102(3): 227–234.

Robbins, W.G. 1997. Landscapes of promise: the Oregon story, 1800-1940. Seattle, WA: University of Washington Press. 392 p.

Rolf, J.M. 2001. Aspen fencing in northern Arizona: In: Shepperd, W.D.; Binkley, D.; Bartos, D.L.; Stohlgren, T.J.; Eskew, L.C., comps. Sustaining aspen in western landscapes. Proceedings RMRS-P-18. Fort Collins, CO: U.S. Department of Agriculture, Forest Service, Rocky Mountain Research Station: 193–196.

Ross, W.D. 1976. Fungi associated with root diseases of aspen in Wyoming. Canadian Journal of Botany. 54: 734–744.

Sakai, A.; Weiser, C.J. 1973. Freezing resistance of trees in North America with reference to tree regions. Ecology. 54(1): 118–126.

Sallabanks, R.; Christofferson, N.D.; Weatherford, W.W.; Anderson, R. 2005. Restoring high priority habitats for birds: aspen and pine in the interior West. Gen. Tech. Rep. PSW-GTR-191. Albany, CA: U.S. Department of Agriculture, Forest Service, Pacific Southwest Research Station: 391–403.

Sallabanks, R.; Marcot, B.G.; Riggs, R.A.; Arnett, E.B.; Mehl, C.A. 2001. Wildlife of eastside (interior) forests and woodlands. In: Johnson, D.H.; O'Neil, T.A., eds. Wildlife-habitat relationships in Oregon and Washington. Corvallis, OR: Oregon State University: 213–238.

Sandberg, D.; Schneider, A.E. 1953. The regeneration of aspen by suckering. Minnesota Forestry Notes 24. St. Paul, MN: School of Forestry, University of Minnesota. 2 p.

Schier, G.A. 1973. Origin and development of aspen root suckers. Canadian Journal of Forest Research. 3(1): 45–53.

Schier, G.A. 1975. Deterioration of aspen clones in the middle Rocky Mountains. Res. Pap. INT-170. Ogden, UT: U.S. Department of Agriculture, Forest Service, Intermountain Forest and Range Experiment Station. 14 p.

Schier, G.A. 1976. Physiological and environmental factors controlling vegetative regeneration of aspen. Gen. Tech. Rep. RM-29. Fort Collins, CO: U.S. Department of Agriculture, Forest Service, Rocky Mountain Forest and Range Experiment Station: 20–23.

Schier, G.A. 1978. Vegetative propagation of Rocky Mountain aspen. Gen. Tech. Rep. INT-44. Ogden, UT: U.S. Department of Agriculture, Forest Service, Intermountain Forest and Range Experiment Station. 13 p.

Schier, G.A.; Campbell, R.B. 1978. Aspen sucker regeneration following burning and clearcutting on two sites in the Rocky Mountains. Forest Science. 24(3): 303–308.

Schier, G.A.; Jones, J.R.; Winokur, R.P. 1985a. Vegetative regeneration. In: DeByle, N.V.; Winokur, R.P., eds. Aspen: ecology and management in the Western United States. Gen. Tech. Rep. RM-119. Fort Collins, CO: U.S. Department of Agriculture, Forest Service, Rocky Mountain Forest and Range Experiment Station: 29–33.

Schier, G.A.; Shepperd, W.D.; Jones, J.R. 1985b. Regeneration. In: DeByle, N.V.; Winokur, R.P., eds. Aspen: ecology and management in the Western United States. Gen. Tech. Rep. RM-119. Fort Collins, CO: U.S. Department of Agriculture, Forest Service, Rocky Mountain Forest and Range Experiment Station: 197–208.

Schier, G.A.; Smith, A.D. 1979. Sucker regeneration in a Utah aspen clone after clearcutting, partial cutting, scarification, and girdling. Res. Note INT-253. Ogden, UT: U.S. Department of Agriculture, Forest Service, Intermountain Forest and Range Experiment Station. 6 p.

Schier, G.A.; Zasada, J.C. 1973. Role of carbohydrate reserves in the development of root suckers in *Populus tremuloides*. Canadian Journal of Forest Research. 3: 243–250.

Shaw, C.G., III; Kile, G.A. 1991. Armillaria root disease. Agric. Handb. 691. Washington, DC: U.S. Department of Agriculture, Forest Service. 233 p.

Shepperd, W.D. 1993. Initial growth, development, and clonal dynamics of regenerated aspen in the Rocky Mountains. Res. Pap. RM-312. Fort Collins, CO: U.S. Department of Agriculture, Forest Service, Rocky Mountain Forest and Range Experiment Station. 8 p.

Shepperd, W.D. 2001. Manipulations to regenerate aspen ecosystems. In: Shepperd, W.D.; Binkley, D.; Bartos, D.L.; Stohlgren, T.J.; Eskew, L.C., comps. Sustaining aspen in western landscapes. Proceedings RMRS-P-18. Fort Collins, CO: U.S. Department of Agriculture, Forest Service, Rocky Mountain Research Station: 355–365.

Shepperd, W.D.; Bartos, D.L.; Mata, S.A. 2001. Above- and below-ground effects of aspen clonal regeneration and succession to conifers. Canadian Journal of Forest Research. 31(5): 739–745.

Shepperd, W.D.; Rogers, P.C.; Burton, D.; Bartos, D.L. 2006. Ecology, biodiversity, management, and restoration of aspen in the Sierra Nevada. Res. Pap. RMRS-178. Fort Collins, CO: U.S. Department of Agriculture, Forest Service, Rocky Mountain Forest and Range Experiment Station. 122 p.

Shirley, D.M.; Erickson, V. 2001. Aspen restoration in the Blue Mountains of northeast Oregon. In: Shepperd, W.D.; Binkley, D.; Bartos, D.L.; Stohlgren, T.J.; Eskew, L.C., comps. Sustaining aspen in western landscapes. Proceedings RMRS-P-18. Fort Collins, CO: U.S. Department of Agriculture, Forest Service, Rocky Mountain Research Station: 101–115.

Skovlin, J.M.; Thomas J.W. 1992. Interpreting long-term trends in Blue Mountain ecosystems from repeat photography. Gen. Tech. Rep. PNW-GTR-315. Portland, OR: U.S. Department of Agriculture, Forest Service, Pacific Northwest Research Station. 102 p.

Soil Survey Division Staff. 1993. Soil survey manual. Agric. Handb. 18. Washington, DC: U.S. Department of Agriculture, Natural Resources Conservation Service.

Soil Survey Staff. 1999. Soil taxonomy: a basic system of soil classification for making and interpreting soil surveys. 2nd ed. Agric. Handb. 436. Washington, DC: U.S. Department of Agriculture, Natural Resources Conservation Service.

Stevens, M.T.; Turner, M.G.; Tuskan, G.A.; Romme, W.H.; Gunter, L.E.; Waller, D.M. 1999. Genetic variation in postfire aspen seedlings in Yellowstone National Park. Molecular Ecology. 8: 1769–1780.

Strain, R.R. 1966. The effect of a late spring frost on the raidal growth of variant quaking aspen biotypes. Forest Science. 12(3): 334–337.

Strothmann, R.O.; Heinselman, M.L. 1957. Five-year results in an aspen sucker density study. Res. Pap. LS-49. St. Paul, MN: U.S. Department of Agriculture, Forest Service, Lake States Forest Experiment Station. 2 p.

Tew, R.K. 1970. Root carbohydrate reserves in vegetative reproduction of aspen. Forest Science. 16(3): 318–320.

Tuskan, G.A.; Francis, K.E.; Russ, S.L.; Romme, W.H.; Turner, M.G. 1996. RAPD markers reveal diversity within and among clonal and seedling stands of aspen in Yellowstone National Park, U.S.A. Canadian Journal of Forest Research. 26: 2088–2098.

U.S. Department of Agriculture, Forest Service [USDA FS]. 2005. Forest inventory and analysis national core field guide. Volume I: field data collection procedures for phase 2 plots, Version 3.0. http://fia fs fed.us/library/field-guides-methods-proc/. (30 July 2008).

U.S. Department of Agriculture, Forest Service [USDA FS]. 2008. Common stand exam users guide, March 2008. http://www fs.fed.us/emc/nris/products/fsveg/index.shtml. (10 Dec 2008).

U.S. Department of Agriculture, Natural Resources Conservation Service [USDA NRCS]. 2007. Monthly precipitation averages—30-Year period. National Water and Climate Center. http://www.wcc.nrcs.usda.gov/snow/30yrprec html. (6 Nov 2007).

U.S. Department of Agriculture, Natural Resources Conservation Service [USDA NRCS]. 2008. The PLANTS Database [Database]. Baton Rouge, LA: National Plant Data Center, 70874-4490 USA. http://plants.usda.gov. (16 April 2008).

U.S. Environmental Protection Agency [USEPA]. 2007. Level III ecoregions of the conterminous United States. Western Ecology Division. http://www.epa.gov/wed/pages/ecoregions/level_iii htm. (29 Jan 2009).

Walker, G.W.; MacLeod, N.S. 1991. Geologic map of Oregon. [1:500,000]. Reston, VA: U.S. Geological Survey.

Wall, T.G.; Miller, R.F.; Svejcar, T.J. 2001. Juniper encroachment into aspen in the northwest Great Basin. Journal of Range Management. 54: 691–698.

Walters, J.W. 1984. An aid to identifying aspen diseases frequently encountered in the Rocky Mountains. Albuquerque, NM: U.S. Department of Agriculture, Forest Service, Southwestern Region, State and Private Forestry, Forest Pest Management. 20 p.

Walters, J.W.; Hinds, T.E.; Johnson, D.W.; Beatty, J. 1982. Effects of partial cutting on diseases, mortality, and regeneration of Rocky Mountain aspen stands. Res. Pap. RM-240. Fort Collins, CO: U.S. Department of Agriculture, Forest Service, Rocky Mountain Forest and Range Experiment Station. 12 p.

Webber, M.G. 1990. Response of immature aspen ecosystems to cutting and burning in relation to vernal leaf-flush. Forest Ecology and Management. 31: 15–33.

Western Regional Climate Center. 2007. Western U.S. Climate Historical Summaries. http://www.wrcc.dri.edu/Climsum.html. (5 Nov 2007).

Williams, K.R. 1972. The relationship of soil temperature and cytokinen production in aspen invasion. Albuquerque, NM: University of New Mexico. 39 p. M.S. Thesis.

Winthers, E.; Fallon, D.; Haglund, J.; DeMeo, T.; Nowacki, G.; Tart, D.; Ferwerda, M.; Robertson, G.; Gallegos, A.; Rorick, A.; Cleland, D.T.; Robbie, W. 2005. Terrestrial ecological unit inventory technical guide: landscape and land unit scales. Gen. Tech. Rep. WO-68. Washington, DC: U.S. Department of Agriculture, Forest Service, Ecosystem Management Coordination Staff. 245 p.

Zasada, J.C.; Schier, G.A. 1973. Aspen root suckering in Alaska: effect of clone, collection date and temperature. Northwest Science. 47: 100–104.

Appendix A: Aspen Stands Sampled as Part of the Blue Mountains Genetics Study

Region[a]	Land status[b]	Drainage	Stand code	Stand number	Number of plants sampled	Number of clones	Area (Hectares)	Latitude (north) (Decimal degrees)	Longitude (east) (Decimal degrees)
BAK	WAW	Dooley Mountain	DO	1	5	4	0.004	44.5924	-118.3520
BAK	WAW	Mason Dam	MD	1	3	2	<0.001	44.6724	-117.9910
BAK	WAW	Stage Gulch	SG1	1	7	2	0.004	44.7338	-118.2323
BAK	WAW	Stage Gulch	SG2	2	4	2	0.004	44.7322	-118.2250
CTUIR	CTUIR	Cabbage Hill	CH	1	3	1	0.025	45.6019	-118.6209
CTUIR	CTUIR	Coyote Flat	CF	1	2	1	0.202	45.6584	-118.4888
CTUIR	CTUIR	Halfmoon Allotment	HA	1	2	1	0.121	45.6081	-118.5551
CTUIR	CTUIR	Kinine Ridge	KR	1	5	2	0.232	45.6284	-118.5025
CTUIR	CTUIR	Minthorn Springs	MS	1	4	1	1.214	45.6742	-118.6067
CTUIR	CTUIR	Pipeline POTR	PP	1	5	3	1.500	45.6164	-118.5195
CTUIR	CTUIR	Sixth Spring	SS	1	7	2	0.081	45.6469	-118.4645
CTUIR	CTUIR	Telephone Ridge	TELR1	1	5	1	0.167	45.6424	-118.4514
CTUIR	CTUIR	Telephone Ridge	TELR2	2	3	1	0.641	45.6321	-118.4462
HP	UMA	Long Prairie	383-50	1	5	1	0.534	44.9859	-119.8154
HP	UMA	Long Prairie	382-49	2	5	3	4.532	44.9861	-119.8224
HP	UMA	Long Prairie	385-46	3	4	2	0.475	44.9829	-119.8199
HP	UMA	Long Prairie	384-48	4	6	2	0.102	44.9840	-119.8212
HP	UMA	Wheeler Point	411-34	1	3	1	0.051	44.9370	-119.8716
HP	UMA	Wheeler Point	409-35	2	6	1	0.128	44.9375	-119.8718
HP	UMA	Wheeler Point	399-39	3	6	2	0.572	44.9545	-119.8499
NFJD East	UMA	Blarney Creek	BLASP1	1	8	1	0.426	45.1566	-118.5977
NFJD East	UMA	Bone Canyon	BCASP1	1	6	2	0.178	44.9830	-119.0125
NFJD East	UMA	Bridge Creek	BRASP1	1	10	1	0.420	45.0630	-118.8549
NFJD East	UMA	Bull Prairie	BPASP1	1	6	1	0.790	44.8666	-118.6918
NFJD East	UMA	Bull Prairie	BPASP2	2	3	1	0.169	44.8657	-118.6879
NFJD East	UMA	Bull Prairie	BPASP3	3	3	1	0.064	44.8649	-118.6868
NFJD East	UMA	Bull Prairie	BPASP4	4	3	1	0.081	44.8640	-118.6864
NFJD East	UMA	Camas Wallow	CAASP1	1	10	2	0.043	45.1713	-118.7121
NFJD East	UMA	Desolation Creek	DEASP1	1	5	1	0.126	44.8302	-118.7059
NFJD East	UMA	Desolation Creek	DEASP2	2	9	2	0.898	44.8144	-118.6660
NFJD East	UMA	Granite Meadow	GRASP1	1	4	1	0.010	44.8323	-118.4145
NFJD East	UMA	Howard Creek	HOASP1	1	18	2	0.544	44.8390	-118.7192
NFJD East	UMA	Lane Creek	LCASP1	1	5	1	0.096	45.2715	-118.8118
NFJD East	UMA	Oriental Springs	OSASP1	1	2	2	<0.001	unknown	unknown
NFJD East	UMA	Park Creek	PKASP1	1	11	1	0.999	44.9134	-118.7815

Appendix A: Aspen Stands Sampled as Part of the Blue Mountains Genetics Study *(continued)*

Region[a]	Land status[b]	Drainage	Stand number	Stand code	Number of plants sampled	Number of clones	Area	Latitude (north)	Longitude (east)
							Hectares	*- - - Decimal degrees - - - -*	
NFJD East	UMA	Trough Creek	1	TCASP1	3	1	0.030	44.8540	-118.4540
NFJD West	UMA	Turpentine Creek	1	WRASEC05	5	1	0.131	45.1600	-119.1647
NFJD West	UMA	Deerlick Creek	1	DCASP1	8	1	0.077	45.1562	-119.0696
NFJD West	UMA	Johnson Creek	1	WRASP40	7	1	0.452	45.2018	-119.1944
NFJD West	UMA	Matlock Creek	1	WRASP135	4	1	0.149	45.1345	-119.1824
NFJD West	UMA	Matlock Creek	2	WRASP129	8	2	0.251	45.1196	-119.1831
NFJD West	UMA	Matlock Creek	3	WRASP124	7	2	0.251	45.1129	-119.1847
NFJD West	UMA	Matlock Creek	4	WRASP121	11	6	0.017	45.1082	-119.1844
NFJD West	UMA	Matlock Creek	5	WRASP78	9	2	0.369	45.0875	-119.1835
NFJD West	UMA	Morsay Creek	1	WRASP185	20	1	0.646	45.1748	-119.1079
NFJD West	UMA	Morsay Creek	2	WRASP44	14	1	0.756	45.1716	-119.1180
NFJD West	UMA	Morsay Creek	3	WRASP24	20	3	0.907	45.1843	-119.1178
NFJD West	UMA	Morsay Creek	4	WRASEC01	7	1	1.376	45.1996	-119.1415
NFJD West	UMA	Morsay Creek	5	WRASP178	6	1	0.170	45.1771	-119.1138
NFJD West	UMA	Rush Creek	1	WRASP66	23	3	0.503	45.0910	-119.1310
NFJD West	UMA	Rush Creek	2	WRASP71	17	8	0.317	45.0770	-119.1351
NFJD West	UMA	Rush Creek	3	WRASP67	6	1	0.195	45.0941	-119.1215
NFJD West	UMA	Silver Creek	5212	WRASP53	9	2	0.196	45.1196	-119.1286
NFJD West	UMA	Silver Creek	5252B	WRASP52	5	1	0.238	45.1219	-119.1313
NFJD West	UMA	Sugar Bowl	1	WRASP26A	18	4	0.860	45.1978	-119.1043
NFJD West	UMA	Sugar Bowl	2	WRASP34	23	6	0.732	45.1933	-119.0880
NFJD West	UMA	Sugar Bowl	3	WRASP37	12	6	0.413	45.1884	-119.0921
NFJD West	UMA	Sugar Bowl	4	WRASEC02	18	7	6.954	45.1814	-119.0913
NFJD West	UMA	Sugar Bowl	5	WRASP47	17	7	2.012	45.1693	-119.0929
NFJD West	UMA	Sugar Bowl	6	WRASEC03	6	1	0.382	45.1671	-119.0952
NFJD West	UMA	Sugar Bowl	7	WRASEC04	21	14	2.648	45.1665	-119.0996
NFJD West	UMA	Sugar Bowl	3A	WRASP35	18	6	2.779	45.1846	-119.0998
NFJD West	UMA	Taylor Creek	1	WRASP143	7	2	0.261	45.1580	-119.2096
NFJD West	UMA	Taylor Creek	2	WRASP137	27	5	1.260	45.1394	-119.1837
NFJD West	UMA	Taylor Creek	3	WRASP150	3	2	0.027	45.1426	-119.1623
NFJD West	UMA	Taylor Creek	4	WRASEC06	8	1	0.836	45.1389	-119.1551
NFJD West	UMA	Taylor Creek	5	WRASP146	24	4	0.068	45.1392	-119.1521
NFJD West	UMA	Taylor Creek	5212C	WRASP49	12	1	0.971	45.1299	-119.1344

Appendix A: Aspen Stands Sampled as Part of the Blue Mountains Genetics Study (continued)

Region[a]	Land status[b]	Drainage	Stand number	Stand code	Number of plants sampled	Number of clones	Area (Hectares)	Latitude (north)	Longitude (east)
								- - - Decimal degrees -----	
NFJD West	UMA	Thompson Creek	1	WRASP83	8	3	0.514	45.0552	-119.1928
NFJD West	UMA	Thompson Creek	2	WRASEC07	12	2	0.538	45.0513	-119.1914
NFJD West	UMA	Thompson Creek	3	WRASP87	43	10	0.104	45.0397	-119.1916
NFJD West	UMA	Thompson Creek	4	WRASP88A	2	1	0.194	45.0343	-119.1937
WW	UMA	Elk Flat	1	POTR0001	19	4	0.113	45.9064	-117.7605
WW	UMA	Jarboe Meadow	1	POTR0053	5	2	0.029	45.8066	-117.8536
WW	UMA	Jarboe Meadow	2	POTR0054	3	1	0.030	45.8099	-117.8559
WW	UMA	Jarboe Meadow	3	POTR0003	6	1	0.167	45.8016	-117.8561
WW	UMA	Lower Brock Meadow	1	061/63	6	2	0.056	45.8110	-117.8690
WW	UMA	Upper Brock Meadow	1	POTR0023	8	1	0.541	45.8163	-117.8626
WW	UMA	Upper Brock Meadow	2	POTR0048	4	2	0.298	45.8143	-117.8617
WW	UMA	Walla Walla RD	1	POTR0016	8	4	1.425	45.7979	-117.8635
WW	UMA	Walla Walla RD	2	POTR0017	7	3	0.410	45.7956	-117.8625
WW	UMA	Walla Walla RD	3	POTR0064	3	1	0.336	45.8052	-117.8699
WW	UMA	Walla Walla RD	4	POTR0073	3	2	0.240	45.8068	-117.8710
WAV	BC	Boise Cascade	1	BC	9	1	1.214	45.5179	-117.2750
WAV	WAW	Cow Camp	1	2J109N99AR03	10	3	1.778	45.3246	-116.8921
WAV	WAW	Harl Butte Lookout	1	2J109N99AR06	5	1	1.027	45.3324	-116.8782
WAV	WAW	Road Canyon Meadow	1	2J109S99ASP4	2	1	0.936	45.3013	-116.9199
WAV	WAW	Road Canyon Meadow	2	2J109S99ASP2	2	2	0.644	45.2997	-116.9192
WAV	WAW	Road Canyon Meadow	3	2J109S99A044	5	3	0.427	45.2969	-116.9210
WAV	WAW	Road Canyon Meadow	4	2J109S99A042	5	3	1.531	45.2986	-116.9255
WAV	WAW	Road Canyon Meadow	5	2J109S99A043	6	4	0.627	45.2992	-116.9269
WAV	WAW	Target Springs	1	2J109S99A055	14	14	2.405	45.2809	-116.9459

[a] Region: BAK = Baker Ranger District, CTUIR = Confederated Tribes of the Umatilla Indian Reservation, HP = Heppner Ranger District, NFJD = North Fork John Day Ranger District (east or west side), WW = Walla Walla Ranger District, WAV = Wallowa Valley Ranger District.

[b] Landstatus: BC = Boise Cascade Corporation, CTUIR = Confederated Tribes of the Umatilla Indian Reservation, UMA = Umatilla National Forest; WAW = Wallowa-Whitman National Forest.

Appendix B: Plant Names Used in This Report

Common name	Code[a]	Latin name and author[b]
Trees:		
Black cottonwood	POTR15	*Populus trichocarpa* Torr. & A. Gray ex Hook.
Douglas-fir	PSME	*Pseudotsuga menziesii* (Mirb.) Franco
Engelmann spruce	PIEN	*Picea engelmannii* Parry ex Engelm.
Grand fir	ABGR	*Abies grandis* (Douglas ex D. Don) Lindl.
Lodgepole pine	PICO	*Pinus contorta* Douglas ex Louden
Mountain hemlock	TSME	*Tsuga mertensiana* (Bong.) Carrière
Ponderosa pine	PIPO	*Pinus ponderosa* C. Lawson
Quaking aspen	POTR5	*Populus tremuloides* Michx.
Subalpine fir	ABLA	*Abies lasiocarpa* (Hook.) Nutt.
Western juniper	JUOC	*Juniperus occidentalis* Hook.
Western larch	LAOC	*Larix occidentalis* Nutt.
Western white pine	PIMO3	*Pinus monticola* Douglas ex D. Don
Yew	TABR2	*Taxus brevifolia* Nutt.
Shrubs:		
Baldhip rose	ROGY	*Rosa gymnocarpa* Nutt.
Big huckleberry	VAME	*Vaccinium membranaceum* Douglas ex Torr.
Big sagebrush	ARTR2	*Artemisia tridentata* Nutt.
Birchleaf spiraea	SPBE2	*Spiraea betulifolia* Pall.
Bitter cherry	PREM	*Prunus emarginata* (Douglas ex Hook.) D. Dietr.
Bitterbrush	PUTR2	*Purshia tridentata* (Pursh) DC.
Black hawthorn	CRDO2	*Crataegus douglasii* Lindl.
Blue elderberry	SACE3	*Sambucus cerulea* Raf.
Cascade mountain ash	SOSC2	*Sorbus scopulina* Greene
Common chokecherry	PRVI	*Prunus virginiana* L.
Common snowberry	SYAL	*Symphoricarpos albus* (L.) S.F. Blake
Creeping Oregon grape	BERE	*Berberis repens* Lindl.
Curl-leaf mountain mahogany	CELE3	*Cercocarpus ledifolius* Nutt.
Elderberry	SAMBU	*Sambucus* L.
Golden currant	RIAU	*Ribes aureum* Pursh
Green rabbitbush	CHVI8	*Chrysothamnus viscidiflorus* (Hook.) Nutt.
Grouse huckleberry	VASC	*Vaccinium scoparium* Leiberg ex Coville
Kinnikinnick	ARUV	*Arctostaphylos uva-ursi* (L.) Spreng.
Lewis' mock-orange	PHLE4	*Philadelphus lewisii* Pursh
Mallow ninebark	PHMA5	*Physocarpus malvaceus* (Greene) Kuntze
Mountain alder	ALIN2	*Alnus incana* (L.) Moench
Mountain snowberry	SYOR2	*Symphoricarpos oreophilus* A. Gray
Nootka rose	RONU	*Rosa nutkana* C. Presl
Oceanspray	HODI	*Holodiscus discolor* (Pursh) Maxim.
Oregon boxwood	PAMY	*Pachistima myrsinites* (Pursh) Raf.
Prickly currant	RILA	*Ribes lacustre* (Pers.) Poir.
Prince's pine	CHUM	*Chimaphila umbellata* (L.) W. Bartram
Red elderberry	SARA2	*Sambucus racemosa* L.
Red-osier dogwood	COST4	*Cornus stolonifera* Michx.
Rocky Mountain maple	ACGL	*Acer glabrum* Torr.
Rose	ROSA5	*Rosa* L.
Scouler's willow	SASC	*Salix scouleriana* Barratt ex Hook.
Shrubby cinquefoil	POFR4	*Potentilla fruticosa* auct. non L.
Snowberry	SYMPH	*Symphoricarpos* Duham.
Snowbrush ceanothus	CEVE	*Ceanothus velutinus* Douglas ex Hook.
Thimbleberry	RUPA	*Rubus parviflorus* Nutt.

Appendix B: Plant Names Used in This Report *(continued)*

Common name	Code[a]	Latin name and author[b]
Twinflower	LIBO3	*Linnaea borealis* L.
Utah honeysuckle	LOUT2	*Lonicera utahensis* S. Watson
Water birch	BEOC2	*Betula occidentalis* Hook.
Wax currant	RICE	*Ribes cereum* Douglas
Western serviceberry	AMAL2	*Amelanchier alnifolia* (Nutt.) Nutt. ex M. Roem.
Western trumpet honeysuckle	LOCI3	*Lonicera ciliosa* (Pursh) Poir. ex DC.
Willow	SALIX	*Salix* L.
Woods' rose	ROWO	*Rosa woodsii* Lindl.
Grasslike plants:		
Baltic rush	JUBA	*Juncus balticus* Willd.
Dewey sedge	CADE9	*Carex deweyana* Schwein.
Elk sedge	CAGE2	*Carex geyeri* Boott
Hood's sedge	CAHO5	*Carex hoodii* Boott
Nebraska sedge	CANE2	*Carex nebrascensis* Dewey
Needle spikerush	ELAC	*Eleocharis acicularis* (L.) Roem. & Schult.
Northwestern sedge	CACO11	*Carex concinnoides* Mack.
Ross' sedge	CARO5	*Carex rossii* Boott
Sedge	CAREX	*Carex* L.
Sierra rush	JUNE	*Juncus nevadensis* S. Watson
Slenderbeak sedge	CAAT3	*Carex athrostachya* Olney
Smallwinged sedge	CAMI7	*Carex microptera* Mack.
Water sedge	CAAQ	*Carex aquatilis* Wahlenb.
Woolly sedge	CALA30	*Carex lanuginosa* auct. non Michx.
Yellow sedge	CAFL4	*Carex flava* L.
Grasses:		
Alaska oniongrass	MESU	*Melica subulata* (Griseb.) Scribn.
Alkali bluegrass	POJU	*Poa juncifolia* Scribn.
Bentgrass	AGROS2	*Agrostis* L.
Blue wildrye	ELGL	*Elymus glaucus* Buckley
Bluebunch wheatgrass	AGSP	*Agropyron spicatum* Pursh
Bluejoint reedgrass	CACA4	*Calamagrostis canadensis* (Michx.) P. Beauv.
Bottlebrush squirreltail	SIHY	*Sitanion hystrix* (Nutt.) J.G. Sm.
Cheatgrass	BRTE	*Bromus tectorum* L.
Columbia brome	BRVU	*Bromus vulgaris* (Hook.) Shear
Common timothy	PHPR3	*Phleum pratense* L.
Creeping bentgrass	AGST2	*Agrostis stolonifera* L.
Fowl mannagrass	GLST	*Glyceria striata* (Lam.) Hitchc.
Idaho fescue	FEID	*Festuca idahoensis* Elmer
Intermediate wheatgrass	AGIN2	*Agropyron intermedium* (Host) P. Beauv.
Kentucky bluegrass	POPR	*Poa pratensis* L.
Meadow foxtail	ALPR3	*Alopecurus pratensis* L.
Mountain brome	BRCA5	*Bromus carinatus* Hook. & Arn.
Orchardgrass	DAGL	*Dactylis glomerata* L.
Pinegrass	CARU	*Calamagrostis rubescens* Buckley
Prairie junegrass	KOCR	*Koeleria cristata* auct. non Pers. p.p.
Quackgrass	AGRE2	*Agropyron repens* (L.) P. Beauv.
Red fescue	FERU2	*Festuca rubra* L.
Rough bentgrass	AGSC5	*Agrostis scabra* Willd.
Spike trisetum	TRSP2	*Trisetum spicatum* (L.) K. Richt.
Tall mannagrass	GLEL	*Glyceria elata* (Nash ex Rydb.) M.E. Jones
Tall trisetum	TRCA21	*Trisetum canescens* Buckley
Tufted hairgrass	DECE	*Deschampsia cespitosa* (L.) P. Beauv.
Western fescue	FEOC	*Festuca occidentalis* Hook.

Appendix B: Plant Names Used in This Report *(continued)*

Common name	Code[a]	Latin name and author[b]
Western needlegrass	STOC2	*Stipa occidentalis* Thurb.
Wheeler's bluegrass	PONE2	*Poa nervosa* (Hook.) Vasey
Forbs:		
American vetch	VIAM	*Vicia americana* Muhl. ex Willd.
Aster	ASTER	*Aster* L.
Bigleaf sandwort	ARMA18	*Arenaria macrophylla* Hook.
Black medick	MELU	*Medicago lupulina* L.
Blue stickseed	HAMI	*Hackelia micrantha* (Eastw.) J.L. Gentry
Brakenfern	PTAQ	*Pteridium aquilinum* (L.) Kuhn
Brown's peony	PABR	*Paeonia brownie* Douglas ex Hook.
Bull thistle	CIVU	*Cirsium vulgare* (Savi) Ten.
California false hellebore	VECA2	*Veratrum californicum* Durand
Canada thistle	CIAR4	*Cirsium arvense* (L.) Scop.
Chamisso arnica	ARCH3	*Arnica chamissonis* Less.
Ciliate bluebells	MECI3	*Mertensia ciliata* (James ex Torr.) G. Don
Cleavers	GAAP2	*Galium aparine* L.
Cluster tarweed	MAGL2	*Madia glomerata* Hook.
Columbian monkshood	ACCO4	*Aconitum columbianum* Nutt.
Common camas	CAQU2	*Camassia quamash* (Pursh) Greene
Common clarkia	CLRH	*Clarkia rhomboidea* Douglas ex Hook.
Common dandelion	TAOF	*Taraxacum officinale* F.H. Wigg.
Common houndstongue	CYOF	*Cynoglossum officinale* L.
Common mullein	VETH	*Verbascum thapsus* L.
Common pearly-everlasting	ANMA	*Anaphalis margaritacea* (L.) Benth.
Common yarrow	ACMI2	*Achillea millefolium* L.
Cowparsnip	HELA4	*Heracleum lanatum* Michx.
Deceptive groundsmoke	GADE2	*Gayophytum decipiens* F.H. Lewis & Szweykowski
Early blue violet	VIAD	*Viola adunca* Sm.
False hellebore	VERAT	*Veratrum* L.
Fendler's waterleaf	HYFE	*Hydrophyllum fendleri* (A. Gray) A. Heller
Few-flowered aster	ASMO3	*Aster modestus* Lindl.
Field mint	MEAR4	*Mentha arvensis* L.
Fireweed	EPAN2	*Epilobium angustifolium* L.
Fragrant bedstraw	GATR3	*Galium triflorum* Michx.
Gairdner's yampah	PEGA3	*Perideridia gairdneri* (Hook. & Arn.) Mathias
Geyer's onion	ALGE	*Allium geyeri* S. Watson
Giant frasera	FRSP	*Frasera speciosa* Douglas ex Griseb.
Globe penstemon	PEGL5	*Penstemon globosus* (Piper) Pennell & D.D. Keck
Golden-pea	THMO6	*Thermopsis montana* Nutt.
Gooseberryleaf alumroot	HEGR8	*Heuchera grossulariifolia* Rydb.
Greater creeping spearwort	RAFL2	*Ranunculus flammula* L.
Green false hellebore	VEVI	*Veratrum viride* Aiton
Heartleaf arnica	ARCO9	*Arnica cordifolia* Hook.
Hotrock penstemon	PEDE4	*Penstemon deustus* Douglas ex Lindl.
Largeleaf avens	GEMA4	*Geum macrophyllum* Willd.
Leafy aster	ASFO	*Aster foliaceus* Lindl. ex DC.
Little buttercup	RAUN	*Ranunculus uncinatus* D. Don ex G. Don
Little sunflower	HEUN	*Helianthella uniflora* (Nutt.) Torr. & A. Gray
Longstalk clover	TRLO	*Trifolium longipes* Nutt.
Lupine	LUPIN	*Lupinus* L.
Missouri goldenrod	SOMI2	*Solidago missouriensis* Nutt.
Mountain phlox	PHAU3	*Phlox austromontana* Coville
Mountain sweet-cicely	OSCH	*Osmorhiza chilensis* Hook. & Arn.

Appendix B: Plant Names Used in This Report *(continued)*

Common name	Code[a]	Latin name and author[b]
Mountain tansymustard	DERI2	*Descurainia richardsonii* O.E. Schulz
Narrowleaf collomia	COLI2	*Collomia linearis* Nutt.
Nettleleaf horsemint	AGUR	*Agastache urticifolia* (Benth.) Kuntze
Nodding chickweed	CENU2	*Cerastium nutans* Raf.
Northern bedstraw	GABO2	*Galium boreale* L.
Nuttall's violet	VINU2	*Viola nuttallii* Pursh
Oregon checker-mallow	SIOR	*Sidalcea oregana* (Nutt. ex Torr. & A. Gray) A. Gray
Phacelia	PHACE	*Phacelia* Juss.
Red baneberry	ACRU2	*Actaea rubra* (Aiton) Willd.
Red columbine	AQFO	*Aquilegia formosa* Fisch. ex DC.
Rocky Mountain iris	IRMI	*Iris missouriensis* Nutt.
Rosy pussytoes	ANMI3	*Antennaria microphylla* Rydb.
Roundleaf alumroot	HECY2	*Heuchera cylindrical* Douglas ex Hook.
Self-heal	PRVU	*Prunella vulgaris* L.
Showy aster	ASCO3	*Aster conspicuus* Lindl.
Shrubby penstemon	PEFR3	*Penstemon fruticosus* (Pursh) Greene
Sierra larkspur	DEGL3	*Delphinium glaucum* S. Watson
Sierran peavine	LANE3	*Lathyrus nevadensis* S. Watson
Silky lupine	LUSE4	*Lupinus sericeus* Pursh
Silverleaf phacelia	PHHA	*Phacelia hastata* Douglas ex Lehm.
Sitka valerian	VASI	*Valeriana sitchensis* Bong.
Skunk-leaved polemonium	POPU3	*Polemonium pulcherrimum* Hook.
Slender cinquefoil	POGR9	*Potentilla gracilis* Douglas ex Hook.
Slim larkspur	DEDE2	*Delphinium depauperatum* Nutt.
Small flowered blue-eyed Mary	COPA3	*Collinsia parviflora* Lindl.
Small flowered penstemon	PEPR2	*Penstemon procerus* Douglas ex Graham
Smallflower nemophila	NEPA	*Nemophila parviflora* Douglas ex Benth.
Spreading dogbane	APAN2	*Apocynum androsaemifolium* L.
St. Johnswort	HYPE	*Hypericum perforatum* L.
Starry false Solomon's seal	SMST	*Smilacina stellata* (L.) Desf.
Sticky geranium	GEVI2	*Geranium viscosissimum* Fisch. & C.A. Mey. ex C.A. Mey.
Stinging nettle	URDI	*Urtica dioica* L.
Straightbeak buttercup	RAOR3	*Ranunculus orthorhynchus* Hook.
Strawberry	FRAGA	*Fragaria* L.
Sulfur penstemon	PEAT3	*Penstemon attenuatus* Douglas ex Lindl.
Sulphur lupine	LUSUS3	*Lupinus sulphureus* Douglas ex Hook. ssp. *subsaccatus* (Suksd.) L. Phillips
Tailcup lupine	LUCA	*Lupinus caudatus* Kellogg
Tall butterweed	SESE2	*Senecio serra* Hook.
Tall cinquefoil	POARC	*Potentilla arguta* Pursh ssp. *convallaria* (Rydb.) D.D. Keck
Tall groundsel	SEFO	*Senecio foetidus* J.T. Howell
Thickleaf groundsel	SECR	*Senecio crassulus* A. Gray
Thinleaf bedstraw	GABI	*Galium bifolium* S. Watson
Thistle	CIRSI	*Cirsium* Mill.
Throughwort	EUOC5	*Eupatorium occidentale* Hook.
Trailplant	ADBI	*Adenocaulon bicolor* Hook.
Trumpet	COLLO	*Collomia* Nutt.
Turpentine cymopterus	CYTEF	*Cymopterus terebinthus* (Hook.) Torr. & A. Gray var. *foeniculatus* (Nutt. ex Torr. & A. Gray) Cronquist
Valerian	VALER	*Valeriana* L.
Varileaf phacelia	PHHE2	*Phacelia heterophylla* Pursh
Violet	VIOLA	*Viola* L.
Western clematis	CLLI2	*Clematis ligusticifolia* Nutt.

Appendix B: Plant Names Used in this Report *(continued)*

Common name	Code[a]	Latin name and author[b]
Western coneflower	RUOC2	*Rudbeckia occidentalis* Nutt.
Western false Solomon's seal	SMRA	*Smilacina racemosa* (L.) Desf.
Western hawkweed	HIAL	*Hieracium albertinum* Farr
Western larkspur	DEOC	*Delphinium occidentale* (S. Watson) S. Watson (pro sp.)
Western meadowrue	THOC	*Thalictrum occidentale* A. Gray
Western mugwort	ARLU	*Artemisia ludoviciana* Nutt.
Western sweetroot	OSOC	*Osmorhiza occidentalis* (Nutt. ex Torr. & A. Gray) Torr.
White hawkweed	HIAL2	*Hieracium albiflorum* Hook.
Wild candytuft	THFE3	*Thlaspi fendleri* A. Gray
Willowherb	EPILO	*Epilobium* L.
Woods strawberry	FRVE	*Fragaria vesca* L.
Wormleaf stonecrop	SEST2	*Sedum stenopetalum* Pursh

[a] Code from the PLANTS database (USDA-NRCS 2008).

[b] Latin names follow Hitchcock and Cronquist (1973). For current synonyms see app. C.

Appendix C: Current PLANTS Database Synonyms for the Names Used in This Report

Hitchcock and Cronquist name[a]			Current synonym[b]	
Latin name	Code[c]	Common name	Latin name	Code[c]
Agropyron intermedium (Host) P. Beauv.	AGIN2	Intermediate wheatgrass	*Thinopyrum intermedium* (Host) Barkworth & D.R. Dewey	THIN6
Agropyron repens (L.) P. Beauv.	AGRE2	Quackgrass	*Elymus repens* (L.) Gould	ELRE4
Agropyron spicatum Pursh	AGSP	Bluebunch wheatgrass	*Pseudoroegneria spicata* (Pursh) A. Löve ssp. *spicata*	PSSPS
Arenaria macrophylla Hook.	ARMA18	Bigleaf sandwort	*Moehringia macrophylla* (Hook.) Fenzl	MOMA3
Aster conspicuus Lindl.	ASCO3	Showy aster	*Eurybia conspicua* (Lindl.) G.L. Nesom	EUCO36
Aster foliaceus Lindl. ex DC.	ASFO	Leafy aster	*Symphyotrichum foliaceum* (Lindl. ex DC.) G.L. Nesom	SYFO2
Aster modestus Lindl.	ASMO3	Few-flowered aster	*Canadanthus modestus* (Lindl.) G.L. Nesom	CAMO32
Berberis repens Lindl.	BERE	Creeping Oregon grape	*Mahonia repens* (Lindl.) G. Don	MARE11
Carex lanuginosa auct. non Michx.	CALA30	Woolly sedge	*Carex pellita* Muhl. ex Willd.	CAPE42
Cornus stolonifera Michx.	COST4	Red-osier dogwood	*Cornus sericea* L. ssp. *sericea*	COSES
Epilobium angustifolium L.	EPAN2	Fireweed	*Chamerion angustifolium* (L.) Holub	CHAN9
Eupatorium occidentale Hook.	EUOC5	Throughwort	*Ageratina occidentalis* (Hook.) King & H. Rob.	AGOC2
Glyceria elata (Nash ex Rydb.) M.E. Jones	GLEL	Tall mannagrass	*Glyceria striata* (Lam.) Hitchc.	GLST
Heracleum lanatum Michx.	HELA4	Cowparsnip	*Heracleum maximum* Bartram	HEMA80
Hieracium albertinum Farr	HIAL	Western hawkweed	*Hieracium scouleri* Hook. var. *albertinum* (Farr) G.W. Douglas & G.A. Allen	HISCA
Koeleria cristata auct. non Pers. p.p.	KOCR	Prairie junegrass	*Koeleria macrantha* (Ledeb.) Schult.	KOMA
Lupinus sulphureus Douglas ex Hook. ssp. *subsaccatus* (Suksd.) L. Phillips	LUSUS3	Sulphur lupine	*Lupinus bingenensis* Suksd. var. *subsaccatus* Suksd.	LUBIS
Osmorhiza chilensis Hook. & Arn.	OSCH	Mountain sweet-cicely	*Osmorhiza berteroi* DC.	OSBE
Poa juncifolia Scribn.	POJU	Alkali bluegrass	*Poa secunda* J. Presl	POSE
Populus trichocarpa Torr. & A. Gray ex Hook.	POTR15	Black cottonwood	*Populus balsamifera* L. ssp. *trichocarpa* (Torr. & A. Gray ex Hook.) Brayshaw	POBAT
Potentilla fruticosa auct. non L.	POFR4	Shrubby cinquefoil	*Dasiphora fruticosa* (L.) Rydb. ssp. *floribunda* (Pursh) Kartesz	DAFRF
Sambucus cerulea Raf.	SACE3	Blue elderberry	*Sambucus nigra* L. ssp. *cerulea* (Raf.) R. Bolli	SANIC5
Senecio foetidus J.T. Howell	SEFO	Tall groundsel	*Senecio hydrophiloides* Rydb.	SEHY
Sitanion hystrix (Nutt.) J.G. Sm.	SIHY	Bottlebrush squirreltail	*Elymus elymoides* (Raf.) Swezey ssp. *elymoides*	ELELE
Smilacina racemosa (L.) Desf.	SMRA	Western false solomon's seal	*Maianthemum racemosum* (L.) Link ssp. *amplexicaule* (Nutt.) LaFrankie	MARAA
Smilacina stellata (L.) Desf.	SMST	Starry false solomon's seal	*Maianthemum stellatum* (L.) Link	MAST4
Stipa occidentalis Thurb.	STOC2	Western needlegrass	*Achnatherum occidentale* (Thurb.) Barkworth	ACOC3

[a] Names used in Hitchcock and Cronquist (1973) and this report.

[b] Recommended synonyms listed in the PLANTS database (USDA-NRCS 2008).

[c] Code from the PLANTS database (USDA-NRCS 2008).

www.ingramcontent.com/pod-product-compliance
Lightning Source LLC
Chambersburg PA
CBHW081220280526
45787CB00006B/2462